D1220465

Understanding
CAFFEINE

Behavioral Medicine and
Health Psychology Series

SERIES EDITOR

J. Rick Turner
Chapel Hill, North Carolina

Behavioral Medicine and Health Psychology brings the latest advances in these fields directly into undergraduate, graduate, and professional classrooms via‘ individual texts that each present one topic in a self-contained manner. The texts also allow health professionals specializing in one field to become familiar with another by reading the appropriate volume, a task facilitated by their short length and their scholarly yet accessible format.

The development of the series is guided by its Editorial Board, which comprises experts from the disciplines of experimental and clinical psychology, medicine and preventive medicine, psychiatry and behavioral sciences, nursing, public health, biobehavioral health, behavioral health sciences, and behavioral genetics. Board members are based in North America, Europe, and Australia, thereby providing a truly international perspective on current research and clinical practice in behavioral medicine and health psychology.

EDITORIAL BOARD

William B. Applegate, M.D., *University of Tennessee, Memphis*
Jacqueline Dunbar-Jacob, Ph.D., R.N., F.A.A.N., *University of Pittsburgh*
Laura L. Hayman, Ph.D., R.N., F.A.A.N., *Case Western Reserve University*
John K. Hewitt, Ph.D., *University of Colorado, Boulder*
Jack E. James, Ph.D., *La Trobe University, Australia*
Marie Johnston, Ph.D., *University of St. Andrews, United Kingdom*
Lynn T. Kozlowski, Ph.D., *Pennsylvania State University*
Laura C. Leviton, Ph.D., *University of Alabama at Birmingham*
Andrew Sherwood, Ph.D., *Duke University*
Shari R. Waldstein, Ph.D., *University of Maryland–Baltimore County*

Books in This Series

Understanding
CAFFEINE

A Biobehavioral Analysis

Jack E. James

Behavioral Medicine & Health Psychology 2

SAGE Publications
International Educational and Professional Publisher
Thousand Oaks   London   New Delhi

Copyright © 1997 by Sage Publications, Inc.
All rights reserved. No part of this book may be reproduced or utilized in any form or by any means, electronic or mechanical, including photocopying, recording, or by any information storage and retrieval system, without permission in writing from the publisher.

For information:

SAGE Publications, Inc.
2455 Teller Road
Thousand Oaks, California 91320
E-mail: order@sagepub.com

SAGE Publications Ltd.
6 Bonhill Street
London EC2A 4PU
United Kingdom

SAGE Publications India Pvt. Ltd.
M-32 Market
Greater Kailash I
New Delhi 110 048 India

Printed in the United States of America

Library of Congress Cataloging-in-Publication Data

James, Jack E.
    Understanding caffeine: A biobehavioral analysis / author, Jack
E. James.
      p. cm. — (Behavioral medicine and health psychology; vol.
2)
    Includes bibliographical references and index.
    ISBN 0-8039-7182-6 (cloth). — ISBN 0-8039-7183-4 (pbk.)
    1. Caffeine—Physiological effect.   I. Title.   II. Series.
QP801.C24J36   1997
615'.785—dc21   96-45893

97 98 99 00 01 02 03 10 9 8 7 6 5 4 3 2 1

Acquiring Editor:	C. Deborah Laughton
Editorial Assistant:	Eileen Carr
Production Editor:	Michèle Lingre
Production Assistant:	Denise Santoyo
Design Director:	Ravi Balasuriya
Typesetter:	Yang-hee Syn Maresca
Cover Designer:	Candice Harman
Print Buyer:	Anna Chin

Contents

To Drifa

Series Editor's Introduction

■ ■ In this very readable volume, Professor James brings together data from
■ ■ human and nonhuman animal studies in order to examine caffeine's
pharmacology and toxicology, its use in contemporary society, and its possible
role in disease etiology. The following chapters document current research
on psychopathology, cardiovascular health, cancer, and pregnancy and perinatal health.

This volume's early inclusion in the series is pleasing for several reasons
over and above its intrinsic merit. First, it employs an alternate approach compared with the lead volume, *Stress and Health: Biological and Psychological
Interactions,* which discussed a broader area of investigation. *Understanding
Caffeine* has a singular focus, the influence of caffeine on health. This
approach facilitates detailed examination of caffeine's possible etiological
role in individual diseases, while also permitting integrative discussion of
social issues pertaining to caffeine use. Both types of volume are important
and informative, and the series will continue to include texts in each category.

Second, inclusion of this volume bears witness to the international
perspective of the series. Dr. James is currently Professor and Head of

Behavioral Health Sciences at La Trobe University, Melbourne, Australia, and is a leading figure in behavioral medicine and health psychology initiatives in his country. He also contributes to the series as a member of its Editorial Board, which contains scientists from three continents.

Dr. James and I first met during the Society for Behavioral Medicine's annual meeting in San Diego in 1995. During our conversations about his research and the development of this project, I was particularly impressed by his multidisciplinary approach to the study of caffeine and health. *Understanding Caffeine* exemplifies this approach, and my thanks are extended to Dr. James for providing an outstanding and timely examination of current research and discourse on this topic.

J. Rick Turner
Chapel Hill, North Carolina

Preface

Caffeine is the most popular drug on Earth. This book was written to promote better understanding of caffeine and its effects and to redress some common misconceptions. The book aims to be comprehensive, while not being excessive in length. Chapter 1 provides a brief account of the history and current use of caffeine. Chapter 2 deals with essential aspects of caffeine pharmacology and toxicology, showing that caffeine in large amounts is toxic, and sometimes fatal, and that acute adverse effects sometimes occur even at moderate levels of intake. Although moderate use of caffeine is commonly believed to assist performance of everyday activities, the scientific evidence presented in Chapter 3 suggests that such benefits are unlikely. Indeed, as described in Chapter 4, with prolonged (i.e., habitual) use, caffeine may undermine psychological well-being, a fact that has led the American Psychiatric Association to formally recognize a number of specific caffeine-induced syndromes.

Chapter 5 traces several lines of scientific evidence, which converge to show that caffeine consumption is a significant cardiovascular risk factor, while Chapter 6 finds no evidence of similar substantial risk for cancer. The main finding of Chapter 7 is that significant potential risk exists in relation to caffeine use during pregnancy, especially in respect of lower birth weight. Notwithstanding many potential adverse effects, caffeine has some beneficial therapeutic and diagnostic applications, and these are described in Chapter 8. The concluding chapter, Chapter 9, provides a tentative analysis of reasons for the high prevalence of caffeine use, taking into account psychopharmacology, interpersonal processes, and the role of the caffeine industry. The main conclusion of the book is that caffeine is a drug of abuse for which there is no safe level of habitual use. The continued widespread use of caffeine confirms the need for better understanding of its effects.

Many people contributed to the completion of this book. In particular, I am grateful to Dr. J. Rick Turner, the Series Editor, for inviting me to undertake the project, and for his unfailing encouragement, enthusiasm, and wise counsel. I thank the staff at Sage Publications, especially C. Deborah Laughton, Senior Editor, and the production team for their thoroughness and willingness to assist. Many helpful comments on earlier drafts of the work were provided by M. Elizabeth Gregg. She also provided vital bibliographic assistance, with help from Natalie Moore. I am grateful to colleagues and students at La Trobe University for their acceptance of the considerable demands the task imposed on my time. Above all, I am indebted to Drifa Hardar Dottir for her constant support and encouragement.

Jack E. James

Caffeine

The Drug and Its Use

Humans possess an extraordinary propensity to consume psychoactive compounds. Of the innumerable "substances" ingested, none is more popular than caffeine. More than 80% of the world's population, irrespective of age, gender, geography, and culture, consumes caffeine daily. As such, caffeine is easily the most widely used drug in the world. Its use far exceeds that of other common drugs such as nicotine and alcohol.

The products of caffeine-bearing plants have been consumed by humans since preliterate times, a fact that has encouraged the *erroneous* belief that caffeine has always been a common and widespread constituent of the human diet. Contrary to this belief, the use of caffeine during ancient times was limited to particular geographic regions, and the means of cultivation and distribution were generally not adequate to maintain continuous supplies. It was not until after European colonization during the 17th and 18th centuries that caffeine products, previously unavailable to most people, came to be distributed universally. Thus, rather than being established in antiquity, widespread and habitual use of caffeine is a relatively recent phenomenon.

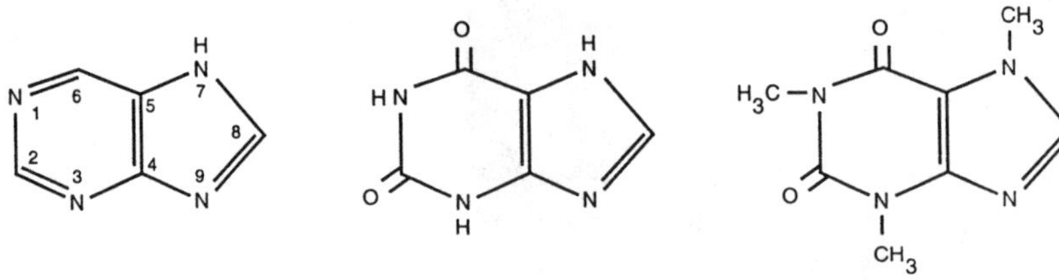

PURINE (Dioxypurine) XANTHINE CAFFEINE (1,3,7-trimethylxanthine)

Figure 1.1. Chemical structure of purine, xanthine, and caffeine.

Sources of Caffeine

Caffeine, also known as trimethylxanthine, is one of a family of methylated xanthines, often referred to as *methylxanthines* or merely *xanthines.* Figure 1.1 depicts the chemical structure of caffeine, xanthine (dioxypurine), and purine, the parent compound of xanthines. In anhydrous form, caffeine is a white odorless powder with a bitter taste. The principal sources of the drug are overwhelmingly coffee and tea, which account for about 90% of dietary use, and the average per capita daily intake varies between about 200 to 400 mg per day (about two to six cups of coffee or tea) (Gilbert, 1984). Most of the remaining 10% is consumed in cola soft drinks, which are an increasingly prominent source of caffeine, especially among children and adolescents. Other sources include cocoa and chocolate, but the caffeine content of these is negligible. Similarly, although the daily caffeine intake from a variety of less common caffeine beverages and products (e.g., maté, miang) peculiar to specific regions may be substantial for individual consumers, the overall intake from these more circumscribed sources accounts for only a small fraction of the global consumption of caffeine. Some medications, both prescribed and over the counter, contain as much as 200 mg (about two to four cups of coffee or tea) per tablet or capsule (Institute of Food Technologists' Expert Panel on Food Safety and Nutrition, 1983) and may represent a major source of caffeine for some individuals. In the general population, however, caffeine-containing medications are typically taken intermittently, if at all, and account for a negligible proportion of total caffeine intake.

Coffee

The coffee tree is of the Rubiaceae family in the *Coffea* genus. There are several species, of which *Coffea arabica* (Arabica) and *Coffea canephora* (Robusta) are the most important. The coffee tree is indigenous to Ethiopia, but its cultivation and use as a beverage appear to have been initiated in Arabia. Of the many legends that describe the discovery of coffee, one of the best-known refers to a goatherd named Kaldi, who observed that his animals "pranced about excitedly" after eating berries from certain wild bushes. Kaldi tried the berries himself and found that they helped him to remain more alert while watching over his herd during the night. Before long, brethren from the local monastery were also using the berries to prevent falling asleep during prayers.

Historical records indicate that coffee plants were transported from Ethiopia to Arabia in the 15th century and cultivated in Yemen, after which consumption flourished. By the early 16th century, the familiar practice of today, whereby a beverage is made by infusing ground roasted beans, was well-established in the Islamic world. The Dutch were the first to cultivate coffee plants outside Arabia. They brought plants to Europe in the early 17th century and established plantations in the Dutch East Indies. Later, France, Spain, and Britain also established extensive plantations in their respective colonies in the West Indies, Latin America, Africa, and India.

Coffeehouses became popular throughout 17th-century Europe. The first English coffeehouse was opened in 1650 in Oxford, and within 25 years, the number had grown to nearly 3,000 throughout England. At times, the introduction and subsequent popularity of coffee occasioned the ire of authorities. In 1675, King Charles II denounced coffeehouses as seditious meeting places. Nevertheless, they prospered, and by 1715, there were over 2,000 in London alone. Coffeehouses became centers of social, political, literary, and commercial life and gave rise to insurance houses, merchant banks, and the London Stock Exchange. The genesis of the world-renowned Lloyd's of London insurance company was Lloyd's Coffee House in Tower Street. Coffee became well-established in America following the War of Independence. In 1773, as a protest against oppression and excessive taxes, British ships moored in Boston Harbor were boarded, and their cargoes of tea were thrown overboard. This episode, the Boston Tea Party, marked the beginning of the rise in popularity of coffee in the United States, which is now the major coffee-consuming nation in the world.

Today, coffee is cultivated in a belt of countries situated between the Tropics of Cancer and Capricorn. Brazil is currently the world's largest coffee producer, followed by Colombia, Indonesia, Ivory Coast, Mexico, and Ethiopia. The major importing countries, besides the United States, are Germany, France, Italy, and Japan. Because of differences in size of population, national consumption does not necessarily give a good indication of per capita consumption. Indeed, import figures consistently show the Nordic countries (Denmark, Finland, Iceland, Norway, and Sweden) as having the highest per capita levels of coffee consumption. Arabica is the most widely grown species and is used for beverages brewed from ground coffee beans, whereas Robusta is used mostly in soluble (i.e., instant) coffees. Arabica is generally regarded as having a superior flavor, even though the caffeine content is typically about half that of Robusta (Spiller, 1984). Instant coffees are usually derived from a combination of Arabica and Robusta beans in proportions determined by the consumer market (Gilbert, 1984). In countries where coffee has not been the traditional predominant hot drink (e.g., the United Kingdom, Japan), the Robusta content of instant coffees may be as high as 50%. In countries that have a strong tradition of coffee drinking (e.g., throughout much of the European continent, the United States), a Robusta content of 20% is more typical (Gilbert, 1984).

Tea

Tea, *Camellia sinesis,* is native to the southern regions of China and parts of India, Burma, Thailand, Laos, and Vietnam. Written accounts of tea and its use appeared in China as early as 350 AD, and it appears to have been introduced to Japan from China around 600 AD. The Dutch were responsible for introducing tea to Europe and America in the 17th century. In England, tea was served in the existing coffeehouses, and its popularity grew to the point where it became the preferred hot beverage of that country. After the British trade monopoly with China expired in 1833, tea cultivation began in India and Sri Lanka (formerly Ceylon). Today, tea is grown in about 30 countries. The major producers and exporters of tea are India, China, and Sri Lanka, and the major importers are the United Kingdom, the United States, and countries of the former Soviet Union. Although it is consumed more widely than coffee, tea is second to coffee as a source of caffeine because tea beverages generally have a lower caffeine concentration than coffee. As a beverage, the consumption of tea worldwide is surpassed only by water (Graham, 1992).

Tea is manufactured in three main forms, black tea, green tea, and oolong tea. Black tea is produced by promoting oxidation of green leaf polyphenols, a process traditionally referred to as *fermentation.* Green tea is a dry product without oxidation, whereas oolong tea, which has an appearance somewhat intermediate between that of black and green tea, is partially oxidized. Black tea accounts for almost 80% of world tea production and is the predominant product outside China, Japan, North Africa, and the Middle East. Green tea accounts for most of the remaining 20%, with oolong tea, which is manufactured primarily in China and Taiwan, accounting for less than 2% (Graham, 1992).

The caffeine concentration of green tea beverage is often less than that of beverages prepared from black tea, although the two are roughly equivalent in caffeine concentration for higher grade green tea (Gilbert, 1984). Notwithstanding the considerable variability in the caffeine content of prepared beverages, an "average" cup of tea may be regarded as containing about one half to two thirds the caffeine content of an equivalent volume of coffee (Barone & Roberts, 1984). Tea also contains small amounts of other methylxanthines, namely, theobromine (about one tenth the caffeine content) and theophylline (less than one fiftieth the caffeine content) (Graham, 1984b). Throughout most of the world, tea is consumed as a hot beverage, although iced tea is preferred in the United States. Tea is sometimes flavored during the production process by spraying flavor extract onto the manufactured tea or by adding stabilized flavors in solid form (e.g., citrus fruit, jasmine) prior to final packaging. Water-soluble powdered extract of tea leaf is also available as instant tea, most of which is manufactured and consumed in the United States.

Soft Drinks

Popular brands of cola drinks contain pharmacologically significant amounts of caffeine. Use of the cola nut, *Cola acuminata,* during manufacture is responsible for some of the caffeine present in the finished product, but it has been estimated that more than 95% of the caffeine in cola drinks is added

(Institute of Food Technologists' Expert Panel on Food Safety and Nutrition, 1983). These drinks are a major, and increasing, source of the caffeine consumed by children. In recent years, the demand for soft drinks derived from guaraná has also increased, especially in Brazil, Japan, and the United States. Guaraná, *Paullinia cupana,* which has long been consumed by indigenous people of South America, has a very high caffeine content (Morton, 1992). The popularity of caffeine foods and beverages has often been explained on the grounds that the drug enhances the taste for sweetness (Schiffman et al., 1986; Schiffman & Warwick, 1989). In addition, as discussed in later chapters, repeated ingestion of caffeine leads to physical dependence. The dual properties of enhanced taste and physical dependence may explain the extraordinary commercial success of cola drinks.

Other Sources

Chocolate and cocoa are obtained from the cacao tree, *Theobromine cacao,* meaning "food of the gods." At the time of the Spanish conquest of the Aztec empire, Cortez learned how cacao beans were used to prepare a foamy beverage called *chocolatl* (from the Aztec word *choco* meaning warm and *atl* meaning drink), and he introduced the beverage to Spain on his return to Europe in 1528. By the middle of the 17th century, drinking chocolate had spread throughout Europe, but it was another 200 years before eating chocolate was developed. The major producers of cacao are low-latitude countries in Africa and South America, and the major consumer countries are France, Germany, Japan, the former Soviet Union, the United Kingdom, and the United States. Theobromine, which has a biological potency substantially less than that of caffeine, is the main methylxanthine in cocoa products, with trace amounts of theophylline also present (Zoumas et al., 1980). The concentration of caffeine in cocoa is about one eighth that of theobromine.

For many people in Argentina, Brazil, Chile, and Uruguay, maté (also known as Paraguayan tea) is the principal source of dietary methylxanthines. Maté is a beverage prepared from the leaves of *Ilex paraguariensis,* a member of the holly family. The caffeine concentration of maté appears to be slightly less than that of tea, and like tea, maté contains small amounts of theobromine and theophylline (Graham, 1984a). Maté is mostly consumed in the same general region of South America in which it is cultivated. Cassina (also known as yaupon, Christmas berry tree, and the North American tea plant) was used by some American Indians and white settlers to prepare a caffeine beverage.

During the American Civil War, when supplies of tea and coffee were blockaded by the Union, cassina became a popular beverage in the Confederacy. Later, during and after World War I, U.S. authorities attempted to popularize cassina as a substitute source of caffeine in the face of high coffee prices.

Substantial quantities of caffeine are also present in certain prescription and patent medicines, including some stimulants, pain relievers, diuretics, cold remedies, and weight-control preparations. In addition to these registered drug products, caffeine is often present in street drugs (Gomez & Rodriguez, 1989; Kaa, 1994). Finally, some caffeine is ingested as part of the practice of miang chewing, which is common in rural northern Thailand (Reichart et al., 1988). Miang is prepared by steaming tea and storing it under moist conditions until it becomes sour and astringent, at which point a pinch of leaves is taken and chewed.

Noncaffeine Constituents

The main dietary sources of caffeine contain a plethora of potentially active compounds, which may be regarded as either endogenous or exogenous. The former occur naturally in the plants from which caffeine foods and beverages are obtained. The latter are "acquired," either intentionally (e.g., flavor additives) or unintentionally (e.g., residues of pesticides used during cultivation). With regard to endogenous compounds, coffee, for example, contains chlorogenic acids, present in a variety of common vegetable foodstuffs, which may stimulate gastric secretion. In addition, coffee contains lipids, which have recently been found to have a cholesterol-raising effect (discussed in Chapter 5). Nevertheless, none of the known actions of the many endogenous constituents of coffee and tea competes for significance with the physiological and psychoactive properties of caffeine. As for exogenous compounds, it is claimed that current manufacturing practice ensures no significant hazard to consumers due to contamination by pesticides used during cultivation and storage (Viani, 1988). Exogenous constituents also include those added by the consumer (e.g., milk and sugar). Once again, when considering the biobehavioral significance of caffeine beverages, these additives are of negligible importance compared to caffeine. That is, the available evidence indicates that caffeine is responsible for the overwhelming majority of the biobehavioral effects of the main caffeine foods and beverages.

▨ Measurement of Caffeine Consumption

The combined biomedical and behavioral impact of caffeine depends on the pattern and extent of exposure to the drug. Consequently, it is important to be able to quantify the caffeine content of beverages and the consumption patterns and levels for individuals and populations.

Caffeine Content of Beverages

Current analytic methods are capable of detecting concentrations of caffeine in liquids at less than 0.1 µg/ml. In addition to measuring the concentration of caffeine in beverages, the most widely used method, high-performance liquid chromatography (HPLC), is also used to measure caffeine in various body fluids, including blood, saliva, urine, breast milk, cerebrospinal fluid, semen, and amniotic fluid. Although HPLC methods are well-advanced, obtaining *standard* estimates of the caffeine content of coffee and tea as typically consumed is complicated by a host of variables that are difficult to control, including plant variety, cultivation methods, and particle size (i.e., fineness of the coffee "grind" or tea leaf cut). Even if a particular manufactured product is assumed to have a consistent caffeine content, there is great variation between consumers with respect to preparation method, including the amount of product used, method of brewing, and brewing or steeping time.

Table 1.1 summarizes standard values for the main dietary sources of caffeine. These values have been derived from published sources (Barone & Roberts, 1984; Bunker & McWilliams, 1979; Burg, 1975) and adjusted for volume of servings for coffee and tea, from 5 ounces, the "industry" standard, to 225 ml (about 7.5 ounces), which is more typical of actual servings (Gilbert et al., 1976; Lelo, Miners, et al., 1986a; Stavric et al., 1988). However, it must be emphasized that these values are merely approximations of the caffeine content of beverages as consumed and that pronounced variations not only exist between individuals, but also for the same individual preparing the same type of beverage under ostensibly the same circumstances (James et al., 1988).

Self-Reported Caffeine Consumption

Numerous studies have examined relationships between caffeine exposure and diverse biobehavioral indices (e.g., blood pressure, headache, anxiety). Typically, caffeine exposure is measured by means of consumer

Table 1.1   Caffeine Content of the Main Dietary Sources of the Drug

Beverage	Serving	Volume (ml)	Caffeine (mg)
Coffee:			
Ground roast ("brewed")	cup	225	125
Instant	cup	225	90
Decaffeinated	cup	225	4.5
Tea (leaf or bag)	cup	225	60
Cocoa, drinking chocolate	cup	225	5
Cola drinks	glass	180	20
	can	360	40
	bottle	1,000	100

self-reports of consumption of caffeine beverages, foods, and/or medications. Two main types of self-report measurements have been employed. The more common of the two types asks respondents to provide retrospective estimates of their usual daily caffeine intake (e.g., James, Bruce, et al., 1989; James et al., 1987). Alternatively, and less commonly, respondents may be asked to maintain diary records of instances of caffeine ingestion throughout a specified period (e.g., 24 hours, 1 week) (James et al., 1988). Both types of self-report measurement may vary considerably in the detail requested of respondents. For example, in its simplest form, the retrospective type might ask respondents merely to answer yes or no to the question, "Do you drink coffee most days?" In general, however, correlations between self-reported intake and objective measurements of caffeine exposure should be increased by more, rather than less, detail. It has been suggested that, as a minimum, self-reports of caffeine consumption should include information on type of beverage and method of preparation (decaffeinated and regular, brewed and instant coffee, tea, soft drinks), and separate reports of consumption for weekdays and weekends (Schreiber, Maffeo, et al., 1988).

Although there have been relatively few empirical studies of the reliability of self-report measurements, the results that have been obtained are encouraging. Good test-retest reliability of retrospective self-reports of caffeine consumption has been found for periods ranging from 1 week to 4 years (Barr et al., 1981; Cumming & Klineberg, 1994b; Ozasa et al., 1994; Schreiber, Maffeo, et al., 1988). In general, however, diary records are likely to be more reliable than retrospective estimates. Whereas retrospective self-reports yielded moderate correlations with salivary caffeine concentration, as measured by HPLC analysis of samples obtained in the late afternoon (James, Bruce, et al., 1989), caffeine diary records were found to be highly correlated with late-afternoon plasma caffeine concentrations (James et al., 1988). Caffeine concentrations measured in blood and saliva are highly correlated (Alkaysi et al., 1988; Soto et al., 1994), and the significance of the sampling being conducted in the late afternoon is that systemic caffeine concentration in habitual consumers typically increases during the day (due to intermittent consumption of caffeine beverages), and plateaus by late afternoon or early evening. Hence, the best single-sample bioassay of daily caffeine intake is provided by samples obtained in the late afternoon (Lelo, Miners, et al., 1986a). A method has been suggested for estimating systemic caffeine concentration based on self-reported caffeine intake over the preceding day or days (Pfeifer & Notari, 1988). The method incorporates several constants representing estimated average values for the pharmacokinetics of caffeine and the caffeine content of foods and beverages. Although vulnerable to self-report errors, the Pfeifer-Notari method offers a possible means by which to achieve greater accuracy than alternative self-report approaches.

Patterns of Caffeine Consumption

Population patterns of caffeine consumption have generally been estimated either by (a) analysis of industry "disappearance" data based on the production and distribution (i.e., export and import) of caffeine products, or (b) interviewing and/or surveying consumers. Although both approaches have particular advantages and disadvantages, they have yielded broadly similar results. One disadvantage of disappearance data, compared to consumer surveys, is that little differentiation is provided regarding subgroups within a population. Conversely, the self-reported information obtained from consumer surveys not only generally lacks objective corroboration but is usually transformed using standard estimates of the caffeine content of foods and beverages and is therefore subject to the measurement errors described in the preceding section.

Disappearance Data

Table 1.2 summarizes the daily per capita consumption of caffeine in Canada, the United States, Sweden, and the United Kingdom, as estimated

Table 1.2 Per Capita Daily Consumption (mg) Estimated on the Basis of Industry Data for Four Major Caffeine-Consuming Countries in North America (Canada, United States) and Europe (Sweden, United Kingdom)

Source	Canada	United States	Sweden	United Kingdom
Coffee	128	125	340	84
Tea	79	35	34	320
Soft drinks	16	35	—	—
Other (e.g., cocoa, medications)	15	16	51	40
Total	238	211	425	444

SOURCE: Adapted from Gilbert (1984).

from industry data (Gilbert, 1984). Although reported more than a decade ago, these estimates provide a good indication of the likely range of contemporary consumption levels for the developed countries of the world. Consumption in developing countries is less clear, because the relevant data are not readily available. Even the estimates in Table 1.2 should be regarded with caution, because wastage, spoilage, and non-food usage are just some of the factors that confound the translation of disappearance data into actual human consumption (Morgan et al., 1982). With regard to broad trends, coffee consumption declined throughout the 20 years from 1962 to 1982 (Masterson, 1983). In particular, in the United States, there was a decline of almost 40% during this period. However, in the mid-1980s, consumption plateaued and then began to increase, and this more recent trend has continued into the 1990s (Heuman, 1994b).

Similarly, record tea sales have been achieved in successive years since 1990, at least in the United States (Richards, 1994). Although global consumption of soft drinks is more difficult to establish precisely, soft drinks are an increasingly important source of caffeine, especially for the young. Gilbert (1984) found that per capita consumption of soft drinks in the United States increased by 231% between 1960 and 1982. Although the same *rate* of increase may not have continued in the United States, or have been equalled in other countries, soft drink consumption has generally continued to increase. Consequently, the estimates in Table 1.2 are probably somewhat conservative with respect to current levels of caffeine consumption, especially in the United States.

Interview and Survey Results

A consistent finding of population surveys is that habitual consumers of caffeine far outnumber abstainers. Because consumer frequencies of more than 90% have been reported in most surveys, global consumer frequency of at least 80% represents a conservative estimate. Broadly, caffeine is consumed habitually by people of all ages and from all walks of life, and almost all of the drug is consumed in the form of coffee, tea, and cola soft drinks. During early adulthood, consumption tends to increase progressively with age, reaching a plateau during middle age and decreasing slightly during old age. Although the *amount* of caffeine consumed is greater in older than in younger children, *exposure* may reach higher levels in younger children because of their lighter weight. The consumption of cola drinks, for example, can lead to caffeine-exposure levels in children equal to or greater than levels experienced by many coffee-drinking adults. Even breast-fed infants receive small amounts of caffeine if the mother is a consumer. Although there appear to be no marked gender differences in consumption for any of the principal dietary sources of caffeine, a slightly higher level of intake for females in most adult age groups has been reported (Barone & Roberts, 1984).

When considering the research findings discussed in later chapters, it is important to recognize that the pattern of exposure experienced by most consumers is very different from what is employed in most laboratory studies of the drug. Caffeine is usually consumed in separate portions throughout the day, with fewer portions consumed later in the day, followed by overnight abstinence. Most laboratory studies, however, involve the administration of a single, comparatively large caffeine "challenge." Furthermore, caffeine consumption, as a behavior, is associated with various other behavioral or lifestyle variables. In particular, caffeine consumption is positively associated with cigarette smoking, and to a lesser extent, alcohol (Berger & Wynder, 1994; Klesges et al., 1994; Kozlowski et al., 1993; Patton et al., 1995; Ungemack, 1994; Weill & Le-Bourhis, 1994), whereas coffee and tea consumption are inversely associated (Klesges et al., 1994; Schwarz et al., 1994).

SUMMARY

Over the past 400 years, there has been relentless growth in worldwide consumption of caffeine foods and beverages, such that a large majority of the world's current population consumes the drug daily. Not only is caffeine the most widely used psychoactive compound, but for most consumers, exposure to the drug is effectively lifelong. Level of exposure is a key factor in assessing the cumulative biobehavioral impact of drug-induced effects. Considering current levels of caffeine use, even small effects, when accumulated across entire populations, may have very important consequences. This point, which should be kept in mind when the epidemiology of caffeine is discussed in later chapters, has parallels in the population impact of cigarette smoking. In the developed countries of the world, the relative risk of death from lung cancer among cigarette smokers is about 14 (i.e., smokers are 14 times more likely to die from lung cancer than nonsmokers). Conversely, the smoking-related relative risk of death from coronary heart disease is only about 1.6. Nevertheless, the number of premature deaths attributable to cigarette smoking is far greater for heart disease than lung cancer. This apparent contradiction is due to the relative frequencies of the events involved. Because coronary heart disease is far more prevalent than lung cancer, the contribution of smoking to premature death is greater for the former than the latter. Caffeine use is near universal. Consequently, even a small increase in the caffeine-related relative risk for a particular outcome variable will have comparatively large absolute effects, especially if the outcomes (e.g., heart disease deaths) are also prevalent.

FURTHER READING

Gilbert, R. M. (1984). Caffeine consumption. In G. A. Spiller (Ed.), *The methylxanthine beverages and foods: Chemistry, consumption, and health effects* (pp. 185-214). New York: Alan R. Liss.

Kaa, E. (1994). Impurities, adulterants, and diluents of illicit heroin: Changes during a 12-year period. *Forensic Science International, 64,* 171-179.

Pfeifer, R. W., & Notari, R. E. (1988). Predicting caffeine plasma concentrations resulting from consumption of food or beverages: A simple method and its origin. *Drug Intelligence and Clinical Pharmacy, 22, 953-959.*

Schreiber, G. B., Maffeo, C. E., Robins, M., Masters, M. N., & Bond, A. P. (1988). Measurement of coffee and caffeine intake: Implications for epidemiologic research. *Preventive Medicine, 17,* 280-294.

Schwarz, B., Bischof, H. P., & Kunze, M. (1994). Coffee, tea, and lifestyle. *Preventive Medicine, 23, 377-384.*

Pharmacology and Toxicology of Caffeine

As discussed in the preceding chapter, global usage of caffeine as a psychoactive substance is unsurpassed. Hence, it is reasonable to ask why caffeine is so popular. Also, what are the biobehavioral consequences of such widespread usage? To answer these questions, it is appropriate to begin by considering the distinctive pharmacological actions of the drug and its toxicological potential.

Pharmacology

Pharmacokinetics

Pharmacokinetics refers to the biological fate of a compound that has been ingested by a living organism, and it is a composite of the processes of absorption, distribution, metabolism, and excretion. Following oral ingestion, caffeine is rapidly absorbed from the gastrointestinal tract into the

14

bloodstream (Arnaud, 1987; Blanchard & Sawers, 1983b). About 90% of the caffeine contained in a cup of coffee is cleared from the stomach within 20 minutes (Chvasta & Cooke, 1971), and peak plasma concentration is typically reached within about 40 to 60 minutes (Rall, 1990a). The rate of absorption may be slowed by the presence of food in the intestine (Arnaud, 1987), and time to reach peak plasma concentration tends to be longer when larger amounts of the drug are ingested (Passmore et al., 1987). In one group of habitual consumers, the highest peak plasma caffeine concentration was found to be about 10 µg/ml, with a mean 24-hour plasma level of about 5 µg/ml (Lelo, Miners, et al., 1986a). In addition, the rate of caffeine absorption appears to be the same for coffee and tea (Marks & Kelly, 1973) but slower for soft drinks (Bonati et al., 1982; Marks & Kelly, 1973), apparently because the pH value of soft drinks is generally lower than that of coffee and tea (Chvasta & Cooke, 1971).

Once ingested, caffeine is readily distributed throughout the entire body (Rall, 1990a). Animal and human studies have shown that there are no significant physiological barriers limiting the passage of the drug through tissues (Bonati & Garattini, 1984), and there is no evidence of its being sequestered in particular body organs (Yesair et al., 1984). Concentrations in blood are highly correlated with those found in saliva (Callahan et al., 1982; Khanna et al., 1982; Setchell et al., 1987; Walther et al., 1983; Zylber-Katz et al., 1984), breast milk (Bailey et al., 1982; Berlin, 1981; Findlay, 1983; Hildebrandt et al., 1983; Stavchansky et al., 1988), amniotic fluid and fetal tissue (Brazier et al., 1983; Van't Hoff, 1982), semen (Beach et al., 1984), and the brain (Somani et al., 1980). In humans, the elimination half-life of caffeine generally varies between about 3 and 7 hours (Rall, 1990a), with an average of about 5 hours (Pfeifer & Notari, 1988). The elimination rate does not appear to be subject to any significant diurnal variation (Hashiguchi et al., 1992).

A number of factors affect rate of elimination, including age, pregnancy, disease, and use of other substances. Premature and full-term newborns show a markedly decreased rate of clearance (Aranda, Collinge, et al., 1979; Parsons et al., 1976), because the enzyme system responsible for metabolizing the drug is underdeveloped during the first 6 to 12 months of life (Cazeneuve et al., 1994; Yesair et al., 1984). Thereafter, the caffeine elimination rate appears to be stable, although a slightly shorter plasma caffeine half-life (i.e., more rapid biotransformation) has been reported for men over 65 years of age compared to those under 25 years (Blanchard & Sawers, 1983a).

The clearance rate may be slightly faster in women than in men (Callahan et al., 1983), and in women it appears that there may be a 25% slower rate of elimination during the luteal phase of the menstrual cycle, when progesterone levels are highest, than in the follicular phase (Lane et al., 1992). The clearance rate for caffeine decreases during the course of pregnancy, resulting in an approximate threefold increase in the plasma half-life of the drug by the third trimester (Aldridge et al., 1981; Knutti et al., 1981; Parsons & Pelletier, 1982). Because caffeine is primarily metabolized by liver enzymes (Berthou et al., 1988; Carrillo & Benitez, 1994; Tassaneeyakul et al., 1994), the rate of caffeine clearance can be compromised by liver disease (Desmond et al., 1980; Scott et al., 1988, 1989; Statland & Demas, 1980; Ullrich et al., 1992) and liver dysfunction associated with acute illness (Wilairatana et al., 1994). Cigarette smoking increases the rate of caffeine elimination by about twofold (Kalow & Tang, 1991; May et al., 1982; Parsons & Neims, 1978), whereas oral contraceptives decrease clearance by about the same order of magnitude (Callahan et al., 1983; Patwardhan et al., 1980). Furthermore, the half-life of caffeine may be significantly decreased at high altitude (Kamimori et al., 1995).

Caffeine Metabolism

The process of biotransformation performed by the liver is regulated by the cytochrome P-450 enzyme system and includes demethylation of caffeine (1,3,7 trimethylxanthine), resulting in three dimethylxanthine metabolites, paraxanthine (1,7-dimethylxanthine), theobromine (3,7-dimethylxanthine), and theophylline (1,3-dimethylxanthine), as shown in Figure 2.1. In adults, caffeine is virtually completely transformed, with less than 2% of the ingested compound being recoverable in urine unchanged (Arnaud, 1987; Somani & Gupta, 1988). Paraxanthine is by far the major metabolite of caffeine in humans. One study reported that paraxanthine accounted for 84% of the demethylations, theobromine for 12%, and theophylline for 4% (Lelo, Miners, et al., 1986b). The abundance of paraxanthine as a caffeine metabolite suggests the need to take account of the actions of this compound when considering the pharmacology of caffeine (Benowitz et al., 1995; Dulloo et al., 1994; Graham et al., 1994). Interspecies comparisons are complicated by marked differences in both kinetic and metabolic profiles. Moreover, kinetic similarity between species does not necessarily indicate metabolic similarity, and vice versa. For example, although the caffeine elimination

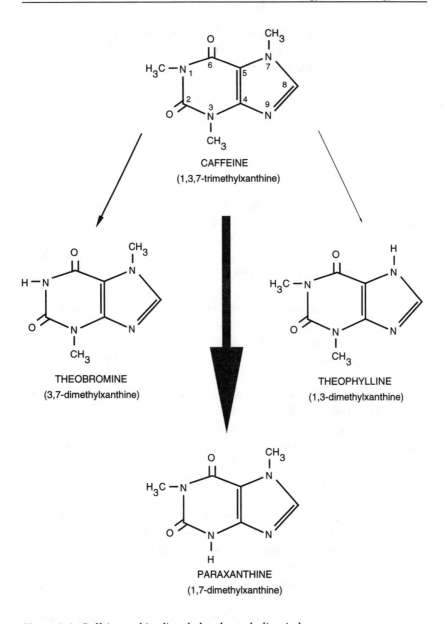

Figure 2.1. Caffeine and its dimethylated metabolites in humans

NOTE: arrow widths indicate relative proportions of the metabolites in plasma.

half-life is similar between humans and some species of monkeys, paraxanthine is the major metabolite in the former, whereas theophylline is the major metabolite in latter. Conversely, paraxanthine is the major metabolite in mice (as in humans), but the clearance rate of caffeine in mice is about one fifth the rate in humans. Interspecies kinetic and metabolic differences serve as a reminder of the need for caution when generalizing findings from animal studies to humans.

Mechanisms of Action

Caffeine exerts a variety of pharmacological actions at diverse sites, both centrally and peripherally. Several mechanisms have been suggested as being responsible for these effects, including translocation of intracellular calcium, and increased levels of cyclic adenosine monophosphate due to inhibition of phosphodiesterase activity. However, these mechanisms only function at systemic levels of caffeine far in excess of those associated with the human consumption of the drug. To explain the effects of caffeine by phosphodiesterase inhibition and calcium translocation, plasma concentrations would need to reach 100 μg/ml and 300 μg/ml, respectively (Fredholm, 1985). Because the plasma concentrations associated with typical patterns of consumption are generally in the order of 0.5 to 3 μg/ml and do not usually exceed 10 μg/ml, phosphodiesterase inhibition and calcium mobilization cannot explain the actions of caffeine as ordinarily consumed, although these mechanisms may contribute to the acute toxic effects of caffeine ingested in large amounts. A consensus has emerged that the most plausible principal mechanism of action, at dose levels achieved during typical usage of caffeine, is competitive blockade of adenosine receptors (Fredholm, 1995).

Adenosine. Caffeine and adenosine have a similar molecular structure. Adenosine is a neuromodulator that acts upon specific cell-surface receptors distributed throughout the body (Bush et al., 1989; Marangos & Boulenger, 1985; Schiffman & Warwick, 1989; Watt et al., 1989). Because adenosine generally functions to inhibit physiological activity, the blockade of adenosine receptors by caffeine has broadly stimulant effects (Biaggioni et al., 1991; Carter et al., 1995; Franchetti et al., 1994; LeBlanc & Soucy, 1994). Caffeine is a nonselective antagonist of two major types of adenosine receptors, A_1 and A_2, which when activated are associated with a host of biological functions, including those summarized in Table 2.1. Recently, the A_2 type has

Table 2.1	Some Acute Biological Effects of Adenosine	
	Biological System	*Effect*
	Central nervous system	Decreased transmitter release
		Sedation
	Cardiovascular	Dilates cerebral and coronary blood vessels
	Renal Antidiuresis	Platelet inhibition
	Respiratory	Bronchoconstriction
	Gastrointestinal	Inhibition of acid secretion
	Metabolic	Inhibition of lipolysis

NOTE: These effects are broadly opposite to those of caffeine.

been differentiated into A_{2A}, and A_{2B}, and a further type, A_3, has been identified (Fredholm, 1995). It appears that A_1 and A_{2A} are the primary targets of caffeine, and both may interact in functionally important ways with dopamine receptors (Ferré, Popoli, et al., 1994; Ferré, Schwarcz, et al., 1994; Garrett & Holtzman, 1994a, 1994b; Josselyn & Beninger, 1991).

■ Toxicology

Notwithstanding the widespread use of caffeine, deaths and near-deaths due to caffeine poisoning do occur, albeit relatively infrequently. The lethal dose for adults has been estimated to be about 10 g (Ritchie, 1975). This estimate approximates the caffeine *index of lethality* (LD_{50}) for several species of animals. In dogs, cats, and rats, the LD_{50} (i.e., the experimentally determined dose sufficient to kill one half of a population of test animals) has been found to be approximately 150 to 200 mg/kg of caffeine ingested orally (Hirsh, 1984; Stavric, 1988a). Because an adult human ingests about 1 to 2 mg/kg of caffeine per beverage, it is virtually impossible for a lethal dose of caffeine to be consumed in one of its usual dietary forms. Nevertheless, of almost 3,000 cases of caffeine "exposure" registered with the American Association of Poison Control Centers in a single year, 0.1% (i.e., three cases) did indeed result in death. Of the many reports of lethal and near-lethal cases of caffeine poisoning, all have involved atypical methods of ingestion.

There have been several reported cases of accidental caffeine poisoning involving children. Most often, the children ingested multiple caffeine-containing prescription or over-the-counter medications (e.g., diuretics, stimulants, and headache preparations). In most cases, recovery occurred within several days, with the children showing no lasting after-effects (Banner & Czajka, 1980; Fligner & Opheim, 1988; Rowland & Mace, 1976; Seger & Schwartz, 1994; Sullivan, 1977; Walsh et al., 1987). However, in at least two cases, poisoning resulted in death. One involved a girl aged 5 years who ingested more than 5 g of caffeine in the form of diuretic tablets (Dimaio & Garriott, 1974), and the other involved a boy aged 15 months who inadvertently received about 18 g of caffeine in solution while undergoing a hospital medical examination (Farago, 1968). There have been many reported cases of caffeine poisoning in adults resulting in death (Caughlin & O'Halloran, 1993; Garriott et al., 1985; Jokela & Vartiainen, 1959; Leson et al., 1988; McGee, 1980; Rejent et al., 1981; Ryall, 1984; Turner & Cravey, 1977), including suicide (Alstott et al., 1972; Bryant, 1981) or near-death (Benowitz et al., 1982; Nagesh & Murphy, 1988; Wrenn & Oschner, 1989; Zimmerman et al., 1985). One recent nonfatal case involved a man who was revived after being admitted to the hospital in a state of unconsciousness, and it was discovered that he had ingested about 500 g of ground coffee (possibly containing as much as 15 g of caffeine) with the stated intention of achieving a "high" (Würl, 1994).

Although there appears to be no characteristic final cause of death following caffeine overdose, there do appear to be some common symptoms of caffeine poisoning, including abdominal cramps and vomiting, convulsions, markedly increased heart rate, and cardiac arrhythmia. Severe vomiting probably contributed to the survival of some individuals (Deng et al., 1983; May et al., 1981; Nagesh & Murphy, 1988; Rowland & Mace, 1976; Sullivan, 1977). Overall, the conventional estimate of 10 g seems to be a reasonable general approximation of the likely oral lethal dose for caffeine, although the reported variation above and below this estimate has been considerable. As little as 5.3 g orally ingested caffeine was reported to have caused the death of a child (Dimaio & Garriott, 1974), whereas a woman aged 21 years was reported to have survived an estimated intake of 106 g (Nagesh & Murphy, 1988). Moreover, caffeine in large amounts is sometimes consumed with illicit drugs (e.g., amphetamine, cocaine), which is likely to increase its toxic potency (Caughlin & O'Halloran, 1993; Derlet et al., 1992; Gomez & Rodriguez, 1989; Lake & Quirk, 1984; Lambrecht et al., 1993). In any event, the many reports of fatal or near-fatal caffeine overdose, most of which have involved ingestion of caffeine-containing medications, demonstrate that it is virtually impossible to ingest acutely life-threatening amounts of the drug in beverage form.

▓ Acute Effects of Caffeine on Major Physiological Processes

Notwithstanding the potentially life-threatening toxic effects of caffeine when it is ingested in unusually large quantities, most consumers do not experience any direct threat of this kind. Most caffeine use is habitual, consisting of modest amounts ingested daily over much of the life span. This book is concerned primarily with effects associated with habitual use. The outline of acute effects, not necessarily toxic, contained in this section provides a foundation for understanding the chronic effects described in later chapters.

Central Nervous System

Caffeine is generally regarded as a central nervous system *stimulant,* although only limited means exist for conducting direct observation of these effects. One approach has been to examine the effects of the drug on electroencephalographic (EEG) records, which show electrical activity in the outermost layers of the cerebral cortex via electrodes attached to the scalp. The findings have generally been taken as broadly indicative of the effects of psychostimulants (Bruce et al., 1986; Clubley et al., 1979; Dimpfel et al., 1993; Gibbs & Maltby, 1943; Goldstein et al., 1963; Hasenfratz & Bättig, 1992; Hasenfratz, Bunge, et al., 1993; Kenemans & Lorist, 1995; Pritchard et al., 1995). Overall, however, there has not been a high level of consistency regarding caffeine-induced EEG patterns reported to date, possibly due to methodological differences, including EEG-measurement protocol, caffeine dose, and the caffeine-consumer status of participants. Alternatively, the low level of consistency may simply indicate that the EEG effects of caffeine are modest.

Autonomic Nervous System

It has sometimes been claimed that caffeine has effects on the autonomic nervous system that mimic those of anxiety. Several studies, for example, have reported that caffeine increases skin conductance, with evidence of a dose-response relationship (Bruce et al., 1986; Davidson, 1991; B. D. Smith et al., 1993; Zahn & Rapoport, 1987). Similarly, studies have reported increases in electromyographic (EMG) activity (James, 1990) and skin temperature (France & Ditto, 1992; Koot & Deurenberg, 1995).

Cardiovascular System

Although some of the autonomic effects of caffeine may be anxiomimetic, the hemodynamic effects of the drug differ from anxiety in one important respect. Whereas anxiety tends to increase heart rate and blood pressure, caffeine in moderate amounts increases blood pressure while generally having little effect on heart rate (France & Ditto, 1992; James, 1990, 1994b; Lane & Williams, 1987; Perkins, Sexton, Epstein, et al., 1994; Smits et al., 1993). If heart rate does change, it is likely to *decrease* slightly (Robertson et al., 1978), possibly due to vagal activity elicited by increased blood pressure. The principal mechanism responsible for the hemodynamic effects of caffeine appears to be antagonism of endogenous adenosine (Smits et al., 1989; Snyder & Sklar, 1984), although actions may also be mediated by catecholamines and possibly by the renin-angiotensin system (Burghardt et al., 1982; Fredholm, 1984). Adenosine dilates coronary and cerebral blood vessels (Biaggioni et al., 1986, 1987; Fuller et al., 1987; Smits et al., 1987), and these effects appear to be mediated by the A_2 subclass of receptors (Fredholm & Sollevi, 1986). Caffeine-induced pressor effects appear to be due primarily to increased vascular resistance rather than increased cardiac output (Biaggioni et al., 1991; France & Ditto, 1988; Pincomb et al., 1988, 1993).

Gastrointestinal System

There is evidence that caffeine is capable of stimulating gastric secretion (Cohen & Booth, 1975; Debas et al., 1971), but it does not appear to be the only constituent of coffee having this effect (Van Deventer et al., 1992). Moreover, it appears that the level of acid production due to coffee is no greater, and may be less, than that due to various noncaffeine beverages (McArthur et al., 1982). Coffee apparently contributes to gastroesophageal reflux (Brazer et al., 1995; Wendl et al., 1994), but again, the effect appears to be due to constituents other than caffeine. Although there is a belief that caffeine beverages are contributory causes of peptic ulcer (Christensen et al., 1994), and there is clinical evidence that coffee (although probably not caffeine per se) may aggravate peptic ulcer bleeding (Lin et al., 1994; Perng et al., 1994), the epidemiologic evidence is contradictory regarding the population association between dietary factors, including coffee, and occurrence of peptic ulcer (Archimandritis et al., 1995; Johnsen et al., 1994).

Renal Function

Consumers often become aware that caffeine beverages stimulate an increased flow of urine, apparently to a greater extent than similar amounts of noncaffeine beverages. Indeed, caffeine does have diuretic effects, which appear to be due to an increase in renal blood flow and increased rate of glomerular filtration (Fredholm, 1984). Again, the diuretic action of caffeine is probably due to antagonism of endogenous adenosine, which is believed to have an antidiuretic regulatory role in renal function (Spielman & Thompson, 1982). Consistent with its diuretic potential, caffeine has been observed to exacerbate urinary incontinence in experimental studies involving particular populations. The drug was found to have contributed to nocturnal enuresis in chronic psychiatric inpatients (Edelstein et al., 1984) and to contribute to daytime and nighttime urinary incontinence in psychogeriatric inpatients (James, Sawczuk, et al., 1989). However, no association was observed between caffeine intake and urinary incontinence in a cross-sectional survey of healthy middle-aged women (Burgio et al., 1991). Caffeine has also been suspected of having a role in renal disease caused by excessive and prolonged use of analgesic compounds (Elseviers & De Broe, 1994). It is believed that physical dependence on caffeine may increase the likelihood of abuse of analgesic compounds, many of which contain caffeine.

Respiration

Caffeine is a respiratory stimulant (Pianosi et al., 1994), although its effects are modest at doses associated with usual patterns of consumption. At larger doses, discussed in Chapter 8, it has been found to be effective in the treatment of neonatal apnea (Brouard et al., 1985; Pearlman et al., 1989). Although caffeine has sometimes been regarded as having less potent bronchodilatory effects than the related methylxanthine, theophylline (Rall, 1990a), Becker et al. (1984) found no differences in airway responsiveness in children when comparing oral administrations of the two drugs. It has been suggested that caffeine use might attenuate the development of chronic bronchitis and pulmonary emphysema in cigarette smokers (Lima et al., 1989).

Neuroendocrine Function

Caffeine has been found to stimulate neuroendocrine activity commonly associated with psychophysiological stress. In particular, caffeine has been reported to increase serum and urinary levels of the catecholamine stress hormones epinephrine and norepinephrine (Bellet, Roman, et al., 1969; Graham & Spriet, 1991; Lane et al., 1990; Levi, 1967; Robertson et al., 1978). Increases in serum cortisol and/or urinary cortisol metabolites have also been reported (Avogaro et al., 1973; Bellet, Kostis, et al., 1969; Lane et al., 1990; Lovallo et al., 1989; Pincomb et al., 1987, 1988). However, findings have not been entirely consistent, especially in relation to cortisol, which several investigators have found to be unresponsive to caffeine (Daubresse et al., 1973; Lane, 1994; Oberman et al., 1975). It may be that these inconsistencies indicate that the typical challenge of about 250 mg (two to three cups of coffee) represents a "borderline dose" to which some people may be unresponsive (Spindel, 1984). Indeed, in one study, 250 mg of caffeine had no effect on cortisol, whereas 500 mg increased plasma cortisol levels (Spindel et al., 1984).

Energy Metabolism

Caffeine has been reported to increase basal metabolic rate (Acheson et al., 1980; Dodd et al., 1991; Jung et al., 1981; Poehlman et al., 1989) and plasma free fatty acid levels (Acheson et al., 1980; Dodd et al., 1991; Jung et al., 1981; Powers et al., 1983; Sasaki et al., 1987). In addition, caffeine has been observed to induce a dose-dependent thermogenic effect (Astrup et al., 1990), which appears to be due to increased lipid and carbohydrate oxidation (Bracco et al., 1995). Caffeine-induced thermogenesis has stimulated interest in the therapeutic potential of the drug as a pharmacological adjuvant in the management of weight loss (see Chapter 8).

Sleep and Insomnia

Caffeine is widely believed to be a cause of sleep disturbances, with many consumers reporting avoidance of caffeine beverages prior to bedtime. Overall, this perception and the behavior it engenders are supported by the scientific findings. Indeed, it has been suggested that insomnia can be modeled in people with normal sleep by administering caffeine close to bedtime (Bonnet & Arand, 1992; Karacan et al., 1976; Okuma et al., 1982). Research on caffeine and sleep can be categorized into three broad groupings, consisting of cross-sectional surveys, experimental studies involving subjective sleep measures, and experimental studies involving objective sleep measures (James, 1991).

Of the three main research approaches that have been used to investigate the effects of caffeine on sleep, cross-sectional surveys have yielded the least consistent results. Whereas some surveys have suggested a positive correlation between caffeine consumption and sleep problems (Hicks, Hicks, et al., 1983; Hicks, Kilcourse, et al., 1983; Pantelios et al., 1989), others reported no such association (e.g., Broughton & Roberts, 1985; Lack et al., 1988). Evidence implicating caffeine as a possible cause of sleep disturbance has been reported for renal dialysis patients, who as a group are known to report frequent sleep complaints (Holley et al., 1992; Walker et al., 1995). More consistent results have been obtained in experimental caffeine-challenge studies involving subjective sleep measures. These have generally found that caffeine is capable of delaying sleep onset and/or adversely affecting quality of sleep (Dorfman & Jarvik, 1970; Forrest et al., 1972; Goldstein et al., 1965; A. P. Smith, Maben, et al., 1993).

The most consistent results concerning caffeine and sleep have been provided by challenge studies conducted under sleep laboratory conditions involving objective measurements (e.g., EEG) of sleep parameters. These leave no doubt about the potential of caffeine to disrupt sleep, especially by increasing sleep onset latency (Bonnet & Webb, 1979; Brezinová, 1975; Karacan et al., 1976; Nicholson & Stone, 1980; Penetar et al., 1993; Rosenthal et al., 1991). Despite strong evidence that caffeine may disrupt sleep, these effects may not necessarily be discernible to the individual. Effects are likely to be most obvious when caffeine is consumed shortly before bedtime by people whose habitual use of the drug is comparatively low. Under such circumstances, the disruptive effects are also likely to be dose-dependent. Although there is evidence that repeated exposure leads to the development of tolerance to the disruptive effects of caffeine on sleep (Zwyghuizen-Doorenbos et al., 1990), it is not clear whether complete tolerance develops. If tolerance is partial, habitual caffeine consumers may suffer chronic caffeine-induced sleep disturbance, even if at a diminished level relative to the acute antisoporific effects of the drug in nonconsumers.

Drug Interaction Effects

Considering the near-universal use of caffeine, it is inevitable that usage of other drugs, taken for either recreational or therapeutic purposes, will often be concurrent with that of caffeine. In the simplest case, the effects of other drugs may be additive to those of caffeine. Alternatively, interactions may occur, whereby one drug moderates the actions of another, resulting in a potentiation or inhibition of the effects of one or both drugs.

Cigarette Smoking

Scores of population surveys have found that cigarette smokers generally consume more caffeine than nonsmokers, and this is consistent with the finding that smoking increases the rate of caffeine elimination (Campbell et al., 1987; Fraser et al., 1983; Hart et al., 1976; Joeres et al., 1988; Kotake et al., 1982; Parsons & Neims, 1978). Thus, smokers need to consume larger amounts of caffeine if they are to achieve plasma levels comparable to nonsmokers. However, at the level of the individual caffeine-consuming smoker, the exact relationship between caffeine intake and smoking frequency remains unclear. Caffeine-consuming smokers have been reported to inhale more nicotine when consuming decaffeinated than caffeinated coffee (Kozlowski, 1976), to smoke more when consuming coffee irrespective of caffeine content (Marshall et al., 1980a, 1980b), and not to smoke more when consuming coffee (Chait & Griffiths, 1983; Lane & Rose, 1995; Ossip et al., 1980). The question has also been raised as to whether attempts by smokers to quit may be affected by caffeine either alleviating or exacerbating smoking-withdrawal effects. However, caffeine intake has been found to be unrelated to smoking relapse rates (Hughes & Oliveto, 1993). Notwithstanding uncertainty concerning the relationship between the behaviors of caffeine consumption and cigarette smoking, there is consistent evidence regarding the cumulative hemodynamic effects when caffeine and nicotine are ingested concurrently. Specifically, caffeine-induced increases in blood pressure are essentially additive to nicotine-induced increases in blood pressure and heart rate (Freestone & Ramsay, 1982, 1983; Freestone et al., 1995; James & Richardson, 1991; Perkins, Sexton, Stiller, et al., 1994; Ray et al., 1986; Rose & Behm, 1991; Smits et al., 1993).

Alcohol

Surveys of caffeine and alcohol use have reported inconsistent results, with the two activities being found to be either positively correlated (Ayers et al., 1976; Cameron & Boehmer, 1982; Klatsky et al., 1973; Thomas et al., 1977; Zavela et al., 1990), negatively correlated (Dawber et al., 1974; Soeken & Bausell, 1989), or unrelated (Carmody et al., 1985; Conway et al., 1981; James et al., 1987; Marchand et al., 1989). A common belief about caffeine is that it can have the effect of counteracting the debilitating effects of alcohol intoxication, but the findings are inconsistent (Fudin & Nicastro, 1988; Nash, 1966). Studies of the effects of caffeine on alcohol-induced decrements in psychomotor and cognitive performance have reported varied results, including attenuation of alcohol-induced decreases in performance (Franks et al., 1975; Hasenfratz, Bunger, et al., 1993b; Moskowitz & Burns, 1981; Newman & Newman, 1956), potentiation (i.e., worsening of alcohol-induced decreases in performance (Oborne & Rogers, 1983), and no effect (Carpenter, 1959; Forney & Hughes, 1965; Nuotto et al., 1982). Overall, however, even when alcohol-induced decreases in performance were observed, effects were generally small and not uniform across different tasks.

Prescription Drugs

Particular concerns arise in relation to possible adverse interactions between caffeine and pharmaceutical drugs given for therapeutic purposes.

Benzodiazepines. The benzodiazepines, including diazepam, oxazepam, and lorazepam, are a widely used group of anxiolytic, sedative-hypnotic, muscle relaxant, and anticonvulsant drugs. Caffeine has been observed to antagonize the anxiolytic effects of widely prescribed benzodiazepines (File et al., 1982; Loke et al., 1985; Mattila et al., 1982; Roache & Griffiths, 1987), with several investigators suggesting that caffeine and the benzodiazepines may interact at the receptor level (Boulenger et al., 1982; Holloway et al., 1985; Marangos et al., 1981; Phillis et al., 1983). However, Roache and Griffiths (1987) have suggested that the lack of uniform antagonism across different functions for given dosage levels might mean that the observed antagonism involves functionally opposing effects rather than pharmacological antagonism. Caffeine has also been reported to attenuate benzodiazepine-induced decrements in learning and performance (Ghoneim et al., 1986; Johnson et al., 1990; Mattila et al., 1992; Roache & Griffiths, 1987; Rush, Higgins, Bickel, et al., 1994; Rush, Higgins, Hughes, et al., 1994). Thus, whatever the mechanism of action, evidence of antagonism is sufficiently consistent to suggest the need for caution whenever benzodiazepines are prescribed.

Fluroquinolones. Fluroquinolones (or simply, quinolones) are a group of broad spectrum antibiotics that have been shown to inhibit the hepatic enzyme system (cytochrome P-450) which is responsible for caffeine metabolism (Marchbanks, 1993; Nicolau et al., 1995; Rodvold & Piscitelli, 1993). Consequently, these drugs can cause as much as a fourfold inhibition of caffeine clearance (Carbó et al., 1989). The resulting accumulation of systemic caffeine is potentially harmful, with nausea and vomiting being prominent among the observed effects (Borcherding et al., 1996).

Adverse interactions with other therapeutic drugs. To date, no comprehensive assessment has been made of adverse drug interactions involving caffeine. In addition to those outlined above, the following have also been reported: Oral contraceptive steroids have been found to inhibit caffeine elimination by about 50% (Abernethy & Todd, 1985; Balogh et al., 1995; Patwardhan et al., 1980), thereby necessitating a decrease in caffeine intake if significantly increased plasma caffeine levels are to be avoided. Concern has been expressed in relation to possible adverse cardiovascular effects arising from the interaction between caffeine and phenylpropanolamine, a common oral decongestant (Bernstein & Diskant, 1982; Horowitz et al., 1980; Lake et al., 1989, 1990; Mueller et al., 1984; Pentel et al., 1982). Abrupt cessation of lithium, used in the treatment of some serious psychiatric conditions (e.g., bipolar disorders), has been found to produce significantly increased lithium blood levels, with an accompanying risk of toxicity (Jefferson, 1988; Mester et al., 1995). Caffeine has also been reported to counteract the sedative effects of the barbiturate hypnotic pentobarbital (Forrest et al., 1972). Finally, concern has also been expressed about adverse reactions to caffeine arising from the use of particular neuroleptic preparations used in the treatment of schizophrenia (Vainer & Chouinard, 1994).

■ Habitual Caffeine Consumption

With few exceptions, studies of the pharmacology of caffeine have employed a methodology involving acute caffeine challenge. Generally, a relatively large caffeine dose (typically equivalent to two to four cups of coffee) is administered after an overnight fast and a period of caffeine abstinence. Notwithstanding the suitability of this classic experimental approach for elucidating acute effects, there is no reason to believe that it has much potential for clarifying the chronic effects of habitual caffeine use, characterized by the daily ingestion of three to five caffeine beverages consumed at intervals. Because much of the present book is concerned with the effects of habitual use, it is important that consideration be given to processes initiated by repeated exposure. The processes of caffeine tolerance and physical dependence are of particular importance.

Tolerance

Drug tolerance refers to the progressive reduction in responsiveness that sometimes accompanies repeated exposure to a drug. It is evidenced by less effect being produced by the same dose, or an increased dose being required to produce the same effect. Tolerance has been demonstrated in a number of animal species (Griffiths & Mumford, 1995b), but it has been most widely studied in relation to the locomotor stimulant effects of the drug in rats (Finn & Holtzman, 1987; Holtzman, 1983; Holtzman & Finn, 1988). Because repeated exposure to caffeine has been reported to increase the number of adenosine receptors in the brain (Daly et al., 1994), it has sometimes been assumed that receptor upregulation is the mechanism underlying caffeine tolerance. However, Holtzman et al. (1991) have questioned the adenosine explanation on both theoretical and empirical grounds, including the fact that repeated exposure to caffeine produces change in several receptor systems, some or all of which may contribute to the observed effects (Daly et al., 1994; Holtzman et al., 1991; D. Shi et al., 1993). Nevertheless, in a recent study that compared the effects of two chronic dose regimens in rats, Lau and Falk (1995) concluded that upregulation of adenosine does explain the development of tolerance to the locomotor stimulant effects of caffeine in these animals.

Caffeine tolerance in humans has been reported in relation to the cardiovascular effects of the drug (Denaro et al., 1991; James, 1994a; Robertson et al., 1981), its subjective effects (Evans & Griffiths, 1992), and its disruptive effects on sleep (Zwyghuizen-Doorenbos et al., 1990). However, although there is little doubt that repeated exposure to caffeine leads to a degree of tolerance to some of its effects, it is highly doubtful whether complete tolerance occurs in the context of typical habitual patterns of consumption. In general, the response magnitude to successive doses is inversely proportional to plasma caffeine level (Smits et al., 1985b). Importantly, overnight abstinence, which characterizes usual patterns of consumption, results in almost complete depletion of systemic caffeine by early morning (Lelo, Birkett, et al., 1986; Pfeifer & Notari, 1988; J. Shi et al., 1993). Converging evidence, especially in relation to the hemodynamic effects of the drug (discussed in Chapter 5), suggests that the pattern of diurnal depletion of systemic caffeine experienced by most consumers ensures that tolerance is typically partial rather than complete. Indeed, the very fact that hundreds of experiments have reported significant caffeine-induced behavioral, physiological, and subjective effects provides convincing evidence that usual patterns of consumption do *not* produce complete tolerance. Most participants in such experiments have been habitual caffeine consumers who arrive at the experimental laboratory after having abstained overnight. Notwithstanding the brevity of the abstinence period, participants are generally observed to be caffeine responsive. Thus, although caffeine ingested during the day produces a progressive diminution in responsiveness to the drug (i.e., tolerance develops) (e.g., Goldstein et al., 1990; Lane & Manus, 1989), consumers begin each day resensitized (at least partially), because systemic caffeine levels are depleted by overnight abstinence (Smits et al., 1985b).

Physical Dependence

Drug physical dependence is indicated by the appearance of a characteristic syndrome of behavioral, physiological, and subjective disruption that is provoked by abrupt abstinence after a period of chronic use. Caffeine withdrawal effects have been demonstrated in animals and include decreased locomotor activity (Holtzman, 1983), decreased operant behavior (Carroll et al., 1989), and increased sleep (Sinton & Petitjean, 1989). As with tolerance, there is incomplete understanding of the mechanism responsible for physical dependence, although adenosine is implicated (Biaggioni et al., 1991; Paul et al., 1993; von Borstel & Wurtman, 1982; von Borstel et al., 1983). Chronic exposure to caffeine is believed to result in an increased number of adenosine receptors and/or enhanced receptor affinity, resulting in hypersensitivity to adenosine after abrupt withdrawal of caffeine. In humans, headache, sleepiness, and lethargy are the most frequent symptoms of caffeine withdrawal (Dreisbach & Pfeiffer, 1943; Goldstein et al., 1969; Greden et al., 1980; Griffiths et al., 1990; Hughes et al., 1991; Silverman et al., 1992; Smith, 1987; van Dusseldorp & Katan, 1990). Cessation of as little as 100 mg (one cup of coffee) per day can produce symptoms, which may begin within about 12 to 16 hours, peak at around 24 to 48 hours, and persist for up to 1 week (Griffiths et al., 1990; Hughes et al., 1993; Hughes, Oliveto et al., 1992). Typically, symptoms are relieved by ingesting caffeine. Several studies have reported caffeine withdrawal headache associated with surgical operations, the application of anesthesia, and other medical procedures (Fennelly et al., 1991; Galletly et al., 1989; Nikolajsen et al., 1994). Because patients are often required to fast (including abstaining from caffeine beverages) preparatory to medical operations, it is important that patients and physicians anticipate the possibility of caffeine withdrawal headache and other dysphoric symptoms. Similarly, a pattern of weekend caffeine withdrawal headache has been reported in people whose consumption of caffeine during weekends is less than during the week (Couturier et al., 1992).

▨ Some Possible Chronic Effects of Habitual Caffeine Use

Although this chapter is concerned primarily with the acute effects of caffeine on various physiological processes, the present section provides an overview of the possible involvement of habitual caffeine use in a variety of somatic syndromes not considered elsewhere in the book. Several cross-sectional surveys have reported an inverse association between self-reported caffeine intake and self-reported health status in adolescents (Hemminki et al., 1988) and adults (Gondola & Tuckman, 1983; James, Bruce, et al., 1989; James & Crosbie, 1987; James et al., 1987; Shirlow & Mathers, 1985). Despite the fact that these studies have generally attempted to control for various potential confounders (e.g., age, gender, cigarette smoking, and alcohol use), caution is needed in interpreting the results. A common problem with population surveys is that the observed relationship between caffeine intake and poorer health may be due to variables other than caffeine consumption that are part of a generalized pattern of poorer health behavior including heavier caffeine use.

Calcium Metabolism and Osteoporosis

Dietary calcium is required for healthy bone development during early life and to maintain skeletal integrity during later life. There is evidence of an increased risk of negative calcium balance (i.e., increased urinary and fecal excretion of calcium) due to caffeine intake (Heaney & Recker, 1982; Massey & Wise, 1984; Schaafsma et al., 1987), although findings have not been entirely consistent (Barger-Lux et al., 1990). Several recent epidemiologic studies have reported a positive association between caffeine consumption and bone fractures and/or decreased bone mass in women (Cummings et al., 1995; Hernandez-Avila et al., 1991, 1993; Kiel et al., 1990). Increased risk of bone fracture has also been reported to be associated with increased consumption of carbonated beverages (a significant proportion of which contain caffeine) in girls and boys (Wyshak & Frisch, 1994). However, several epidemiologic studies have reported little or no increased risk of fractures associated with increased caffeine consumption (Cooper et al., 1992; Cumming & Klineberg, 1994a; Johansson et al., 1992; Kreiger et al., 1992; Tavani et al., 1995). It has been suggested that some of the contradictory findings can be explained in terms of age of the cohort under study and dietary caffeine levels (Massey & Whiting, 1993). Overall, the available evidence suggests that lifelong consumption of caffeine may have progressively adverse effects on bone health and that such effects are most evident in older women whose calcium intake is low (Barrett-Connor et al., 1994; Bunker, 1994; Harris & Dawson-Hughes, 1994; Massey et al., 1994; Massey & Whiting, 1993). It has also been suggested that increased calcium excretion due to habitual caffeine consumption should be taken into account when formulating recommended levels of daily calcium intake (Schaafsma, 1992).

Miscellaneous Syndromes and Effects

Caffeine consumption has been associated with various dysfunctions for which too little literature exists to allow firm conclusions. These conditions include lower extremity arterial disease in elderly women (Vogt et al., 1993), increased risk of type 1 diabetes mellitus in children (Virtanen et al., 1994), urticaria or "hives" (Caballero et al., 1993; Pola et al., 1988), multiple sclerosis (Tola et al., 1994), and Raynaud's syndrome (Whitaker & Kelleher, 1994). In addition, caffeine-beverage consumption may entail risks not attributable to caffeine directly. For example, the tea plant is unusual in that it accumulates aluminum, which is potentially neurotoxic and has been implicated in the development of Alzheimer's disease (Duggan et al., 1992; Flaten & Ødegård, 1988). Moreover, it has been found that beverages (e.g., cola soft drinks) have a higher aluminum content when packaged in aluminum cans than when packaged in glass containers (Duggan et al., 1992; Jorhem & Haegglund, 1992). There is evidence, however, that only a small proportion of aluminum in tea is absorbed by the body (Drewitt et al., 1993; Fairweather-Tait et al., 1991; Powell et al., 1993). In addition, there are health risks associated with the production of caffeine beverages. These occupational hazards relate mainly to allergic symptoms of the eyes, nose, and respiratory system (De Zotti et al., 1988; Johansen & Viskum, 1987; Romano et al., 1995; Shirai et al., 1994; Uragoda, 1988; Zuskin et al., 1993).

SUMMARY

Much is known about the absorption, distribution, and metabolism of caffeine in humans. Although the mechanisms of action have still to be fully elucidated, it is generally accepted that antagonism of endogenous adenosine is the major mechanism. Through this mechanism, caffeine is capable of influencing a wide range of organ systems and physiological processes. If consumed in amounts greatly in excess of usual dietary levels, caffeine can have dangerous, even fatal, toxic effects. Although the longer term consequences of habitual consumption of typical dietary levels of caffeine are less clear, extensive experimentation has shown that even moderate intake has discernible acute effects on the central nervous system, the autonomic nervous system, the cardiovascular system, the gastrointestinal system, renal function, respiration, neuroendocrine function, energy metabolism, and sleep processes. Although the study of the effects of concurrent use of caffeine and other psychoactive compounds is underdeveloped, as is true of drug-interaction phenomena generally, numerous adverse interactions have been reported with other drugs taken for either recreational or therapeutic purposes. Overall, these findings provide strong justification for concern about the near-universal use of caffeine. Specific major concerns are treated in detail in the chapters that follow.

FURTHER READING

Fredholm, B. B. (1995). Adenosine, adenosine receptors, and the actions of caffeine. *Pharmacology and Toxicology, 76,* 93-101.

Harris, S. S., & Dawson-Hughes, B. (1994). Caffeine and bone loss in healthy postmenopausal women. *American Journal of Clinical Nutrition, 60,* 573-578.

Hughes, J. R., Higgins, S. T., Bickel, W. K., Hunt, W. K., Fenwick, J. W., Gulliver, S. B., & Mireault, G. C. (1991). Caffeine self-administration, withdrawal, and adverse effects among coffee drinkers. *Archives of General Psychiatry, 48,* 611-617.

Lane, J. D. (1994). Neuroendocrine responses to caffeine in the work environment. *Psychosomatic Medicine, 546,* 267-270.

Shi, J., Benowitz, N. L., Denaro, C. P., & Sheiner, L. B. (1993). Pharmaco-kinetic-pharmacodynamic modeling of caffeine: Tolerance to pressor effects. *Clinical Pharmacology and Therapeutics, 53,* 6-14.

Psychopharmacology of Caffeine

Scientific interest in the effects of caffeine on psychological processes began more than 100 years ago (Bridge, 1893; Hollingworth, 1912a, 1912b), and has persisted throughout the 20th century. Unfortunately, however, many fundamental aspects of the psychopharmacology of caffeine remain unclear. This situation is partly attributable to current limitations in the wider discipline of psychopharmacology, which has been criticized for not making adequate use of basic psychometric principles (Parrott, 1991a, 1991b, 1991c). A related criticism is that many of the psychometric tests commonly used by psychopharmacologists have unacceptably low reliability (Bittner et al., 1986). Lack of psychometric sophistication is evident in many studies of the psychopharmacology of caffeine, especially studies of the drug's effects on psychomotor and cognitive performance.

▨ Psychomotor and Cognitive Performance

Animal Studies

Studies of operant behavior in laboratory animals (e.g., learned bar pressing in rats) have provided important opportunities for examining the effects of drugs. In an early study, Skinner and Heron (1937) reported an increase in the rate of schedule-controlled operant responding in rats following administration of caffeine. Subsequent studies, however, have shown that the rate of responding tends to increase only when the initial rate is low, whereas higher response rates are typically decreased by caffeine (Ando, 1975; Davis et al., 1973; Goldberg et al., 1985; McKim, 1980; Meliska & Brown, 1982; Wayner et al., 1976; Webb & Levine, 1978). Another important tool for assessing drug effects has been the study of open-field behavior in animals, and increased spontaneous activity after caffeine has been reported in a variety of species, including dogs (Kusanagi et al., 1974), gerbils (Pettijohn, 1979), and race horses (Fujii et al., 1972). In rodents, spontaneous locomotor activity has been reported to increase in a dose-dependent manner for doses up to about 25 mg/kg (Calhoun, 1971; Gilbert, 1976; Holloway & Thor, 1983, 1984), but for doses above this level, activity is more likely to be depressed (File et al., 1988).

Although there is a degree of consistency in the effects of acute caffeine challenge on locomotor activity, the effects of chronic exposure to the drug appear to be less uniform. For example, chronic ingestion of caffeine was found to reduce locomotor exploratory activity in mice (Nikodijevic et al., 1993), whereas rats treated chronically appear to develop tolerance to the motor stimulant effects of the drug (Garrett & Holtzman, 1994a). In any event, it is unclear what implications caffeine-induced effects on relatively undifferentiated motor activity might have for more complex behavior. The empirical evidence suggests that performance of complex tasks is unlikely to be improved. For example, caffeine has been reported as having no effect on operant avoidance learning in mice (Sansone et al., 1994), no effect on motor control involving force discrimination in rats (Falk & Lau, 1991), and either no effect (Molinengo et al., 1994) or a disruptive effect (Kant, 1993) on maze learning in rats.

"Simple" Motor and Psychomotor Activity in Humans

Although locomotor activity has been a focus of interest in animal research on caffeine, there has been little research on the effects of the drug on locomotor activity in humans. Rapoport et al. (1981) reported increased gross motor activity, as measured by an ambulatory accelerometer, in children following ingestion of caffeine. In adults, effects depended on caffeine-consumer status. Compared to placebo, no significant changes in motor activity were observed in a low caffeine-consumer group, whereas activity was increased significantly after 10 but not 3 mg/kg of caffeine in a high consumer group (Rapoport et al., 1981). However, it appears that withdrawal from caffeine during a pre-experimental abstinence period may have produced decreased levels of motor activity in the high consumers and that subsequent exposure to caffeine may only have restored activity to pre-abstinence levels. In other words, the findings suggest that caffeine abstinence may produce decreased motor activity in habitual consumers.

Of the many indices of human performance that have been included in studies of caffeine, the most consistent results have been obtained in relation to what would appear to be one of the simplest of motor activities, namely, of tremor. Numerous studies have reported that caffeine increases tremor or *psychomotor agitation* (Gilliland & Bullock, 1984), particularly as measured by decreased hand steadiness (Chait & Griffiths, 1983; Franks et al., 1975; Ghoneim et al., 1986; Gilliland & Nelson, 1939; Hull, 1935; James, 1990; Lehmann & Csank, 1957; Loke et al., 1985; Richardson et al., 1995; Smith et al., 1977; Thornton et al., 1939; Wharrad et al., 1985). The practical implications of this effect are unclear, other than suggesting that caffeine might disrupt activities requiring precise motor control (Calhoun, 1971). With more complex behaviors, however, the findings have been considerably less consistent. The results have been inconsistent even for tapping (e.g., rapid movement of a stylus between two adjacent discs, depressions of a telegraph key), a behavior that superficially, at least, would appear to be as simple a "voluntary" act as any. There have been reports of increased tapping rate following caffeine (Fagan et al., 1988; Hollingworth, 1912a; Horst, Buxton, et al., 1934; Horst, Robinson, et al., 1934; Thornton et al., 1939), no effect (Alder et al., 1950; Flory & Gilbert, 1943), and decreased rate (Gilliland & Nelson, 1939).

Similarly, studies of reaction time have produced mixed results. Some studies have reported reduced (i.e., improved) reaction times after caffeine (Cheney, 1935, 1936; Gilliland & Nelson, 1939; Smith et al., 1977; Thornton et al., 1939); others have reported increased reaction times (Eddy & Downs, 1928; Hawk, 1929; Schilling, 1921), and still others have reported no change (Alder et al., 1950; Lehmann & Csank, 1957; Seashore & Ivy, 1953). Wenzel and Rutledge (1962) suggested that some of the inconsistencies may have been due to the use of different caffeine doses in different studies. For example, Horst and Jenkins (1935) found that 3 mg/kg of caffeine reduced reaction time, whereas the effects of 2 mg/kg were variable, and Jacobson and Edgley (1987) found that reaction time was reduced after 300 mg but was unaffected by 600 mg of caffeine. In a similar vein, Roache and Griffiths (1987) found that reaction time was improved more by a 400-mg dose of caffeine than by either 200 or 600 mg. Conversely, Zahn and Rapoport (1987) observed no effect on reaction time following administration of 3 and 10 mg/kg of caffeine, and Richardson et al. (1995) found that 70 mg reduced reaction time, but 250 mg had no effect. One explanation for these variable results is that reaction time, and hence measures of reaction time, are not as simple as might appear. Distinctions are sometimes made between a number of components, including "simple" reaction time, movement time, and choice reaction time, with each component possibly being affected differently by caffeine. Furthermore, reaction time is subject to influence by a variety of other factors that may or may not interact with caffeine, including the sense modality involved (e.g., auditory, visual), stimulus intensity, and the performer's precaffeine level of arousal (Estler, 1982; Wenzel & Rutledge, 1962).

Cognitive Performance

There is a long history of scientific interest in the effects of caffeine on cognitive performance, as measured by a wide variety of tasks involving a host of different information-processing demands, including memory span (Cattell, 1930), arithmetic addition (Barmack, 1940; Gilliland & Nelson, 1939), numerical reasoning (Franks et al., 1975; Lienert & Huber, 1966), reading speed and comprehension (Flory & Gilbert, 1943), learning of nonsense syllables (Hull, 1935), and solving of chess problems (Holck, 1933). One consequence of the diversity of measurements evident in these and subsequent studies is that systematic comparison between studies has been impeded. To the extent that reasonable comparisons can be made, they reveal a high level of inconsistent findings. An exhaustive account of these inconsistencies could easily occupy a whole chapter (if not an entire book). Table 3.1 provides a summary of just a few of the apparently inconsistent results. In addition to diversity in measurement, research on the cognitive effects of caffeine has also shown great diversity in other methodological features (e.g., caffeine dose, time of day, age, gender, and caffeine-consumer status of participants). Although methodological diversity has provided researchers with a seemingly endless source of speculative reasons for explaining discrepancies between their own and others' findings, no particular set of differences between studies provides an obvious explanation of the numerous inconsistencies.

One popular explanation of the many null results (a small sample of which is cited in Table 3.1) is that these could have been due to studies having insufficient statistical power (Type II error), attributable primarily to small sample size and proportionately large measurement error. Conversely, it should be noted that the overwhelming majority of studies included multiple cognitive tests, with individual measures typically being treated as separate dependent variables in the absence of appropriate statistical methods (e.g., multivariate analysis of variance, Bonferroni adjustment) for controlling experiment-wise error. Thus, it could be argued that the positive studies are more likely to have been in error, because of the unacceptably high risk of Type I error that would have existed in many studies.

Some Possible Patterns of Caffeine-Induced Performance Effects

Notwithstanding the confusing array of inconsistent findings, particular patterns of caffeine effects have been claimed in relation to a number of variables, including arousal, personality, and fatigue.

Arousal. In the field of psychopharmacology, there is a long history of interest in the relationship between psychophysiological arousal and performance (Parrott, 1991c). There is a general principle, embodied in the Yerkes-Dodson (1908) function, which states that the relationship between arousal and performance efficiency takes the form of an inverted U. That is, performance tends to be optimal at intermediate levels of arousal and less than optimal when persons are underaroused (e.g., bored, fatigued) or overaroused (e.g., anxious, "stressed"). Caffeine has provided interest be-

Table 3.1   Summary of Some of the Inconsistent Reports of the Effects of Caffeine on Various Performance Tasks

Task	Reported Effect on Performance	Authors
Digit-symbol substitution	None	Bruce et al., 1986; Lieberman, Wurtman, Emde, & Coviella, 1987; Lieberman, Wurtman, Emde, Roberts, et al., 1987; Rush, Higgins, Bickel, et al., 1994; Rush, Higgins, Hughes, et al., 1994
	Improved	File et al., 1982
Stimulus recognition	None	Linde, 1995; Pritchard et al., 1995; Rush, Higgins, Bickel, et al., 1994; Rush, Higgins, Hughes, et al., 1994
	Improved	Bättig & Buzzi, 1986; Yu et al., 1991
Vigilance	None	Bonnet & Arand, 1992; Linde, 1995; Loke & Meliska, 1984
	Improved	Fagan et al., 1988; Fine et al., 1994; Lieberman, Wurtman, Emde, & Coviella, 1987; Lieberman, Wurtman, Emde, Roberts, et al., 1987; Lorist et al., 1994; Smith et al., 1990, 1992; A. P. Smith, Maben, et al., 1994
Memory	None	Clubley et al., 1977; Erikson et al., 1985, males but not females; File et al., 1982; Loke et al., 1985; Rush, Higgins, Bickel, et al., 1994; Rush, Higgin, Hughes, et al., 1994
	Improved	Anderson & Revelle, 1994; Arnold et al., 1987, females but not males; Smith et al., 1992, 1993; A. P. Smith, Maben, et al., 1994
	Impaired	Arnold et al., 1987, males but not females; Erikson et al., 1985, females but not males; Terry & Phifer (1986)
Stroop test	None	Foreman et al., 1989, "low" caffeine dose
	Improved	Hasenfratz & Bättig, 1992
	Impaired	Foreman et al., 1989, "high" caffeine dose

cause of its purported membership in the class of drugs said to have stimulant properties (e.g., amphetamines, nicotine). Thus, many studies of the performance effects of caffeine have been conducted within the general framework of theory concerned with the relationship between arousal and performance.

Revelle, Anderson, Humphreys, and colleagues (Anderson & Revelle, 1982, 1983; Bowyer et al., 1983; Craig et al., 1979; Gilliland, 1980; Gilliland & Andress, 1981; Revelle et al., 1976, 1980) have conducted a series of experiments in which caffeine has been used to manipulate arousal. The findings of these various studies led Humphreys and Revelle (1984) to propose a general model of information processing. A central assumption of the model is that arousal (including that induced by caffeine) facilitates performance on tasks involving low memory load (e.g., simple information recognition or transfer) while hindering performance on tasks that place high demands on short-term memory functions (e.g., prose memory, word-list recall). Because many tasks involve a combination of information transfer and short-term memory, the overall relationship between performance and arousal is predicted to be curvilinear, in accordance with the inverted U pattern enshrined in the Yerkes-Dodson principle. This model could help to explain some of the inconsistent findings concerning the effects of caffeine on performance. For example, the null results in some caffeine studies may have been due to the use of tasks that combine information transfer and modest demands on memory processes. According to the Humphreys-Revelle model, the information transfer component of such tasks should be facilitated by caffeine-induced arousal, whereas the memory component should be affected adversely. Thus, depending upon the dose, the net effect could conceivably be an increase, a decrease, or no effect at all on overall performance on the task. However, one problem with trying to interpret the research findings on caffeine in this way is that it ignores the fact that inconsistent results have been frequent, even between studies that appear to have used similar tests of performance (see Table 3.1).

Personality. Interest in the effects of arousal (and, therefore, caffeine) on performance stems in part from Eysenck's (1967) theory of personality, which states that physiological arousal is a major differentiating factor between introverts and extroverts (Anderson & Revelle, 1983). To the extent that caffeine influences arousal, Eysenck's theory suggests that introverts should reach a point of optimal arousal at lower levels of intake than extroverts. Although there is some supportive evidence (Gilliland, 1980; Keister & McLaughlin, 1972; Meyer et al., 1983), Revelle et al. (1980) found that the impulsivity subscale of the Eysenck Personality Inventory was a more sensitive measure of trait arousal than introversion/extroversion and that the personality-caffeine interaction was influenced by the time of day at which participants were tested. Specifically, performance in high-impulsive persons was said to be facilitated by caffeine in the morning but impaired by caffeine in the evening, whereas performance in low-impulsive persons was impaired by caffeine in the morning and facilitated in the evening (Revelle et al., 1980). Although the originators of the proposed moderating influence of impulsivity on caffeine-induced performance effects have continued to obtain empirical results consistent with their thesis (Anderson & Revelle, 1994), other investigators have had less success. Partial confirmation has been reported by some (Gupta, 1991, 1993; Gupta et al., 1994; A. P. Smith, Maben, et al., 1994; A. P. Smith et al., 1991), whereas others have found the effects of caffeine on performance to be related to neither introversion/extroversion (Bättig & Buzzi, 1986) nor impulsivity (Erikson et al., 1985).

Fatigue. There has long been interest in the question of whether caffeine is capable of producing absolute improvements in psychomotor and cognitive performance or whether effects are limited to alleviating deficits caused by fatigue. In their influential review, Weiss and Laties (1962) suggested that the reports of caffeine-induced enhancement of performance were not restricted to performance that was already degraded by factors such as muscular fatigue, sleep deprivation, and boredom. While this general observation has been supported by some subsequent investigators (Baker & Theologus, 1972; Bättig & Buzzi, 1986; Kerr et al., 1991; Lieberman, Wurtman, Emde, & Coviella, 1987; Lorist et al., 1994; Regina et al., 1974), others have suggested that caffeine mostly reverses declines in performance on tasks of long duration (i.e., tasks likely to induce fatigue and boredom) (Fagan et al., 1988; Yu et al., 1991).

Caffeine dose and other moderators. To the extent that caffeine influences arousal, the Yerkes-Dodson principle would predict that any beneficial effects of the drug should be limited to amounts that induce optimum arousal levels. In turn, the amount of caffeine needed to produce optimum arousal may depend on other factors, such as wakefulness and fatigue, personality factors, and the consumer's history of caffeine use. Table 3.2 summarizes a number of task, performer, and setting characteristics that have been claimed to moderate the performance effects of caffeine. Lieberman and colleagues (Lieberman, Wurtman, Emde, & Coviella, 1987; Lieberman, Wurtman,

Table 3.2   Some Possible Moderators of Caffeine-Induced Performance Effects

Factor	Possible Moderators
Person	Age and gender Biobehavioral condition—fatigued; alcohol intoxicated Personality—introversion/extroversion; impulsivity Caffeine-consumer status—nonusers versus habitual consumers; "high" versus "low" usage Expectancies—expected effects of improvement versus impairment
Task	Stimulus type—auditory; visual Task demands—stimulus recognition; motor coordination; reaction time; memory Complexity—simple and repetitive motor and psychomotor responses versus varying and demanding cognitive tasks Familiarity—well-practiced versus novel Length—short versus long duration
Setting	Time of day Stimulus rich versus stimulus deprived

NOTE: The "moderators" summarized here are essentially speculative. It remains an open question whether caffeine has *any* reliable effects on performance (see text).

Emde, Roberts et al., 1987) reported significant enhancement of performance after as little as 32 mg of caffeine (less than a half cup of coffee) on tests of auditory vigilance and reaction time, but effects have only rarely been reported for such small amounts. Although there is little consistency in what constitutes the upper limit of an effective dose (a "large" dose in one study may be considered "moderate" in another), acute amounts in excess of 500 mg are unlikely to be beneficial (Hasenfratz & Bättig, 1994). It is widely believed that performance on "easy" tasks is more likely to be improved than performance on "complex" tasks (e.g., Snel, 1993), and this is consistent with the model of information processing proposed by Humphreys and Revelle (1984), which postulates that an individual's position on the arousal curve may enhance or impair performance depending upon task complexity. However, the empirical evidence for an association between caffeine dose and performance is not consistent for either relatively simple psychomotor tasks (Wenzel & Rutledge, 1962) or more complex cognitive tasks (see Table 3.1).

Expectancy. There is evidence that knowing whether or not caffeine has been ingested may influence the effects of the drug on performance (Fillmore & Vogel-Sprott, 1992; Fillmore et al., 1994; Mitchell et al., 1974). For example, Fillmore and Vogel-Sprott (1992) found that the performance effects of caffeine depended on what participants were led to expect. Of three groups that received placebo disguised as strong coffee, one group was led to expect that performance on a rotor pursuit task would be enhanced, a second group was led to expect that performance on the task would be impaired, and the third group received no information. A fourth (control) group received no beverage and therefore had no expectations about any effect on performance. Level of performance was consistent with what participants had been led to expect. Those who received no information performed no differently than the controls, whereas participants who received positive information performed significantly better and those who received negative information performed significantly worse than the controls.

Does Caffeine Merely Restore Performance Degraded by Abstinence?[1]

In light of the many inconsistencies between studies, even when positive caffeine-induced performance effects are reported, not to mention the numerous null results and the not uncommon reports of caffeine-induced impairment of performance, most reviewers have concluded that any enhancement of performance by caffeine is, at most, likely to be small and unstable. For example, Dews (1984) concluded that caffeine's effects on performance are too unreliable and capricious to be of any real importance. Similarly, Stavric (1988a) concluded that the effects are no more than "very slight and subtle" (p. 655), and James (1991) found that "caffeine bestows little if any benefit on cognitive and psychomotor performance" (p. 272). Moreover, most of the studies of caffeine and performance conducted over the past several decades contain a fundamental methodological flaw that has generally gone unnoticed until recently. The problem in question arises from the fact that (a) most people are caffeine users, and (b) experimental studies of caffeine (as with drug trials in general) typically require participants to be free of the drug under examination (caffeine in this instance) for a period immediately preceding the trial. Because caffeine abstinence produces a variety of withdrawal effects in habitual users, improvements in performance following the experimental administration of caffeine may simply involve restoration (to normal) of performance that has been degraded during the pretrial period of caffeine abstinence. A similar flaw has also recently been identified in much of the psychopharmacological research on nicotine (Heishman & Henningfield, 1994; Heishman et al., 1993; Hughes, 1991).

This general problem can be illustrated by reference to a recent series of studies by A. P. Smith and colleagues (Smith, Brockman, et al., 1993; Smith et al., 1990, 1991, 1992). These authors claim to have demonstrated great and global benefits of caffeine (A. P. Smith, Brockman, et al., 1993), and have described their experimental approach as a model that others should emulate (A. P. Smith, Brockman, et al., 1993; Smith et al., 1991, 1992). In a recent study, A. P. Smith, Brockman, et al. (1993) examined 24 student volunteers who were tested under three conditions: decaffeinated coffee with 1.5 or 3 mg/kg caffeine added, decaffeinated coffee only, and fruit juice. Measurements were taken during two 8.5-hour shifts (one during the day and one overnight), and included a number of tests of psychomotor performance. Generally, performance was better, and subjects reported increased alertness during both the day and night, after caffeine (both doses), than after either decaffeinated coffee or juice, with no difference between the two caffeine-free conditions. On the basis of this general pattern of results, the authors concluded that caffeine enhances performance. However, this interpretation is open to challenge, because the participants were all moderate coffee drinkers (two to four cups per day). The question arises as to whether the superior performance observed during the caffeine condition was due to actual enhancement by caffeine, or whether the observed differences between the conditions were due to performance and alertness being degraded by caffeine withdrawal in the two caffeine-free conditions.

As discussed elsewhere in this book, there is extensive literature showing that caffeine withdrawal has significant adverse effects (e.g., Griffiths & Mumford, 1995a; Griffiths & Woodson, 1988a). Typically, abstinence results in reports of headache and other dysphoric symptoms, including drowsiness, irritability, impaired concentration, and lethargy (Hughes et al., 1991; Silverman et al., 1992; van Dusseldorp & Katan, 1990). Considering the severity of the dysphoric effects reported by some individuals (e.g., "extreme," "totally incapacitating"; Griffiths & Mumford, 1995a), it is to be expected that some aspects of performance might also be impaired. However, although relatively few studies have examined the effects of withdrawal on objective indices of performance (compared to the number that have studied subjective effects), withdrawal-induced performance impairments have been reported in relation to a variety of psychomotor, vigilance, and cognitive tasks

(Bruce et al., 1991; Fine et al., 1994; Griffiths et al., 1986; Horst, Buxton, et al., 1934; Hughes et al., 1991; Mitchell & Redman, 1992; Rizzo et al., 1988; Silverman et al., 1992).

Caffeine-consumer status. One alternative to the strategy of measuring performance after a period of caffeine abstinence is to compare people who differ in terms of their habitual use of caffeine. A cross-sectional survey of a representative sample of over 9,000 British adults showed a dose-response relationship to improved cognitive performance for each of four separate cognitive tests (Jarvis, 1993). These results not only suggest the possibility that habitual caffeine consumption might enhance overall cognitive performance, but that such improvements are also resistant to the development of tolerance. However, findings have not been consistent (Jacobson & Thurman-Lacey, 1992; Loke & Meliska, 1984; Richardson et al., 1995). For example, Loke and Meliska (1984) found that on a vigilance task, high users made significantly fewer hits and more false alarms, but responded faster, than low users. Recently, Richardson et al. (1995) found that acute caffeine intake affected performance similarly in habitual consumers experiencing caffeine withdrawal, consumers not experiencing withdrawal, and infrequent consumers. Notwithstanding the inconsistencies, it is difficult to assess the implications of results showing consumer-associated performance differences. Caffeine use is self-selected, and performance differences between consumers and nonconsumers may be due to factors other than (but associated with) caffeine use. Moreover, it is conceivable that caffeine has different effects on people who choose to consume the drug and those who do not, which in turn may influence whether a person becomes a consumer.

Caffeine pretreatment. In a recent study, Warburton (1995) sought to determine whether improved performance following ingestion of caffeine is absolute or due to restoration of abstinence-induced impairment. Eighteen healthy, young, nonsmoking, habitual coffee consumers participated in three laboratory sessions during which they ingested either placebo, or 75 or 150 mg of caffeine. One hour before each session, subjects were pretreated with 75 mg of caffeine (equivalent to a weak cup of coffee) in order that they would be "without caffeine abstinence" at the time of testing in the laboratory. Relative to the placebo condition, performance was found to be improved following ingestion of caffeine. However, the claim that the study shows that caffeine has absolute performance-enhancing effects not attributable to restoration of impaired performance is unwarranted. The main design flaw was that pretreatment consisted of a fixed amount of caffeine (i.e., 75 mg) for all participants, on the apparent assumption that abstinence effects would be eliminated uniformly. However, if it is assumed that level of habitual caffeine use varied between participants (we are told only that participants consumed "more than three cups per day"), it seems unlikely that abstinence effects would have been uniformly affected. Pretreatment might only have been partially effective in eliminating abstinence effects. This shortcoming could possibly have been overcome by measuring participants' usual systemic caffeine levels at times designed to coincide with the experiment, and by ensuring that equivalent systemic levels were induced by the pretreatment regimen.

Systematic manipulation of habitual consumption. Considering the well-documented subjective effects of caffeine withdrawal (e.g., Griffiths & Mumford, 1995a; James, 1991), it is clear that unconfounded caffeine-induced enhancement of performance cannot be demonstrated by the drug-challenge approach used in the overwhelming majority of studies conducted to date. Similarly, although studies of the relationship between performance and caffeine-consumer status are useful, they are limited by the fact that user status is self-selected rather than experimenter-controlled. Although the pretreatment strategy described by Warburton (1995) may have promise, a more effective strategy would be to manipulate habitual consumption directly. Specifically, studies are needed in which "run-in" periods are employed whereby participants either maintain their usual daily intake of the drug or remain caffeine-free. Each run-in period would need to continue for at least 1 week, in order to allow tolerance to develop and reach steady state during the caffeine-intake period, and for withdrawal effects to abate during the abstinent period. This type of protocol has been used to examine the chronic effects of habitual caffeine consumption on blood pressure (James, 1994b, see Chapter 5), but no such studies have been reported in relation to the effects of caffeine on performance.

Caffeine and Performance in Everyday Life

There is evidence that caffeine is sometimes used in the workplace to manage diurnal fluctuations in arousal (e.g., Dekker et al., 1993), although the effect of the drug on the quality of sleep in shiftworkers remains unclear.

Dekker et al. (1993) reported that caffeine use and reported sleep length in shiftworkers were inversely correlated, whereas others observed no association between these variables (Greenwood et al., 1996; Phillips & Danner, 1995). Notwithstanding these mixed findings, several authors have suggested that caffeine could serve as a useful antidote to sleepiness in shiftworkers (Bonnet & Arand, 1994a, 1994b; A. P. Smith, Brockman, et al., 1993; Walsh et al., 1990). However, for both scientific and health reasons, the use of caffeine as a prophylactic in the workplace is unwarranted. Most of the evidence on caffeine and sleep (reviewed in Chapter 4) concerns the effects of relatively large single doses administered after periods of caffeine abstinence. Comparatively little is known about the effects of *habitual* caffeine consumption on sleep, although it appears that the antisoporific effects of the drug are at least partially diminished by acquired tolerance (e.g., Bonnet & Arand, 1992). The benefits, if any, to be derived from the use of caffeine in relation to shiftwork may be offset by associated adverse withdrawal effects, especially when rotating shifts are involved. Above all, the habitual use of caffeine is contraindicated because of potential adverse health consequences (described in later chapters), including cardiovascular risks, threats to the reproductive health of women, and possible adverse interactions with other substances including prescribed medications. For these various reasons, attempts to promote the prophylactic use of caffeine in the workplace should be regarded as contrary to the occupational health and safety of the workers involved.

In addition to the potential general harm to health described elsewhere in this book, habitual use of caffeine could be harmful in ways specific to the settings in which it is used. For example, U.S. aviators whose job it was to patrol the "No Fly Zone" in southern Iraq following the Gulf War were provided with caffeine tablets to use during missions. The dosing regimen also included advice to avoid caffeine for 24 to 48 hours before missions, so as to maximize in-flight "benefits" (Belland & Bissell, 1994). It may be assumed that abstinence would have caused some aviators to experience caffeine-withdrawal headache, impaired attention, and other dysphoric effects, possibly undermining the effectiveness of crucial preflight preparation, with potentially disastrous results during missions. Moreover, processes of state-dependent learning (e.g., Lowe, 1988) could further undermine retrieval of vital information acquired during preflight preparation (caffeine abstinent) to inflight operations (caffeine sated). A more mundane example, but one having no less potentially disastrous outcomes, is Operation Coffee

Break, a scheme introduced in some parts of Australia, whereby rest bays, equipped with facilities dispensing free coffee, have been constructed at intermittent points on long stretches of highway. Notwithstanding the possible benefits of rest stops (with or without coffee), ready access to caffeine could exacerbate the fatigue and inattention experienced during stages of a long journey involving highways not equipped with free coffee-dispensing facilities. Indeed, the *Diagnostic and Statistical Manual of Mental Disorders* (*DSM-IV*; American Psychiatric Association, 1994) refers specifically to a disorder involving sleepiness between doses of caffeine, which may occur as the immediate stimulant effect wanes.

Subjective Effects

To the extent that caffeine has subjective effects, it is conceivable that the putative performance effects of the drug are an indirect effect of changed mood rather than the result of the drug acting directly on information-processing centers in the brain. Certainly, many of the studies of caffeine and performance reviewed above also reported significant change on a variety of subjective indices. However, this also means that the methodological shortcomings described in the preceding section may also apply to studies of the subjective effects of caffeine. Nevertheless, it is interesting to note that mood changes appear to have been reported more consistently than performance effects. For example, Goldstein et al. (1965) found that adult consumers who abstained from caffeine beverages throughout the day rated themselves more alert and physically active after caffeine, despite showing no improvement on objective tests of performance. In a later study, Goldstein et al. (1969) compared the effects of caffeine and placebo in two groups, one of which reported drinking no coffee while the other reported drinking five cups or more daily. In the experiment, before drinking coffee, habitual consumers reported feeling less alert, less active, less content/at ease, more sleepy, and more irritable than the abstainers, but these differences were removed after caffeine was consumed. On days placebo was consumed, the differences persisted, with the habitual consumers also reporting more frequent headache and feeling more jittery/nervous/shaky than nonconsumers.

Although reports of positive subjective effects of the kind observed by Goldstein et al. (1965, 1969) have been numerous (e.g., Bruce et al., 1986;

Chait & Johanson, 1988; Griffiths et al., 1990; Griffiths & Woodson, 1988a; Lieberman, Wurtman, Emde, & Coviella, 1987; Lieberman, Wurtman, Emde, Roberts, et al., 1987; Silverman & Griffiths, 1992; Smith et al., 1992, A. P. Smith, Brockman, et al., 1993, A. P. Smith, Kendrick, et al., 1994; Stern et al., 1989; Warburton, 1995), null findings have also been reported (e.g., King & Henry, 1992; Rush, Higgins, Bickel, et al., 1994; Svensson et al., 1980), as have dysphoric effects such as increased ratings of anxiety, tension, anger/hostility, and jitteriness (Chait & Griffiths, 1983; Charney et al., 1984; Evans & Griffiths, 1991; Loke, 1988; Loke et al., 1985; Oliveto et al., 1993; Richardson et al., 1995; Roache & Griffiths, 1987). As with research on caffeine and performance, the overwhelming majority of studies on the subjective effects of caffeine have included multiple measurements of mood. Consequently, the risk of Type I error was probably unacceptably high in the many studies that did not employ appropriate statistical methods to control error rates. Indeed, when Christensen et al. (1991) applied Bonferroni correction to the results of a study of caffeine-induced changes in mood, effects that had previously been apparent no longer reached the minimum conventional level of statistical significance.

Expectancy and Subjective Effects

Just as studies described above showed that the performance effects of caffeine may be influenced by expectations, it appears that expectations may also influence subjective effects. Goldstein (1964) observed that participants who were informed that they had received caffeine were less likely to report wakefulness than those who did not know whether they had received the drug or a placebo. Similar findings have been reported by Kirsch and his colleagues (Kirsch & Rosadino, 1993; Kirsch & Weixel, 1988). In the more recent study, subjective ratings of alertness and tension were compared for participants who received coffee that was either caffeinated (caffeine group) or decaffeinated (placebo group). Within both groups (caffeine versus placebo), participants were told that the beverage contained either (a) caffeine, (b) no caffeine, or (c) either caffeine or no caffeine (double-blind condition). Increased ratings of alertness were reported following caffeine (whether or not participants were told that they had received the drug), and further increases in alertness were reported when subjects were correctly informed that they had received caffeine. In addition, participants reported increases in alertness when they thought they might receive caffeine, whether caffeine was administered or not (double-blind condition). Conversely, participants reported increased tension only when they were told that they had received caffeine and they actually did. Increased tension was not reported when caffeine was disguised as placebo.

The level of consistency in the pattern of subjective effects reported in many studies is suggestive of a real (albeit subtle) effect. This effect is typically reported as a slight increase in general alertness, which most consumers apparently experience as mild enhancement of mood. However, consumer perceptions of the mood-enhancing properties of caffeine may be somewhat misleading, because changes in mood induced by caffeine are probably often partly due to alleviation of withdrawal-induced dysphoric effects. Nevertheless, reports of reliable subjective effects in consumers who were maintained on an otherwise caffeine-free diet (Griffiths & Mumford, 1995b) suggest that not all (although possibly most) of the subjective effects of caffeine ingestion by habitual consumers can be explained in terms of alleviation of withdrawal effects. Moreover, when caffeine is consumed in amounts exceeding that which is typical of caffeine beverages (or in excess of that which the individual habitually consumes), effects may be experienced as aversive anxiety, jitteriness, or nervousness (Griffiths & Mumford, 1995b).

Children

There is evidence that children are less likely than adults to report subjective effects following ingestion of caffeine (Elkins et al., 1981; Hale et al., 1995; Rapoport et al., 1981). It is unclear, however, whether this difference suggests less susceptibility to caffeine in children. Hale et al. (1995) canvassed a number of possible explanations, namely, that children actually experience fewer caffeine-induced subjective effects, children report subjective effects less reliably than adults, or the self-report scales that have been used are less sensitive to subjective effects in children. A further possible explanation is suggested by the finding (discussed below) that ability to discriminate the subjective effects of caffeine can be greatly improved by practice (Evans & Griffiths, 1991; Griffiths et al., 1990; Oliveto et al., 1992, 1993; Silverman & Griffiths, 1992). Having fewer years of experience as caffeine consumers, children will generally have had fewer opportunities than most adults to learn to discriminate the effects of the drug.

Stimulus Properties of Caffeine

There is a long tradition of research, often animal based, on the stimulus properties of self-administered drugs, the results of which are important in understanding the potential that different drugs may have for fostering dependence and/or abuse. For present purposes, there are two main stimulus features of interest with respect to self-administered drugs, *discrimination* and *reinforcement.*

Discriminative Stimulus Properties

A typical drug discrimination paradigm involves training animals or humans to choose between one of two available responses, one of which has been associated with the drug while the other has been associated with placebo. Overton (1973) found that rats required to make left or right turns in a T-maze in order to escape electric shock failed to discriminate whether they had or had not received caffeine, even after extensive training. In contrast, the same T-maze discrimination was readily learned when amphetamine was used. Somewhat more success has been achieved in discrimination studies with humans. Blount and Cox (1985) found that caffeine in doses of 200, 400, and 600 mg, in either capsule form or coffee, could be reliably discriminated from no caffeine. In addition, Chait and Johanson (1988) found that only a minority of participants could discriminate the presence of a 100-mg dose, whereas the majority succeeded in discriminating a 300-mg dose. The combined findings of Blount and Cox (1985) and Chait and Johanson (1988) suggest that the threshold for discriminating caffeine lies between 100 and 200 mg received as a single dose (i.e., between one and two cups of coffee). Even so, the 300-mg caffeine dose used by Chait and Johanson (1988) was discriminated considerably less well than amphetamine, which was correctly identified by all participants.

It is clear that ability to discriminate caffeine generally increases as dose increases (Griffiths & Mumford, 1995b). However, recent studies have also shown that the ability to discriminate caffeine varies considerably between individuals and that training can improve discrimination markedly (Evans & Griffiths, 1991; Griffiths et al., 1990; Oliveto et al., 1992, 1993; Silverman & Griffiths, 1992). In one study, for example, participants earned money for correctly guessing whether a capsule that had been ingested contained caffeine (Silverman & Griffiths, 1992). Initial training led to the majority of participants being able to reliably discriminate capsules containing 178 mg of caffeine. Further training resulted in some participants being able to discriminate amounts ranging from 32 to 100 mg and one individual being able to discriminate as little as 18 mg of caffeine (about one fifth of a cup of coffee).

Although not expressly designed to examine the discriminative stimulus properties of caffeine, several studies have provided data on the accuracy with which participants in caffeine experiments involving double-blind procedures were able to guess whether they had received caffeine. The results of these studies provide useful information about the discriminability of caffeine. In a number of studies, the majority of participants accurately guessed when they had received the drug rather than placebo (Loke et al., 1985; Loke & Meliska, 1984; Uematsu et al., 1987). However, these studies generally employed a single moderate-to-strong acute caffeine challenge, and the findings may not be representative of everyday caffeine use. In a recent study that more closely resembled the conditions under which caffeine is ordinarily consumed, the drug was poorly discriminated (James, 1994b). The study, described in more detail in Chapter 5, continued for 4 weeks, during which participants alternated between caffeine and placebo under double-blind conditions. Participants' success in guessing whether they had received caffeine or placebo was found to be no better than chance. Thus, although high levels of discrimination can be achieved with training, it appears that under ordinary circumstances the majority of consumers may not discriminate moderate amounts of the drug much above chance levels, if at all.

Reinforcing Properties

A reinforcer is any behavior-contingent consequence that maintains behavior. The behavior of ingesting certain beverages (e.g., coffee and tea) has the consequence of delivering to the body a modest amount of caffeine. Given that caffeine is the most widely self-administered drug in the world, it seems likely that the consumption of the beverages in which it occurs is reinforced by its presence. It is only recently, however, that caffeine's reinforcing properties have been systematically investigated. Self-injection studies have shown that caffeine is a weak and inconsistent reinforcer in rats and nonhuman primates, and is certainly less robust than prototypic or "classic" drugs of abuse (e.g., alcohol, amphetamines, cocaine, opioids) in these animals (Griffiths & Woodson, 1988b; Heishman & Henningfield,

1994). In humans, several studies using choice and/or self-administration procedures involving moderate caffeine users found that caffeine functioned as a reinforcer in only a minority of participants (Griffiths & Woodson, 1988a; Hale et al., 1995; Hughes et al., 1991; Hughes, Hunt, et al., 1992; Oliveto et al., 1992). Somewhat stronger evidence of caffeine reinforcement has been demonstrated by Griffiths and his colleagues in studies involving heavy consumers (Griffiths et al., 1986, 1989), although more recent studies by this group have also demonstrated caffeine reinforcement in a majority of participants who were moderate consumers (Evans et al., 1994; Silverman et al., 1994). In one study, participants not only demonstrated consistency in choosing caffeine over placebo but also showed enhanced preference for caffeine when a vigilance activity was to be performed following ingestion of the drug (Silverman et al., 1994).

Evans et al. (1994) examined caffeine versus placebo in moderate consumers over a 24-week period. Each week consisted of three consecutive daily sessions (2 sampling days followed by a choice day), during which participants were required to abstain from dietary sources of caffeine. On each sampling day, participants ingested one capsule every 2 hours over 8 hours. Capsules contained placebo on one sampling day and caffeine on the other, each being associated with a different color code. At the beginning of the choice day, participants chose one of the two color-coded capsules they wished to consume on that day. They ingested one capsule and thereafter ingested up to six additional capsules of the same color during the remainder of the day. Caffeine was chosen by a majority of subjects on a majority of occasions they were permitted to choose between caffeine and placebo. One important feature of this study was that participants maintained their usual caffeine intake on nonexperimental days, suggesting that habitual consumption may be a contributing factor in the development of caffeine reinforcement.

Specifically, it appears that caffeine reinforcement is potentiated by the effects of caffeine withdrawal (Hughes et al., 1993, 1995; Rogers et al., 1995). For example, Hughes et al. (1995) found that the occurrence of withdrawal effects (e.g., increased headache and drowsiness) predicted caffeine reinforcement, as indicated by participants' choice of caffeine over placebo. Similarly, Rogers et al. (1995) investigated caffeine reinforcement by assessing changes in preference for a novel drink (fruit juices specially prepared so as to be distinctive in flavor and color while also being palatable) consumed with and without caffeine. Caffeine had no significant effects on drink preference (or mood) in participants whose habitual level of caffeine consumption was low. In moderate users, however, overnight caffeine abstinence effects were alleviated by the drug, and these participants also showed a distinct preference for the drinks that contained caffeine. Overall, then, it appears that caffeine generally functions as a weak and inconsistent positive reinforcer. However, in habitual consumers, the reinforcing properties of the drug are markedly potentiated by a period of abstinence. Under these circumstances, caffeine appears to function as a reliable *negative* reinforcer, whereby aversive withdrawal effects are ameliorated by ingesting the drug (Hughes et al., 1993, 1995; Rogers et al., 1995).

SUMMARY

Knowing whether caffeine enhances performance is important theoretically, because the existence of consistent and reliable effects would reveal something about the essential nature of human information processing. Unfortunately, however, the available empirical evidence falls short of permitting firm conclusions about whether caffeine has *any* consistent beneficial effects on human performance. The persistent assertion that caffeine produces "a more rapid and clearer flow of thought" (Ritchie, 1975; Rall, 1985, 1990a) cannot be sustained. Whatever benefits do exist are almost certain to be small, unstable, and essentially inconsequential for most practical purposes. The not uncommon suggestion that a sustained performance advantage (e.g., in the workplace) can be obtained through the habitual consumption of caffeine is ill-founded, particularly in light of the associated health risks discussed in the chapters that follow. The fact that commercial interests representing the caffeine industry have committed substantial resources to promoting the message that coffee and tea are beneficial (see Chapter 9) is further cause for maintaining a skeptical stance with respect to such claims (James, 1994a, 1995a, 1995b). Even the more modest suggestion that habitual use of caffeine might smooth out transient dips in arousal (and, therefore, performance) during the normal waking state (Bättig & Welzl, 1993; Davidson, 1991; Dews, 1984) is dubious. An equally strong argument can be put that diurnal variability in arousal is likely to be exacerbated by habitual caffeine use, because in addition to arousal "highs," daily periods of abstinence (e.g., overnight) might exacerbate arousal lows.

The presence or absence of subjective effects is the probable basis upon which individuals judge whether or not a drug has been ingested. As such, the existence of caffeine-induced subjective effects is supported by objective evidence of caffeine discrimination. In general, it appears that without special training the presence of caffeine in moderate amounts is only weakly discriminated (if at all) by most people, thereby supporting the conclusion that the drug produces subjective effects that are generally experienced as comparatively slight and subtle. In this respect, caffeine is certainly quantitatively (if not qualitatively) different from classic drugs of abuse (e.g., alcohol, amphetamines, cocaine, opioids). That is, it has psychoactive effects, but these are comparatively slight and not well-discriminated. Furthermore, the findings for caffeine as a reinforcer are consistent with studies of the discriminative stimulus and subjective effects of the drug. That is, whereas the psychoactive, discriminative stimulus, and reinforcing properties of caffeine are weak in the absence of habitual consumption, each of these properties is enhanced when the drug is consumed following a period of abstinence.

Finally, it is well to remember that whatever effects might be demonstrated on tests of performance currently used in psychopharmacology laboratories, little is known about the relevance of such tests to performance in everyday settings. As Parrott (1991c) explained, "although many tests can be seen as measures of 'information processing,' the inference that they provide indices of 'real-life performance' can rarely be made on current evidence" (p. 197). Thus, future studies of caffeine should seek to assess the effects of the drug in natural settings, paying due regard to patterns of habitual usage (dosage, repeated intermittent exposure) and including an appropriate time frame to allow for the separate assessment and control of caffeine tolerance and withdrawal.

■ Note

1. This section is based in part on a previously published commentary (James, 1994c) and associated correspondence (James, 1995a; Smith, 1995).

FURTHER READING

Fillmore, M. T., Mulvihill, L. E., & Vogel-Sprott, M. (1994). The expected drug and its expected effect interact to determine placebo responses to alcohol and caffeine. *Psychopharmacology, 115,* 383-388.

Griffiths, R. R., & Mumford, G. K. (1995). Caffeine reinforcement, discrimination, tolerance, and physical dependence in laboratory animals and humans. In C. R. Schuster, S. W. Gust, & M. J. Kuhar (Eds.), *Pharmacological aspects of drug dependence: Towards an integrated neurobehavioral approach. Handbook of experimental pharmacology.* New York: Springer-Verlag.

Heishman, S. J., & Henningfield, J. E. (1992). Stimulus functions of caffeine in humans: Relation to dependence potential. *Neuroscience and Behavioral Reviews, 16,* 273-287.

Hughes, J. R., Oliveto, A. H., Bickel, W. K., Higgins, S. T., & Badger, G. J. (1995). The ability of low doses of caffeine to serve as reinforcers in humans: A replication. *Experimental and Clinical Psychopharmacology, 3,* 358-363.

Parrott, A. C. (1991). Performance tests in human psychopharmacology (1): Test reliability and standardization. *Human Psychopharmacology, 6,* 1-9.

Caffeine and Psychopathology

In the previous chapter, mention was made of the fact that caffeine may elicit reports of anxiety, jitteriness, and nervousness when the drug is ingested in amounts that exceed the individual's usual intake. On such occasions, the dysphoria is typically mild and transient, abating when plasma caffeine concentration returns to levels that are usual for that individual. The present chapter is concerned with caffeine-associated acute and/or chronic psychological effects that are so pronounced as to warrant clinical attention.

Caffeine-Induced Mental Disorders

The apparent decline in the formerly used term, *caffeinism*, is reflected in the terminology employed in successive editions of the American Psychiatric Association's influential *Diagnostic and Statistical Manual of Mental Disorders*. The revised third edition, *DSM-III-R* (American Psychiatric Association, 1987), offered *caffeine intoxication* and *caffeinism* as synonyms. Although the coverage for caffeine has been expanded substantially in the most recent edition, *DSM-IV* (1994), the term *caffeinism* has been dropped.

The main *DSM-IV* entry for caffeine is *caffeine intoxication,* which appears in the section on "caffeine-related disorders" within the broader category of substance-related disorders. The section includes two additional caffeine diagnoses, *caffeine-induced anxiety disorder* and *caffeine-induced sleep disorder.* A fourth diagnosis, *caffeine-related disorder not otherwise specified,* is included in an appendix of *DSM-IV.*

Caffeine Intoxication

The *DSM-IV* (1994) criteria for the diagnosis of caffeine intoxication are shown in Table 4.1. Criterion A indicates that the diagnosis may be made even when relatively moderate amounts of caffeine are involved, namely, an amount *usually* exceeding 250 mg (e.g., more than two to three cups of brewed coffee). As such, there appears to be a contradiction between the signs and symptoms listed under Criterion B in Table 4.1 and the empirical findings reviewed in Chapters 2 and 3. With the possible exception of cases involving significantly compromised liver function, the clinical cases described in Chapter 2 involved amounts of caffeine substantially larger than 250 mg. Indeed, the large volume of literature summarized in Chapter 3 indicates that most people experience only mild effects when ingesting caffeine up to about 400 mg (even when taken as a single dose). Thus, notwithstanding possible rare cases of peculiar sensitivity, there is little evidence that caffeine at the lower amounts specified in *DSM-IV* has effects that could reasonably be described as indicative of intoxication.

Further problems with the *DSM-IV* (1994) diagnosis of caffeine intoxication occur in relation to the particular symptoms that are purported to be involved. Although the attempt to specify observable (i.e., objective) diagnostic signs and symptoms is to be applauded, the criteria listed in Table 4.1 are nevertheless arbitrary and inexact, as was argued previously (James, 1991) in relation to a very similar set of criteria contained in *DSM-III-R* (1987). For example, it is not clear what constitutes restlessness, nervousness, and excitement, and how these signs differ from one another. Moreover, in the absence of further information, it is unclear whether muscle twitching, "rambling flow of thought and speech," periods of inexhaustibility, and psychomotor agitation are themselves indicators of anything other than restlessness, nervousness, and excitement. That is, it appears that these seven criteria, with the possible addition of the criterion of insomnia, are overlapping manifestations of a general process of cognitive and psychomotor

Table 4.1   *DSM-IV* Criteria for the Diagnosis of Caffeine Intoxication

A. Recent consumption of caffeine, usually in excess of 250 mg (e.g., more than 2 to 3 cups of brewed coffee).

B. Five (or more) of the following signs, developing during, or shortly after, caffeine use:
   (1) restlessness
   (2) nervousness
   (3) excitement
   (4) insomnia
   (5) flushed face
   (6) diuresis
   (7) gastrointestinal disturbance
   (8) muscle twitching
   (9) rambling flow of thought and speech
   (10) tachycardia or cardiac arrhythmia
   (11) periods of inexhaustibility
   (12) psychomotor agitation

C. The symptoms in Criterion B cause clinically significant distress or impairment in social, occupational, or other important areas of functioning.

D. The symptoms are not due to a general medical condition and are not better accounted for by another mental disorder (e.g., an Anxiety Disorder).

SOURCE: Reprinted with permission from the *Diagnostic and Statistical Manual of Mental Disorders*, Fourth Edition. Copyright 1994 American Psychiatric Association.

overstimulation. Although it may be useful to acknowledge that caffeine can induce such effects, it is apparent that the suggested distinction between many of the stated signs is both arbitrary and unclear. As such, there is a misleading level of precision implied in the specification that "five or more" symptoms must be identified before the diagnosis can be applied.

The remaining symptoms are also largely arbitrary. Flushed face, in particular, does not appear in the literature as a distinguishing feature of caffeine ingestion. *DSM-IV* (1994) states that the first seven symptoms listed in Table 4.1 can appear following the ingestion of "as little as 100 mg of caffeine per day" (p. 212), whereas the remaining five symptoms "generally appear at levels of more than 1 g per day" (p. 212). However, although it is conceivable that caffeine may contribute to gastrointestinal disturbance, tachycardia or cardiac arrhythmia, and diuresis, it is doubtful whether these signs and symptoms could be attributed specifically to caffeine in the individual case. Furthermore, *DSM-IV* specifies that the individual under examination must have recently consumed caffeine. However, except where unusually large amounts of the drug have been ingested, the recent consumption criterion is unlikely to be helpful, because the majority of the population consumes caffeine daily. To some extent, this dilemma is circumvented in *DSM-IV* with the assertion that caffeine intoxication "is usually seen in infrequent users or in those who have recently increased their caffeine intake by a substantial amount" (p. 214). However, the frequency with which caffeine intoxication actually occurs among such people, and the reliability with which it can be diagnosed using *DSM-IV* criteria, are matters that await empirical confirmation. Until then, the diagnosis should be regarded with some skepticism.

Other Caffeine-Induced Disorders

Two "other" *DSM-IV* (1994) diagnoses are specified, caffeine-induced anxiety disorder and caffeine-induced sleep disorder. In both instances, symptoms must be in excess of those usually associated with caffeine intoxication and severe enough to warrant independent clinical attention. As can be seen from Table 4.2, the two diagnoses share a generic set of criteria, expressed as signs and symptoms of anxiety and sleep, respectively. Caffeine-induced anxiety disorder should be diagnosed if caffeine intoxication or withdrawal have contributed to symptoms of pronounced anxiety, panic attacks, or obsessions or compulsions, whereas caffeine-induced sleep disorder should be diagnosed if caffeine intoxication or withdrawal have contributed to the development of symptoms of pronounced disturbance in sleep. In the latter case, it is said that the typical disturbance is insomnia (including prolonged sleep latency and increased wakefulness), although some individuals may present with a complaint of hypersomnia and daytime sleepiness related to withdrawal. As with caffeine intoxication, there is little objective support for the existence of these other caffeine-induced disorders as discrete clinical syndromes. However, empirical evidence (reviewed below) does suggest that caffeine may exacerbate anxiety and sleep disorders. More important, the inclusion of caffeine "disorders" in *DSM-IV* draws attention to the fact that, with relatively little effort, practitioners can assess the clinical implications of caffeine in individual cases by introducing a period of caffeine abstinence and noting whether symptoms abate. In such circumstances, however, the clinician must take care in relation to the patient's condition possibly being temporarily aggravated by withdrawal symptoms.

Table 4.2   *DSM-IV* Criteria for Caffeine-Induced Anxiety and Sleep[a] Disorder

A. Prominent anxiety, panic attacks, or obsessions or compulsions predominate in the clinical picture. [A prominent disturbance in sleep that is sufficiently severe to warrant independent clinical attention.]

B. There is evidence from the history, physical examination, or laboratory findings of either (1) or (2):
(1)   the symptoms in Criterion A developed during, or within 1 month of, Caffeine Intoxication or Withdrawal
(2)   medication use is etiologically related to the disturbance

C. The disturbance is not better accounted for by an Anxiety [Sleep] Disorder that is not caffeine induced. Evidence that the symptoms are better accounted for by an Anxiety [Sleep] Disorder that is not caffeine induced might include the following: The symptoms precede the onset of the caffeine use; the symptoms persist for a substantial period of time (e.g., about a month) after the cessation of acute withdrawal or severe intoxication or are substantially in excess of what would be expected given the amount of caffeine used or the duration of use; or there is other evidence suggesting the existence of an independent non-caffeine-induced Anxiety [Sleep] Disorder (e.g., a history of recurrent non-caffeine-related episodes).

D. The disturbance does not occur exclusively during the course of a delirium.

E. The disturbance causes clinically significant distress or impairment in social, occupational, or other important areas of functioning.

NOTE: These diagnoses should be made instead of a diagnosis of Caffeine Intoxication or Caffeine Withdrawal only when the anxiety [sleep] symptoms are in excess of those usually associated with the intoxication or withdrawal syndrome and when the anxiety [sleep] symptoms are sufficiently severe to warrant independent clinical attention.
a. Specific references to sleep are shown in square brackets.
SOURCE: Adapted and reprinted with permission from the *Diagnostic and Statistical Manual of Mental Disorders,* Fourth Edition. Copyright 1994 American Psychiatric Association.

Caffeine Withdrawal (Physical Dependence)

The fourth and final caffeine diagnosis in *DSM-IV* (1994) is caffeine-related disorder not otherwise specified, which is reserved for disorders that are associated with the use of caffeine but do not satisfy the criteria for any of the other three diagnoses. Only one specific example is cited, *caffeine withdrawal,* which Hughes, Oliveto, et al. (1992) argued should be included in *DSM-IV.* Although caffeine withdrawal was included, it is described as being a "proposed," rather than official category, due to insufficient information and the need for further research. This is an ironic position, because there is substantially more empirical evidence for the existence of caffeine withdrawal as a specific syndrome than for any of the other three caffeine diagnoses contained in *DSM-IV*. The essential criteria for diagnosing caffeine withdrawal are abrupt cessation of caffeine use, or reduction in the amount of caffeine used, closely followed by headache and one or more of the following: marked fatigue or drowsiness, marked anxiety or depression, or nausea or vomiting. Cessation of caffeine use must have occurred in the context of a history of prolonged daily use of the drug, and symptoms must be such as to cause "clinically significant distress" or impairment in social, occupational, or other important areas of function. The diagnosis also requires that symptoms not be attributable to a concurrent medical or mental disorder. Finally, symptoms should be accompanied by a strong desire for caffeine and worsened cognitive performance (especially on vigilance tasks), with the possibility that individuals may seek medical treatment for these symptoms without realizing they are due to caffeine withdrawal.

The suggestion that caffeine withdrawal be included as a formal diagnosis in *DSM-IV* (1994; Hughes, Oliveto, et al., 1992) is supported by an extensive literature describing a range of dysphoric effects including headache, sleepiness, and lethargy (e.g., Griffiths & Mumford, 1995a, 1995b; Griffiths & Woodson, 1988a). Because not all individuals abstaining from caffeine report all of the common symptoms, the definition of caffeine withdrawal provided by *DSM-IV* may be regarded as conservative. The diagnosis is supposed to be applied only when caffeine abstinence is followed by headache *and* one or more of the other symptoms specified above. By excluding cases of withdrawal-induced headache not accompanied by other symptoms, and cases where symptoms are experienced without headache, it is likely that only the more serious cases of caffeine withdrawal will come to be diagnosed as such. This may be appropriate, considering that the stated main purpose of *DSM-IV* is to assist clinical diagnosis.

Caffeine Dependence and Abuse

Apart from intoxication and withdrawal, *DSM-IV* (1994) has two additional generic diagnoses associated with substance use. These are *dependence* and *abuse,* which the manual recommends are not applicable to caffeine. However, in light of the anomalies and inconsistencies concerning the *DSM-IV* account of caffeine intoxication and withdrawal (discussed above), it is appropriate to consider the recommended proscription on the classification of caffeine use as either dependence or abuse, the criteria for which are summarized in Table 4.3. Studies of the psychoactive, discriminative stimulus, and reinforcing properties of caffeine, reviewed in Chapter 3, provide an objective basis for determining whether caffeine possesses any potential for dependence and/or abuse. This is because all drugs of dependence and abuse have psychoactive effects that are discriminated by, and are reinforcing for, the user (Heishman & Henningfield, 1992). As discussed in Chapter 3, caffeine has psychoactive effects, but in the absence of a history of use leading to physical dependence, these effects are slight and subtle. Consequently, in the absence of special training, effects are not well-discriminated, nor are they strongly reinforcing. In these respects, caffeine is quantitatively (although not qualitatively) different from classic drugs of abuse (e.g., alcohol, amphetamines, cocaine, opioids). However, it is well-established that habitual caffeine use leads to physical dependence, and it appears that the psychoactive, discriminative stimulus, and reinforcing properties of caffeine are potentiated by habitual use. In a study involving cigarette-smoking coffee drinkers, Hughes et al. (1991) found that the reinforcing effects of cigarettes and coffee were comparable. Thus, the question arises as to whether the potentiating effects of habitual use can give rise to caffeine dependence and/or abuse.

Caffeine Dependence

Heishman and Henningfield (1992) reviewed the psychoactive, discriminative stimulus, and reinforcing properties of caffeine and concluded that although caffeine shares features common to classic drugs of dependence, its dependence potential is relatively low. Conversely, Strain et al. (1994) argued that caffeine dependence should be recognized as a clinical syndrome. They based their conclusions on a study of respondents to advertisements that called for volunteers who believed themselves to be "psychologically or physically dependent" on caffeine. Of a total of 99 respondents, 16 were identified on the basis of psychiatric interview as satisfying the *DSM-IV* (1994) diagnosis for substance dependence (see Table 4.3). It is interesting, however, that 13 of the 16 participants also had a history of other psychiatric

Table 4.3	*DSM-IV* Criteria for Substance Dependence and Substance Abuse

Dependence

A maladaptive pattern of substance use, leading to clinically significant impairment or distress, as manifested by three (or more) of the following, occurring at any time in the same 12-month period:

(1) tolerance, as defined by either of the following:
  (a) a need for markedly increased amounts of the substance to achieve intoxication or desired effect
  (b) markedly diminished effect with continued use of the same amount of the substance

(2) withdrawal, as manifested by either of the following:
  (a) the characteristic withdrawal syndrome for the substance (refer to Criteria A and B of the criteria sets for Withdrawal)
  (b) the same (or a closely related) substance is taken to relieve or avoid withdrawal symptoms

(3) the substance is often taken in larger amounts or over a longer period than was intended

(4) there is a persistent desire or unsuccessful efforts to cut down or control substance use

(5) a great deal of time is spent in activities necessary to obtain the substance (e.g., visiting multiple doctors or driving long distances), use the substance (e.g., chain-smoking), or recover from its effects

(6) important social, occupational, or recreational activities are given up or reduced because of substance use

(7) the substance use is continued despite knowledge of having a persistent or recurrent physical or psychological problem that is likely to have been caused or exacerbated by the substance (e.g., current cocaine use despite recognition of cocaine-induced depression, or continued drinking despite recognition that an ulcer was made worse by alcohol consumption)

Abuse

A. A maladaptive pattern of substance use leading to clinically significant impairment or distress, as manifested by one (or more) of the following, occurring within a 12-month period:

(1) recurrent substance use resulting in a failure to fulfill major role obligations at work, school, or home (e.g., repeated absences or poor work performance related to substance use; substance-related absences, suspensions, or expulsions from school; neglect of children or household)

(2) recurrent substance use in situations in which it is physically hazardous (e.g., driving or operating a machine when impaired by substance use)

(3) recurrent substance-related legal problems (e.g., arrests for substance-related disorderly conduct)

(4) continued substance use or interpersonal problems caused or exacerbated by the effects of the substance (e.g., arguments with spouse about consequences of intoxication, physical fights)

B. The symptoms have never met the criteria for Substance Dependence for this class of substance.

SOURCE: Reprinted with permission from the *Diagnostic and Statistical Manual of Mental Disorders,* Fourth Edition. Copyright 1994 American Psychiatric Association.

conditions, which were diagnosed as concurrent in two of the participants and as in remission in the remaining 11. Moreover, because the screening procedures relied primarily on participants' self-reports, there is no way of knowing from this study whether participants' pre-existing beliefs regarding their own "dependence" on caffeine may have influenced diagnostic outcomes.

Caffeine Abuse

The substance-abuse criteria shown in Table 4.3 raise further doubts (additional to those mentioned above) concerning the validity of the diagnosis of caffeine intoxication, as well as doubts concerning more general distinctions between substance use disorders as defined by *DSM-IV* (1994). Any psychoactive substance that is capable of producing significant intoxicating effects has the potential to satisfy one or more of the four abuse criteria shown in Table 4.3. That is, use of the drug produces intoxication sufficient to interfere with role obligations, be physically hazardous, cause legal problems, and/or cause social or interpersonal problems. As such, intoxication appears to be a necessary condition for substance abuse. Indeed, all the substance classes in *DSM-IV* that are classified as substances of abuse are also classified as substances of intoxication (i.e., alcohol, amphetamines, cannabis, cocaine, hallucinogens, inhalants, opioids, phencyclidine, and sedatives). With one exception, the reverse is also true (i.e., all substances of intoxication are also classified as substances of abuse). The one exception is caffeine. The other critical feature of abuse is that use (and associated intoxication-induced problems) must be recurrent. Patterns of caffeine use are clearly recurrent. No other psychoactive drug competes with caffeine for longevity of repeated use. Thus caffeine's position in *DSM-IV* is unique. Of the many varieties of recurrent substance use, caffeine alone has one, but not the other, of the classifications of intoxication and abuse. Considering the relationship between intoxication and abuse (as defined in *DSM-IV*), this special treatment of caffeine appears contradictory.

▇ Schizophrenia and Other Serious Psychiatric Disorders

Considerable attention has been given to the possibility that caffeine consumption may either precipitate or exacerbate schizophrenia and other serious psychiatric disorders. Many case reports illustrate the possible involvement of caffeine in a wide range of disorders, including, for example, paranoid schizophrenia (Mackay & Rollins, 1989) and depersonalization disorder (Stein & Uhde, 1989). Psychiatric patients may be especially vulnerable to caffeine, either because of increased sensitivity or because of increased exposure to the drug. Exposure is facilitated by the common practice within psychiatric institutions of permitting unrestricted access to sources of caffeine (tea, coffee, and cola drinks). Moreover, it has been suggested that the stimulating effects of caffeine may serve to counteract the boredom engendered by institutional routine and the unpleasant side effects of certain antipsychotic medications (De Freitas & Schwartz, 1979; Procter & Greden, 1982; Winstead, 1976). As a group, psychiatric patients have been reported to consume caffeine at about twice the rate of nonpatients matched for sex and age (Furlong, 1975).

Psychosis

Of the literature implicating caffeine as a variable in the development of psychological dysfunction, the most dramatic accounts concern several reports of alleged caffeine-induced *psychosis* (McNanamy & Schube, 1936; Mikkelsen, 1978; Shen & D'Souza, 1979; Stillner et al., 1978; Zaslove et al., 1991). A distinguishing feature of these reports compared to most other accounts of caffeine-related psychological effects is the intensity and nature of the reported symptoms. The individuals described in these reports were not only observed to be markedly distressed (e.g., intense anxiety, extreme agitation), but each was also reported to have experienced hallucinations (a defining feature of psychosis). The case of a truck driver who reported encountering "unidentified flying objects" appears fairly characteristic (Druffel, 1988). The driver complained of having been harassed by several white balls of light during an overnight cross-country trip and of having been inexplicably "possessed." He was seriously sleep-deprived at the time and had consumed the approximate equivalent of eight cups of coffee in the form of *No-Doz* tablets and an unspecified number of coffee and cola drinks within a period of several hours.

The anecdotal nature of the case reports of the possible involvement of caffeine in psychotic episodes, and the unusually large quantities of caffeine that have typically been involved, casts doubt on the generality of the reported effects. The same may be said about a study by Lucas et al. (1990), who administered a caffeine challenge to 13 schizophrenic patients. Ratings of patients' behavior indicated that following caffeine, symptoms of psychosis and mania worsened, although mood, "energy," and social involvement improved. The generality of the results is limited by the amount of caffeine that was administered. Subjects received a single dose of 10 mg of caffeine per kg of body weight, the approximate equivalent of eight cups of coffee consumed at once.

Inpatient Access to Caffeine

Several studies have sought to demonstrate the potential effects of habitual caffeine consumption by systematically manipulating inpatient access to caffeine. After substituting decaffeinated coffee for regular coffee, Podboy and Mallory (1977) reported that aggressive outbursts and nocturnal awakenings decreased in a group of 15 intellectually handicapped girls, and De Freitas and Schwartz (1979) reported decreases in anxiety, irritability, suspiciousness, and hostility in a group of 14 chronic psychiatric patients. Similarly, Zaslove et al. (1991) compared the frequency of aggressive behavior before and after a ban on caffeine beverages was introduced in a 1,200-bed public hospital. Comparison of data before and after the ban showed that assaults against other patients and assaults against staff decreased by 25% or more and that episodes of property destruction were halved. However, an attempt by Koczapski et al. (1989) to replicate the study by De Freitas and Schwartz (1979) was largely unsuccessful. After regular coffee was replaced by decaffeinated coffee, Koczapski et al. (1989) found no significant improvements in patients' behavior, nor was any deterioration in behavior observed when regular coffee was reinstated.

Largely null results were also reported by Shisslak et al. (1985) in a study that compared two groups of acute psychiatric inpatients, one of which was switched to decaffeinated coffee while the other continued to receive the usual beverage. No significant differences between the two groups were observed in relation to ratings of psychological adjustment, ward behavior, or response to treatment. Similarly, in a double-blind crossover study of 26 long-stay schizophrenic patients, Mayo et al. (1993) reported no effect on patient mood or behavior when caffeine-containing coffee and tea supplies were replaced by decaffeinated alternatives. Searle (1994) also reported that

removal of caffeine for a period of 2 weeks had no effect on the behavior of 31 psychiatric inpatients, but behavior disturbances increased when caffeine was reintroduced. Unfortunately, however, none of these studies (including those that reported significant effects and those that did not) provided reliability data for the observational measures of patient behavior. As such, there is no sound basis for resolving the discrepant findings. In this regard, it is interesting to note that Shisslak et al. (1985) found that the regular-coffee group were prescribed higher dosages of phenothiazines. That is, in contrast to the observational measures that were performed, a significant difference was found in relation to the comparatively objective measure of prescribed medication.

Positive improvements following removal of caffeine have also been reported in studies in which outcome variables were specific rather than general. Edelstein et al. (1984) examined the effects of sustained caffeine withdrawal on nocturnal enuresis, insomnia, and behavior "requiring physical or pharmacological restraint" among inpatients of a large psychiatric hospital. Compared to baseline levels, improvements were reported for all three problem behaviors. Although the reported reductions in the severity of enuresis are consistent with the known diuretic effect of caffeine (Fredholm, 1984), these reductions could actually have been due to patients reducing their intake of liquids following the removal of regular coffee. This potential confound was controlled by James, Sawczuk, et al. (1989) in a study of urinary incontinence in a group of psychogeriatric inpatients. Incontinence episodes were recorded day and night throughout the 13 weeks of the study, which consisted of alternating double-blind phases of caffeine exposure and abstinence. Comparing caffeine and caffeine-free phases, frequency of incontinence was reduced by 34% during the day and 21% at night. Importantly, the reductions in incontinence occurred despite overall increases in total fluid intake. Thus, the results suggest that caffeine consumption may exacerbate urinary incontinence problems in older persons and that such problems may be partially alleviated by removal of caffeine from the diet.

Anxiety

As mentioned above, it is recommended in *DSM-IV* (1994) that the diagnosis of caffeine-induced anxiety disorder be used when caffeine use

contributes to pronounced symptoms of anxiety, panic attacks, or obsessions or compulsions (see Table 4.2). Apart from a specific clinical diagnosis involving caffeine, there is concern that caffeine may also contribute more generally to anxiety levels in the population. However, it is important to remember that caffeine use is self-selected and that people who are adversely affected by the drug may avoid it (Boulenger et al., 1984; Lee et al., 1985). At the population level, avoidance would decrease the likelihood of a positive association, possibly giving rise to no association, or even an inverse association. Indeed, the actual population association remains unclear (Eaton & McLeod, 1984; Hire, 1978; Lynn, 1973).

Psychiatric patients have attracted particular attention, because their use of caffeine has been observed to be higher than that of the general population (Greden et al., 1978; James & Crosbie, 1987; Winstead, 1976). Caffeine use among patients has also been found to be positively associated with self-reported anxiety as measured by standard psychometric tests (Greden et al., 1978; Winstead, 1976). However, these findings are open to alternative interpretation, because of inadequate control of potentially important confounders, including participant expectations (heavier users in these studies may have been inadvertently led to expect adverse effects) and the fact that caffeine use is positively correlated with other known variables, especially cigarette smoking. Consequently, James et al. (1987) attempted to control for patient expectations and usage of other substances (cigarettes, alcohol, prescription and nonprescription medication) in a survey of 173 psychiatric inpatients. Although heavier caffeine users reported more somatic symptoms, no significant association was found between caffeine consumption and anxiety. In a subsequent study, James and Crosbie (1987) sought to further examine the association between caffeine and psychological well-being in the context of unusually heavy habitual use, while simultaneously controlling for concurrent substance use. Ninety-six subjects were divided into three groups of equal size, matched on age and sex, consisting of psychiatric patients, university students, and members of the general public (contacted through newspaper publicity) who were chosen specifically because of their habitually high caffeine intake. The results indicated that caffeine use contributed to increased anxiety only in the heavy user group, whose self-reported mean caffeine intake was at the exceptionally high level of more than 2 g per day.

Particular attention has also been given to the anxiogenic potential of caffeine in patients with panic disorder. Boulenger et al. (1984), for example, compared patients diagnosed as having either panic disorder or a significant

depressive condition and a group of matched control subjects, finding that the panic-disordered group reported greater sensitivity to the effects of caffeine than the other two groups. Breier et al. (1986), for example, found that of 48 agoraphobic patients who reported being caffeine consumers, 26 reported that caffeine generally exacerbated their anxiety symptoms. Similarly, Lee et al. (1988) found that patients with panic disorder attributed more anxiety, palpitations, and tachycardia to caffeine beverages than nonpsychiatric patients. These results are consistent with the finding by Charney et al. (1985) that patients with panic disorder reported significantly greater increases in anxiety than control subjects when both groups were administered a caffeine challenge. More recently, Uhde et al. (1991) reported that patients with panic disorder showed more severe anxiogenic responses to a caffeine challenge than socially phobic patients, who in turn showed a more marked response than nonphobic participants.

Notwithstanding the apparent support for the suggestion that patients with anxiety disorders may have an exaggerated sensitivity to caffeine (Boulenger et al., 1984; Breier et al., 1986; Charney et al., 1985; Lee et al., 1988), most of the available evidence is based on subjects' self-reports of adverse effects and is thereby open to an alternative interpretation. Specifically, the patients are not necessarily experiencing more intense effects but might be more inclined than nonpatients to label the psychoactive effects of caffeine as symptoms of anxiety. However, using a novel taste test, DeMet et al. (1989) found objective evidence of exaggerated sensitivity to caffeine, in patients with panic disorder. Previous research had shown that the ability to taste quinine is enhanced if caffeine is present in the solution (Schiffman et al., 1986). Compared to normal controls and patients with post-traumatic stress disorder, panic disorder patients were found to have an exaggerated response to a caffeine challenge. This finding, which has been independently replicated (Apfeldorf & Shear, 1993), has been interpreted as evidence of the involvement of adenosine as part of the causal mechanism of panic disorder. It has been suggested either that panic disorder patients may have an increased number of adenosine receptors or that adenosine mechanisms in these people may have a greater affinity for caffeine (Apfeldorf & Shear, 1993; DeMet et al., 1989; Klein et al., 1991). As such, suppression by caffeine of the adenosine receptor system is consistent with accounts of pronounced caffeine-induced anxiogenic effects reported by patients with panic disorder (Breier et al., 1986; Charney et al., 1985; Lee et al., 1988).

Depression

Occasional uncontrolled case reports have given rise to the suspicion that caffeine may be involved in depressive disorders (e.g., Tondo & Rudas, 1991). Attempts to clarify the relationship using cross-sectional surveys of patient groups and others have been only partially successful. Moderate to high caffeine intake in psychiatric patients was found to be positively associated with depression by Greden et al. (1978) but unrelated by James et al. (1987). Conversely, unusually high intake among a nonpsychiatric sample was found by James and Crosbie (1987) to be associated with increased self-reported levels of depression. Jacobsen and Hansen (1988) provided a brief account of the association between coffee intake and "mental problems" in 143,000 Norwegian men and women. A positive correlation was found between coffee consumption and depression, which was interpreted as indicating that "coffee consumption is probably part of a lifestyle associated with mental problems" (p. 291). Indeed, it has been suggested that certain subgroups may increase their intake of caffeine during periods of depression (Leibenluft et al., 1993). This action has been interpreted as "self-medication" under-taken to combat lethargy and other symptoms. In this context, it is interesting to note that the existence of a positive correlation between caffeine and anxiety has sometimes been cited as evidence that caffeine may *cause* anxiety (e.g., Greden et al., 1978), whereas a positive correlation between caffeine and depression tends to be interpreted as suggesting that caffeine consumption may be an *effect* of depressed mood (Leibenluft et al., 1993; Neil et al., 1978). Clearly, both interpretations are speculative, as correlation provides no proof of causation, let alone causal direction.

Eating Disorders

A purported common practice among people with anorexia nervosa is to consume large quantities of caffeine, either in low-calorie caffeine beverages (e.g., diet cola, black coffee) or caffeine-containing medications (Shaul et al., 1984; Sours, 1983). It appears that the ingestion of caffeine may provide a convenient means by which to lessen appetite (especially if consumed in large quantities as a beverage) while maintaining alertness and minimizing lethargy. Also, as mentioned in Chapter 2, caffeine may increase metabolic rate, thereby possibly assisting the efforts of people wishing to control weight or to effect weight loss. Furthermore, citing previous accounts of occasional transient psychotic episodes among anorexic patients (Grounds, 1982; Hsu et al., 1981), Shaul et al. (1984) suggested that such episodes may be manifestations of excessive caffeine consumption. More recently, Krahn et al. (1991) speculated whether food deprivation in patients with eating disorders, including bulimia nervosa and anorexia nervosa, might itself stimulate increased caffeine intake. Increased severity of symptoms did indeed appear to be related to increased caffeine consumption. However, whether caffeine contributed to increased severity of symptoms or vice versa, or whether both variables were correlated co-effects of other factors, remains unclear.

▦ Aggression

Reports of decreased aggression and hostility in psychiatric patients whose access to caffeine beverages has been curtailed (e.g., De Freitas & Schwartz, 1979; Edelstein et al., 1984; Podboy & Mallory, 1977) suggest that caffeine consumption may exacerbate aggressive behavior. However, the effect (if any) of caffeine on aggression is unclear. Results from animal studies suggest that caffeine may decrease aggression (e.g., Hansen et al., 1985), and these results are consistent with suggestions of a possible common neuro-chemical mechanism by which caffeine exacerbates anxiety while simultane-ously moderating aggression (Cherek et al., 1983, 1984). Aggressive respond-ing in the laboratory was elicited by deducting money from research participants and attributing this action to another (fictitious) participant. Caffeine compared to placebo (Cherek et al., 1983), and regular coffee compared to decaffeinated coffee (Cherek et al., 1984) produced decreases in the experimentally defined aggressive responses. Further research is needed to resolve the apparent discrepancy between the effects of caffeine on discrete responses elicited in the experimental laboratory and the more general behavior of psychiatric patients in naturalistic settings. Variables to be considered in the natural environment include the amount of caffeine consumed (markedly different amounts may have qualitatively different effects), the duration of exposure (a single caffeine challenge may not adequately represent the effects of repeated ingestion), possible interactions with other substances (e.g., therapeutic drugs, illicit drugs), and consumption pattern (caffeine withdrawal effects may be more marked than the psychoactive effects induced by the drug).

▩ Sleep Disorders

Studies reviewed in Chapter 2 show that although caffeine may disrupt sleep, these effects are not necessarily readily discernible. On the other hand, if such effects are apparent and pronounced, *DSM-IV* (1994) recommends that the diagnosis of caffeine-induced sleep disorder be applied (see Table 4.2). However, the likely population distribution of such disorders remains unclear. For example, whereas a positive association was observed between caffeine consumption and prevalence of insomnia in an epidemiologic study conducted in Australia (Shirlow & Mathers, 1985), no such relationship was found for either "difficulties inducing sleep" or sleep latency in a recent epidemiologic study conducted in Belgium, Iceland, and Sweden (Janson et al., 1995). Concern has been expressed regarding the possible involvement of caffeine in high rates of sleep complaints among renal dialysis patients. Again, however, the evidence is inconsistent, with one study reporting that caffeine intake was associated with more "sleep-wake complaints" (Walker et al., 1995), whereas the other found that caffeine was unrelated to "sleep problems" (Stepanski et al., 1995).

Overall, there is a puzzling inconsistency between the strength of the laboratory findings regarding the disruptive effects of caffeine on sleep and the paucity of evidence implicating caffeine as a factor in the etiology of sleep disorders. Because most of the laboratory studies examined the acute effects of caffeine, more needs to be learned about whether tolerance to the antisoporific effects of caffeine develops with habitual use. In one study, participants were examined over a period of 7 consecutive nights during which caffeine was consumed daily, and partial tolerance was observed (Bonnet & Arand, 1992). In addition, more attention needs to be given to the possible influence of patterns of caffeine consumption on sleep problems. Whereas caffeine is typically administered immediately before bedtime in the sleep laboratory, most consumers reduce their caffeine intake during the latter part of the day. Thus, although caffeine has demonstrated potential to disrupt sleep, its actual role in either precipitating or exacerbating sleep disorders remains unclear.

▓ Children

It is obvious from casual observation that children are often the targets of marketing activities to promote the consumption of caffeine foods and beverages (especially cola drinks), and caffeine is indeed widely consumed by children (Barone & Roberts, 1984). Moreover, compared to adults, patterns of caffeine consumption tend not to be as firmly fixed or routine in children. Consequently, children may be at particular risk of experiencing intermittent episodes of caffeine withdrawal. Certainly, headache, irritability, inattention, and tiredness are common in children, and these also happen to be the main symptoms of caffeine withdrawal. It is surprising, therefore, that comparatively little research has been conducted on the effects of caffeine in children.

In one of the few available studies, Rapoport et al. (1984), found that level of habitual caffeine intake was a reliable predictor of child behavior during experimental periods of abstinence and re-exposure to caffeine. In particular, "high" consumers had higher scores on an anxiety questionnaire and scored lower on measures of autonomic arousal when deprived of caffeine. Conversely, "low" consumers were reported by their parents as more emotional, inattentive, and restless during periods of caffeine exposure. Although the response of the high consumers has the appearance of a withdrawal effect, Rapoport et al. (1984) dismissed this possibility. They argued that as all the children were on low-caffeine diets for 2 weeks prior to caffeine challenge, the effects they observed are indicative of an underlying physiological difference between high and low caffeine-consuming children.

The suggestion that children who have had differing levels of exposure to caffeine may also show subtle physiological differences draws attention to a potentially important but neglected area of caffeine research. It is well-known that most mothers-to-be continue to consume caffeine during pregnancy, thereby raising questions as to whether caffeine may contribute to congenital abnormalities. To date, the search has been primarily concerned with gross morphological abnormalities, and the general opinion is that caffeine does not contribute significantly to such defects in humans (see Chapter 7). The question of whether maternal use of caffeine might have more subtle effects, especially with respect to *postnatal* physiology and behavior, has been largely ignored. A longitudinal study by Streissguth et al. (1980), which was only partly concerned with caffeine, provides one of the few relevant human studies. The investigators found that alcohol is a behavioral teratogen (i.e., capable of producing congenital abnormalities) with detectable effects in children at 8 months and that nicotine also has teratogenic effects detectable in the behavior of children at 4 years (Streissguth et al., 1984). Caffeine was not found to be teratogenic in the earlier study, nor apparently in the later one (although no specific data were presented). However, in view of the fact that nicotine was not identified as a teratogen at 8 months but was found to be teratogenic at 4 years, the possibility exists that maternal caffeine may have effects that are detectable in children older than 4 years. This possibility is all the more plausible in light of the fact that, over the past decade, strong evidence has emerged of an inverse association between caffeine and birth weight (see Chapter 7). As such, important questions arise in relation to the possible effects of maternal caffeine use on fetal growth and subsequent behavioral and psychological development in the children of caffeine-consuming mothers.

■ Treating Physical Dependence on Caffeine

Despite increased interest and concern that caffeine may be harmful to health, few reports exist of systematic efforts to assist habitual consumers to reduce their caffeine consumption. Using a single-subject experimental design, Foxx and Rubinoff (1979) reported favorable results for three participants who received a program of behavioral intervention based on nicotine and cigarette "fading" methods that had been developed for smokers (e.g., Foxx & Axelroth, 1983; Foxx & Brown, 1979). Interestingly, almost a century earlier, Bridge (1893) advised that adverse withdrawal effects could be avoided by a gradual reduction of caffeine. Foxx (1982) obtained additional follow-up data from the three original participants and reported that the reduced intake of all three was substantially maintained 40 months following the termination of treatment. In essence, treatment consisted of a combination of self-monitoring and a series of predetermined stepwise reductions in daily caffeine consumption in the direction of a specified terminal goal of reduced daily intake. Similar procedures were used with a single subject by Bernard et al. (1981), who also reported favorable results. These generally promising initial findings were confirmed in a larger study by James et al. (1985) in which 27 chronic heavy caffeine consumers were monitored before and during a 4-week treatment program and at 6 and 18 weeks follow-up. However, because the results of these caffeine-reduction studies were expressed solely in terms of participant self-reports, the reliability of the findings is open to question. This problem is not unique to the assessment of caffeine use. Just as bioanalytic techniques for directly quantifying levels of drug exposure have become an integral part of research into other dependence-producing substances (e.g., alcohol, nicotine), objective methods of quantification are needed to advance understanding of caffeine use.

Accordingly, James et al. (1988) reported plasma concentrations of caffeine and its primary demethylated metabolites (paraxanthine, theophylline, and theobromine) as well as self-reported caffeine intake during the course of a caffeine-fading regimen similar to that employed by James et al. (1985). Overall, the 12 subjects, each with a history of heavy caffeine use, provided highly reliable self-reports of caffeine intake during the course of the 18-week program. However, although the general efficacy of the caffeine-fading procedure was also supported, there were indications that maintenance effects may not necessarily be as good as had been reported in previous studies. Unlike the earlier studies, participants in the James et al. (1988) study showed signs of relapse at 12 weeks follow-up. It has long been known that the accuracy of self-reports is enhanced when subjects are aware that their behavior may be independently checked (e.g., Lipinsky et al., 1975; Nelson et al., 1975). Hence, the independent measure provided by the plasma assays may have encouraged subjects to be more accurate than the subjects of previous studies in reporting follow-up caffeine intake. If accurate and generalizable, the relapse reported by James et al. (1988) is consistent with generally reported therapy outcomes for substances of dependence. Although the reasons for the relapse observed by James et al. (1988) remain unclear, it would not appear to have been due to the influence of withdrawal effects, because the resumption of higher levels of consumption did not occur until many weeks after the original treatment goal had been achieved.

SUMMARY

The inclusion of several caffeine-associated clinical syndromes in *DSM-IV* has been important in raising awareness of the drug's potential to undermine psychological well-being. However, the main *DSM-IV* classification of caffeine intoxication is not well-supported empirically. In contrast, the syndrome of caffeine withdrawal (i.e., physical dependence) has strong empirical support but a tentative status in *DSM-IV* as a proposed classification. Whereas there is little direct support for the *DSM-IV* classifications of caffeine-induced anxiety disorder and caffeine-induced sleep disorder, there is consistent evidence that caffeine is capable of exacerbating existing problems of anxiety (especially panic disorder) and that it may interfere with sleep. Although in several important respects caffeine is not qualitatively different from classic drugs of abuse, the drug is presented in *DSM-IV* as having neither dependence nor abuse potential.

It is unclear whether caffeine has any involvement in depression and aggression, and apart from some exceptional circumstances, there is little evidence that caffeine contributes to schizophrenia and other serious psychiatric disorders. The exceptional circumstances described in individual case reports have involved unusually large amounts of caffeine, and the presence of other factors (e.g., extreme fatigue) capable of undermining psychological function, which when combined may result in transient hallucinations and delusions. In addition, there is evidence that people with anorexia nervosa sometimes consume large amounts of caffeine to suppress hunger and/or elevate mood. However, issues concerning the effects of caffeine on psychological well-being in children have been largely neglected. Similarly, little attention has been given to the possible effects of maternal caffeine use on postnatal behavioral development. Finally, regarding habitual caffeine use by adults, it appears that good success may be achieved by people motivated to reduce high levels of intake, although the prospects for long-term maintenance remain unclear. Provided withdrawal is achieved by graded steps, substantial reductions in intake may be achieved without significant untoward abstinence effects.

FURTHER READING

American Psychiatric Association. (1994). Substance-related disorders. In *Diagnostic and statistical manual of mental disorders* (4th ed., pp. 173-272). Washington, DC: Author.

Griffiths, R. R., Evans, S. M., Heishman, S. J., Preston, K. L., Sannerud, C. A., Wolf, B., & Woodson, P. P. (1990). Low-dose caffeine physical dependence in humans. *Journal of Pharmacology and Experimental Therapeutics, 255,* 1123-1132.

Heishman, S. J., & Henningfield, J. E. (1992). Stimulus functions of caffeine in humans: Relation to dependence potential. *Neuroscience and Biobehavioral Reviews, 16,* 273-287.

Hughes, J. R., Oliveto, A. H., Helzer, J. E., Higgins, S. T., & Bickel, W. K. (1992). Should caffeine abuse, dependence, or withdrawal be added to DSM-IV and ICD-10? *American Journal of Psychiatry, 149,* 33-40.

Strain, E. C., Mumford, G. K., Silverman, K., & Griffiths, R. R. (1994). Caffeine dependence syndrome: Evidence from case histories and experimental evaluations. *Journal of the American Medical Association, 272,* 1043-1048.

Caffeine and Cardiovascular Health

■

 Cardiovascular disease is a major cause of mortality and morbidity throughout the world and *the* major cause of these events in the developed countries (Houston, 1989). The causes of cardiovascular disease are known to be complex and multifactorial, involving aspects of behavior and lifestyle (e.g., Grundy, 1982; Kannel & Schatzkin, 1983; Shekelle et al., 1981). Of the many controversies concerning the role of lifestyle factors in cardiovascular disease, few have been more persistent than the debate about the possible involvement of caffeine. Concern about caffeine and cardiovascular health is understandable, considering the known pharmacological properties of the drug and its near-universal use. The large research literature on caffeine and cardiovascular health that has accumulated over the past several decades can be loosely divided on the basis of the two main methodological approaches that have been used. On one hand, *epidemiologic* studies have sought to quantify the naturally occurring relationship between caffeine and cardiovascular disease in populations. On the other hand, *experimental* studies have generally aimed to measure the cardiovascular effects of controlled exposure to caffeine.

▧ Epidemiology of Caffeine and Cardiovascular Health

Since the early 1960s, almost 100 epidemiologic studies, involving hundreds of thousands of participants in more than a dozen countries, have examined the relationship between habitual caffeine consumption and cardiovascular function, morbidity, and/or mortality. Most of the research can be assigned to one of two broad categories, studies concerned primarily with either the relationship between caffeine and manifest disease (e.g., myocardial infarction, angina pectoris) or the relationship between caffeine and cardiovascular risk factors. Most of the latter group is composed of two subgroups of studies concerned with blood lipid levels and blood pressure, respectively. A previous work by this author provided a critical review of studies published prior to 1990 (James, 1991). The present section integrates the main conclusions of that earlier review with the findings of subsequent studies summarized in Table 5.1. The overall findings can be best understood if, in the first instance, several key methodological issues are considered, including the measurement of caffeine exposure, the influence of confounders, and the selection of controls.

Epidemiology of Caffeine and Cardiovascular Health: Key Methodological Issues

One of the most striking features of the large literature on the epidemiology of caffeine and cardiovascular health is the extent of the many inconsistencies in the reported findings. For example, LaCroix et al. (1986) found a "dose-responsive" association between coffee consumption and coronary disease that was independent of age, baseline serum cholesterol, and cigarette smoking; Klatsky et al. (1990) found a "weak independent" association that was statistically significant only in people who consumed more than three cups of coffee per day; and Grobbee et al. (1990) found no association at all between coffee consumption and risk of coronary heart disease. Another striking feature of the epidemiology of caffeine and cardiovascular health is the dearth of conceptual and methodological innovation. Although there have been some laudable exceptions, investigators (and journal editors) have generally continued to repeat the flaws of previous studies. This intellectual sterility is nowhere more evident than in relation to the measurement of the central variable of interest, caffeine exposure.

Table 5.1 Summary of Recent Epidemiologic Studies of Caffeine and Cardiovascular Disease and Cardiovascular Risk Factors of Serum Cholesterol and Blood Pressure

Investigators	Date	Results	Country	Comments
Cardiovascular disease:				
Linsted et al.	1992	Positive	United States	Coffee in men. Main outcome variables were ischemic heart disease (IHD), "other" cardiovascular diseases, and "all causes of death."
Brown et al.	1993	Null	United Kingdom	Coffee and tea in men and women. Main outcome variable was coronary heart disease (CHD).
Gartside & Glueck	1993	Null	United States	Coffee and decaffeinated coffee in men and women. Main outcome variable was CHD. A positive association for decaffeinated coffee was interpreted as indicating that participants switched from caffeine/coffee *after* CHD was diagnosed.
Klatsky et al.	1993	Positive	United States	Coffee and tea (not significant) in men and women. Significant association observed in consumers of four or more cups per day. Authors concluded no "overall relation to mortality risk," because coffee consumption was inversely associated with liver cirrhosis and suicide.
Klag et al.	1994	Positive	United States	Coffee in men. Main outcome variable was CHD. Association observed in both smokers and nonsmokers.
Gyntelberg et al.	1995	Null	Denmark	Coffee and tea in men. Main outcome variable was IHD.
Palmer et al.	1995	Positive	United States	Coffee and decaffeinated coffee (not significant) in women. Significant association observed only for intake of five or more cups per day.
Serum cholesterol:				
Salvaggio et al.	1991	Positive	Italy	Coffee in men and women.
Green & Harari	1992	Positive	Israel	Coffee and tea (not significant) in men and women.
Kalandidi et al.	1992	Positive	Greece	Coffee in men and women. Significant association evident only for "excessive" coffee intake.
Berndt et al.	1993	Positive	Germany	Coffee in men.
Carson et al.	1993	Null	United States	Coffee, tea, and cola in elderly women.

Study	Year	Result	Country	Description
D'Avanzo et al.	1993	Inconsistent	Italy	Coffee and decaffeinated coffee in men and women. Cholesterol levels higher in non-coffee drinkers than moderate drinkers, but there was a significant positive correlation between cholesterol and intake among drinkers.
El Shabrawy Ali & Felimban	1993	Positive	Arabia	Arabic coffee in men and women.
Jossa et al.	1993	Positive	Italy	Coffee in men. Significant association evident in smokers only.
Lewis et al.	1993	Null	United States	Coffee, tea, and cola in black and white men and women.
Mensink et al.	1993	Positive	Germany	Coffee and tea (not significant) in men and women.
Nylander et al.	1993	Null	United States	Coffee in middle-aged women
Lancaster et al.	1994	Null	United Kingdom	Coffee and decaffeinated coffee in men and women.
Lane et al.	1994	Positive	United States	Coffee in men and women.
Gyntelberg et al.	1995	Positive	Denmark	Coffee and tea (not significant) in men. Participants consumed filtered coffee—positive result obtained despite earlier findings that filters retain putative lipid-increasing agents contained in coffee.
Jensen et al.	1995	Positive	Serbia	Turkish coffee in men.
Blood pressure:				
Salvaggio et al.	1990	Inverse	Italy	Coffee in men and women. Blood pressure (BP) was measured after participants had fasted.
Burke et al.	1992	Positive	Australia	Coffee and tea (not significant) in elderly men and women. No information provided on whether subjects fasted prior to BP measurement.
Salvaggio et al.	1992	Inverse	Italy	Coffee in men and women. BP was measured after participants had "fasted for 8 hours."
Lewis et al.	1993	Inverse	United States	Coffee, tea, and cola in black and white men and women. BP was measured after participants had fasted.
Kirchhoff et al.	1994	Inverse	Denmark	Coffee in men and women. BP was measured after most participants (two thirds) had fasted.
Lancaster et al.	1994	Null	United Kingdom	Coffee and decaffeinated coffee in men and women. BP was measured in nonfasted state.
Gyntelberg et al.	1995	Inverse	Denmark	Coffee and tea (not significant) in men. BP was measured after participants "had fasted for at least 12 h."

NOTE: This table includes studies published since the review by James (1991).

The caffeine measurement problem. In an early critical commentary, Gilbert (1976) identified "the arbitrary nature of the classifications of coffee consumption" (p. 140) as a major problem in epidemiologic research on caffeine and cardiovascular health. More than 20 years later, this pivotal problem remains, unresolved and largely ignored. Striking inconsistencies exist between the measurement techniques used to quantify relevant outcome variables and the measurement of caffeine consumption. That is, although sensitive to questions of reliability and validity when diagnosing clinical manifestations of cardiovascular disease, quantifying blood lipid levels, and measuring blood pressure, investigators have often shown cavalier disregard for the integrity of measures of caffeine consumption. One early example of the contrast between the marked imbalance of attention given to outcome variables versus caffeine consumption can be seen in a widely cited study by Klatsky et al. (1973) that examined the relationship between caffeine and heart disease. On one hand, the diagnosis of myocardial infarction was "documented by careful review of the hospital chart, with rigidly applied clinical, electrocardiographic, and serum enzymatic criteria" (Klatsky et al., 1973, p. 540). In contrast, caffeine intake was measured by having subjects respond to a questionnaire that "included a single question relating to coffee drinking ('Have you usually, in the past year, drunk more than six cups of coffee per day?')" (p. 540). Given that participants who reported consuming no coffee at all were grouped together with those who consumed as many as six cups per day, a significant association between coffee and coronary disease would surely have been unlikely, and none was observed.

The caffeine measurement problem is exacerbated by the paucity of detail provided in many studies. Wilson et al. (1989), for example, stated only, "coffee intake was recorded" (p. 1169). Although the measurement of caffeine exposure has advanced to the extent that participants are now usually asked to report caffeine beverage consumption as number of cups consumed per day (earlier investigators sometimes used simple dichotomous yes/no responses regarding caffeine-beverage use), much more could be achieved with little additional effort. At the very least, beverage consumption (including coffee, tea, and cola drinks) should be converted into caffeine equivalents (e.g., James, Bruce, et al., 1989), thereby enabling ready examination and comparison between beverages and overall intake. More importantly, objective measurements based on HPLC analysis of blood or saliva should be obtained whenever possible. The absence of objective measurement is all the more disappointing, given that in at least half of all the studies published to date (and this includes *all* studies in which lipid levels were measured), blood samples were collected. Despite the fact that these samples could have been used to conduct bioassays of systemic caffeine levels, no epidemiologic study has done so.

In recognition of the minimal detail reported in most studies, Schreiber, Maffeo, et al. (1988) recommended that information be obtained on amount of regular and decaffeinated coffee consumed on weekdays and weekends, the size of the container used, the method used to brew coffee, and the amount of caffeine consumed as tea and soft drinks. In addition, use should be made of the Pfeifer and Notari (1988) method, described in Chapter 1, for predicting caffeine plasma concentrations on the basis of records of food and beverage intake. The method offers a convenient, economic, and potentially reliable means by which to quantify caffeine exposure with respect to habitual use, as well as estimating the systemic levels of participants at the time other measurements are taken (e.g., serum cholesterol, blood pressure).

In the epidemiologic literature, measurement error is often referred to as *misclassification*. Considering the crude methods that have been used, it follows that there is likely to have been a high rate of misclassification of caffeine exposure among epidemiologic studies conducted to date. The question arises as to what effect this misclassification is likely to have had. It has been common to suggest that misclassification of caffeine consumption might explain the many positive findings that have been reported. For this to be true, it would have to be argued that the measurement of caffeine exposure has not only often been biased, but that this bias has also often been correlated with the outcome variable of interest (e.g., myocardial infarction, serum cholesterol). In most instances, these conditions are unlikely to have prevailed. It is more likely that the methods commonly used to measure caffeine consumption will have resulted in undifferentiated errors (i.e., distributions of estimates that are approximately evenly balanced in terms of the frequency and size of over- and underestimates). It has been shown that undifferentiated (i.e., unbiased) misclassification of an exposure variable (caffeine in the present context) diminishes the strength of its association with outcome variables (Copeland et al., 1977; Greenland, 1980). That is, spurious null results (Type II error) are likely to have been more frequent than spurious positive results (Type I error). In other words, the association between caffeine and adverse cardiovascular outcomes is likely to be *stronger* than is suggested by the pattern of results summarized in Table 5.1.

The caffeine confounder myth. A major myth concerning the epidemiology of caffeine and cardiovascular health is that there has been widespread neglect of *confounders.* These are variables to which subjects may be exposed that are predictive of the disease under investigation, while also being associated with the primary exposure variable. The most common specific expression of the caffeine confounder myth is that positive findings (e.g., coffee consumption predicts myocardial infarction) are due to the failure to control for cigarette smoking. Although a small number of early studies failed to control for smoking (Kasanen & Forsström, 1966; Paul et al., 1963), this variable has been routinely taken into account for more than 20 years. The list of confounders considered in studies that have reported positive findings includes age, gender, cigarette smoking, alcohol consumption, body mass index, dietary factors, serum cholesterol, blood pressure, medical history (e.g., evidence of diabetes and hypertension), use of oral contraceptives, family history of heart disease, physical activity, personality, region of residence, education level, and religion. Moreover, studies that have reported a positive association between caffeine and cardiovascular disease cannot be distinguished, with respect to the extent and quality of control of confounders, from those that have reported no association. Although an unidentified confounder may yet exist to explain the reported positive results, it is a possibility that seems fairly unlikely. Apart from smoking, age, gender, and diet, few variables have accounted for any significant caffeine-associated variance in cardiovascular disease.

Schreiber, Robins, et al. (1988) specifically examined the associations between a wide range of disease risk factors (potential confounders) and coffee/caffeine intake. Information on more than 30 relevant risk factors, as well as coffee and caffeine intake, was obtained through telephone interviews of 2,714 adult males and females ages 25 to 74 years. Only cigarette smoking and gender were found to be important potential confounders of caffeine and coffee intake. Whereas smoking accounted for 11% and 15% of the variation in coffee/caffeine consumption by men and women, respectively, none of the remaining variables considered by Schreiber, Robins, et al. (1988) explained more than 1% of the variation for either men or women. Thus, the control of confounders in studies of caffeine and cardiovascular disease would generally appear to have been adequate. Indeed, it has been suggested that there has been a tendency toward overadjustment for confounder effects (LaCroix et al., 1987; La Vecchia, Gentile, et al., 1989; Rosenberg et al., 1988). A general principle states that a factor should not be regarded as a confounder if it is "an intermediate variable in the causal pathway" (Greenland & Robins, 1985, p. 495). Violations of this rule appear to have been widespread. Many studies of caffeine and manifest cardiovascular disease have adjusted for blood pressure and serum cholesterol, and there is evidence (discussed below) that caffeine/coffee-induced elevations in blood pressure and cholesterol may contribute directly to the development of cardiovascular disease.

Selection of controls. Epidemiologic approaches to the study of caffeine and cardiovascular health have been varied and have included cohort, case-control, and cross-sectional studies. Some early case-control studies (Boston Collaborative Drug Surveillance Program, 1972; Jick et al., 1973) were criticized for selecting chronically ill hospital patients to serve as controls. There was concern that chronically ill patients might consume less coffee than the general population. Using such persons as controls, and comparing their caffeine consumption to cases involving recently diagnosed cardiovascular disease, could lead to spurious conclusions about a positive association between caffeine and cardiovascular disease. Indeed, there is evidence that chronically ill persons do, on average, consume less caffeine-containing beverage than either the general population or patients hospitalized for acute conditions (Klatsky et al., 1973; Rosenberg et al., 1981; Silverman et al., 1983). Thus, there is agreement that chronically ill patients should *not* be enlisted as controls, and the practice appears to have ceased. Studies employing more appropriate controls have reported both positive findings (e.g., Rosenberg et al., 1987, 1988) and null results (e.g., Hennekens et al., 1976; Klatsky et al., 1973, 1974). A further suspicion that people with recently diagnosed illnesses might be inclined to overestimate their premorbid coffee intake, has not been supported (Silverman et al., 1983). As such, it would appear that the overall pattern of inconsistent findings cannot be attributed to biased selection of controls.

Epidemiology of Caffeine and Cardiovascular Health: Main Findings

The inconsistencies in the main findings of the studies summarized in Table 5.1 are characteristic of the research in this field. However, despite the many inconsistencies among individual studies, there are discernible trends regarding the overall findings.

Manifest cardiovascular disease. About 40 studies have investigated the population association between caffeine and manifest cardiovascular disease (see James, 1991, and Table 5.1 here). Conclusions have been roughly evenly divided between caffeine having no relationship with relevant outcome variables and there being a positive caffeine-disease association (i.e., increased consumption is predictive of increased mortality and morbidity). Considering the apparent shortcomings in relation to the measurement of the key variable of caffeine consumption, doubt exists over the veracity of at least some of the many studies that reported null results. Because some studies reported a pattern of results in which the association with cardiovascular disease was significant for coffee but not for tea, the specific involvement of caffeine has been questioned (e.g., Klatsky et al., 1990). However, this doubt may be countered. First, given that tea contains less caffeine than coffee, insensitive measurement of caffeine exposure may simply have resulted in studies having insufficient statistical power to detect effects for tea, even when effects were evident for coffee.

Second, as mentioned in Chapter 1, population studies have consistently found coffee and tea consumption to be negatively correlated, with tea consumption appearing to be specifically associated with aspects of lifestyle that are disease preventive (Schwarz et al., 1994). Therefore, even if caffeine is harmful, the harm caused by the caffeine in tea may be countered by health-promoting behaviors associated with tea consumption. Third, several studies have reported that tea contains noncaffeine factors that may be health-promoting. Specifically, it has been suggested that polyphenols in tea, which have known antioxidant properties, may reduce the risk of atherosclerosis (Abe et al., 1995; Hertog et al., 1993; Imai & Nakachi, 1995; Miura et al., 1994). Indeed, a significant inverse association between tea consumption and mean serum cholesterol was observed in a population study conducted in Norway (Stensvold et al., 1992). Thus, apart from being difficult to detect in its own right, any potentially adverse effect of the caffeine in tea could be more than offset, either by the tendency among tea drinkers to engage in more health-promoting behavior than coffee drinkers or by a direct protective action of tea polyphenols.

Overall, the epidemiologic literature supports the conclusion that caffeine is a risk factor for cardiovascular disease, and this conclusion is consistent with two recent meta-analyses (Greenland, 1993; Kawachi et al., 1994). Both analyses showed an overall modest caffeine-disease association. An earlier meta-analysis, which reported no caffeine-disease association

(Myers & Basinski, 1992), was shown by Greenland (1993) to have been "improperly conducted and interpreted" (p. 372). Both Greenland (1993) and Kawachi et al. (1994) found that the caffeine-disease association was consistently more pronounced in case-control studies than in cohort studies. However, neither epidemiologic approach was found to have any specific strengths or shortcomings that would satisfactorily explain the difference in results (e.g., neither approach has been superior regarding the control of potential confounders). Finally, the central conclusion that caffeine contributes to cardiovascular disease has high biological plausibility, especially in relation to the known hemodynamic properties of the drug. These properties are discussed in the context of relevant experimental studies described below.

Population serum cholesterol. Table 5.1 suggests that of the three areas of research focus (i.e., manifest disease, serum cholesterol, and blood pressure), a positive association has been most consistently observed for studies of the relationship between coffee and cholesterol. This pattern has a long history, being evident in the large number of studies published before 1990 (James, 1991). It is possible that this consistency is due to the use of superior methods for measuring habitual caffeine consumption. Studies of caffeine and cholesterol have typically examined a variety of dietary variables, and there has been a tendency for investigators in these studies to employ more detailed, and possibly more accurate, measurement procedures. Consequently, statistical power may have been improved, thereby reducing the risk of Type II errors. Indeed, strong support for a causal relationship between coffee and serum cholesterol is provided by experimental evidence discussed below.

Population blood pressure. Of the 7 studies summarized in Table 5.1, and a further 11 published before 1990, 5 reported no association (Bertrand et al., 1978; Dawber et al., 1974; Lancaster et al., 1994; Medeiros, 1982; Stanton et al., 1978), 6 reported a significant positive association for either systolic or diastolic blood pressure (Birkett & Logan, 1988; Burke et al., 1992; Lang, Bureau, et al., 1983; Lang, Degoulet, et al., 1983; Miner et al., 1985; Shirlow et al., 1988), and 7 reported an inverse association (Gyntelberg et al., 1995; Kirchhoff et al., 1994; Lewis et al., 1993; Periti et al., 1987; Salvaggio et al., 1990, 1992; Stensvold et al., 1989). This diversity of outcomes appears daunting. Consequently, it is not surprising that many commentators have stated that the epidemiologic findings on caffeine and blood pressure are too

---

Table 5.2 Experimental Studies Confirming Acute Caffeine-Induced Increases in Blood Pressure

Casiglia et al., 1991	Conrad et al., 1982
France & Ditto, 1988, 1989, 1992	Goldstein & Shapiro, 1987
Greenberg & Shapiro, 1987	Greenstadt et al., 1988
Horst, Robinson, et al., 1934	Horst & Jenkins, 1935
Horst et al., 1936	Izzo et al., 1983
James, 1990	James & Richardson, 1991
Lane, 1982	Lane et al., 1990
Lane & Williams, 1985, 1987	Lovallo et al., 1989, 1991
Myers et al., 1989	Perkins, Sexton, Stiller, et al., 1994
Passmore et al., 1987	Pincomb et al., 1987, 1991, 1993
Ray et al., 1986	Robertson et al., 1978
Rose & Behm, 1991	Smits et al., 1983, 1985a, 1985b, 1986, 1993
Strickland et al., 1989	Sung et al., 1990, 1994
Whitsett et al., 1984	

---

inconsistent to permit any sensible conclusions. Yet, it will be argued here that careful consideration of the experimental evidence (discussed below) not only implicates caffeine as a persistent pressor agent but also helps to explain the seemingly inconsistent findings of two decades of epidemiologic research.

■ Experimental Studies of Caffeine and Blood Pressure

It has been shown conclusively that caffeine has the potential to elevate blood pressure (see Table 5.2). Caffeine-induced elevations in blood pressure peak within a range of 5-15 mm Hg systolic and 5-10 mm Hg diastolic, may last several hours, and have been observed across a wide age range, in both normotensive and hypertensive men and women. Herein lies a dilemma. If caffeine is a significant pressor agent, it would be reasonable to expect elevated blood pressure to emerge as a stable epidemiologic outcome of habitual caffeine use. Contrary to this expectation, as discussed above, there has been great diversity in the epidemiologic findings for caffeine and blood pressure. This pattern of inconsistencies is especially intriguing and can be traced to the failure of investigators to take account of the processes of caffeine tolerance and withdrawal in the context of the habitual consumption of the drug.

The Myth of Hemodynamic Tolerance

Considering the apparent inconsistencies between the epidemiologic findings and the proven acute pressor effects of caffeine, it is useful to reiterate a point made in Chapter 3, namely, that most of what is known about the pharmacological effects of caffeine in humans has been provided by studies that have employed a methodology involving acute caffeine challenge. Generally, a relatively large caffeine dose is administered after an overnight fast and a period of caffeine abstinence, despite the fact that most caffeine use is characterized by the daily ingestion of relatively small doses consumed at intervals. In respect to the cardiovascular effects of caffeine, the relative absence of experimental protocols that more closely match habitual patterns of caffeine use appears to be attributable, in part, to the long-held belief that habitual use leads to the development of hemodynamic tolerance. If frequency of citation is any guide, then one important source of this belief has been a study by Robertson et al. (1981). Although important, the study contains a number of shortcomings (see James, 1991, pp. 112-113), including the fact that the conclusions regarding tolerance were based on analyses of data obtained from only nine subjects. Considering the small sample size (and consequently compromised statistical power), persistent hemodynamic effects, indicative of incomplete tolerance, were unlikely to be apparent (i.e., there was a high risk of Type II error). Indeed, it is interesting to note that small sample size (five to eight participants) is also a feature of several subsequent studies that claimed to have demonstrated hemodynamic tolerance (Casiglia et al., 1992; Debrah et al., 1995; Haigh et al., 1993).

In fact, the overall evidence suggests that habitual use of moderate amounts of caffeine leads to partial rather than complete tolerance. Of several converging lines of evidence, the studies referred to in Table 5.2 provide strong inferential support for the suggestion that habitual consumers are not immune to the pressor effects of caffeine. Although individual studies were designed to investigate reactivity to acute caffeine challenge, participants in the studies cited in Table 5.2 represent the entire spectrum of caffeine users, ranging from nonusers to consumers of higher than average amounts. Despite the overall similarity of method (caffeine challenge after a brief period of caffeine abstinence), no systematic differences in consumer-associated reactivity to caffeine are evident in the overall results. Moreover, in the minority of studies in which caffeine consumer status was used as an explicit criterion for selecting participants representing high and low habitual consumers, no systematic differences in caffeine reactivity were observed between the different user groups (e.g., James, 1990; Lane et al., 1990). This is contrary to what would be expected, if habitual consumers develop tolerance.

More specifically, a few studies have examined the effects of repeated caffeine doses, rather than employing a single caffeine dose (characteristic of the large majority of experimental studies). It has been found that the magnitude of caffeine-induced pressor effects is inversely related to plasma caffeine concentration at the time the drug is ingested, irrespective of prior history of use (Smits et al., 1985b). Consequently, a second cup of coffee, for example, ingested within 1 or 2 hours of an earlier cup, produces a discernible but smaller pressor effect (a phenomenon known as tachyphylaxis) than that caused by the first cup (Goldstein et al., 1990; Lane & Manus, 1989; Ratliff-Crain et al., 1989). As plasma levels fall, the hemodynamic effects of the drug increase in both consumers and nonconsumers (Smits et al., 1985b). Of the various factors that influence plasma caffeine level, elimination half-life and time since the drug was last consumed are generally the main determinants. Given that the half-life of caffeine in humans is typically about 5 hours (Pfeifer & Notari, 1988), and that the drug is usually consumed in separate portions throughout the day (with fewer portions consumed later in the day followed by overnight abstinence), plasma caffeine concentration is typically highest in the late afternoon and lowest on awakening in the morning (Denaro et al., 1991; Lelo, Miners, et al., 1986a). Overnight abstinence of 10 to 12 hours is characteristic of the consumption patterns of the majority of consumers and leads to almost complete depletion of systemic caffeine by early morning (Lelo, Miners, et al., 1986b; Pfeifer & Notari, 1988; J. Shi et al., 1993). This, in turn, renders the consumer sensitive to the hemodynamic effects of the drug when reexposure next occurs (typically, shortly after awakening) (Denaro et al., 1991; D. Shi et al., 1993; Smits et al., 1985b).

Pressor Effects of Habitual Caffeine Consumption

Among the comparatively few studies that have examined the effects of caffeine exposure resembling usual patterns of habitual consumption, there is evidence that modest sustained decreases in blood pressure occur when caffeine beverages are either removed from the diet (Bak & Grobbee, 1990) or are replaced by decaffeinated alternatives (van Dusseldorp et al., 1989).

Similar results were obtained in a number of recent studies in which ambulatory monitoring was used to measure blood pressure level for extended periods. To date, there have been seven such studies, four of which reported persistent caffeine-induced pressor effects (Green & Suls, 1996; James, 1994b; Jeong & Dimsdale, 1990; Superko et al., 1994), and three reported no effect (Eggertsen et al., 1993; MacDonald et al., 1991; Myers & Reeves, 1991). Interestingly, the seven studies are distinguishable on the basis of the length of the time epochs used to analyze results (James, 1993, 1997). Readings were averaged across shorter time periods in the four positive studies, and longer time periods in the three negative studies. Because the hemodynamic effects of caffeine generally peak within about 1 hour postingestion, and are substantially diminished within about 3 hours (Robertson et al., 1978), significant pressor effects were probably obscured in the three negative studies because blood pressure readings were averaged across inappropriately long epochs.

Figure 5.1(a) summarizes results averaged across 2-hour epochs for ambulatory blood pressure measured over 24-hour periods in healthy normotensive men and women who were maintained on a habitual regimen of moderate caffeine intake equivalent to one to one and a half cups of coffee consumed three times daily (morning, mid-morning, and mid-afternoon) (James, 1994b). The 2-hour blood pressure levels correlated well with systemic caffeine levels. Increases in blood pressure peaked at 6 mm Hg systolic and 5 mm Hg diastolic by late morning, whereas increases of 2-4 mm Hg persisted for several hours of the day. Compared to the effects of caffeine ingested after a sustained period of abstinence, habitual caffeine consumption diminished peak pressor effects by only 25% (James, 1994b). That is, habitual use of the drug produced partial (rather than complete) caffeine tolerance.

Withdrawal following habitual consumption. In addition to confirming the presence of persistent postingestion increases in blood pressure, 24-hour monitoring revealed modest blood pressure decreases during times of the day when participants had been caffeine-abstinent for several hours (see Figure 5.1(a)). These findings are consistent with recent studies of the pharmacokinetics and pharmacodynamics of caffeine, which indicate that sensitivity to the pressor effects of the drug is fully regained after as little as 20 hours of abstinence (D. Shi et al., 1993). Furthermore, Figure 5.1(b) shows that the transient hypotensive effects that accompany overnight abstinence persist throughout most of the following day when abstinence is extended.

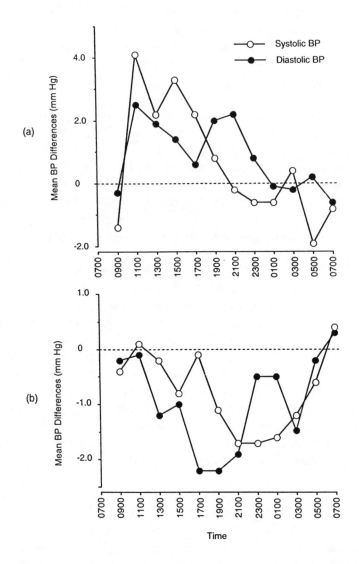

Figure 5.1. Mean differences in ambulatory systolic (SBP) and diastolic (DBP) blood pressure obtained during a double-blind caffeine-free regimen versus (a) caffeine (equivalent to 1 to 1.5 cups of coffee) three times daily, and (b) abrupt withdrawal of caffeine.

Difference scores were obtained by subtracting mean blood pressures obtained during the caffeine-free condition from pressures obtained at the same time of day during the caffeine condition.

SOURCE: Adapted from results reported previously in James, 1994.

Population Caffeine and Blood Pressure: An Integration

The results summarized in Figure 5.1 shed new light on the epidemiologic findings reported above. The apparent inconsistencies in the association between caffeine consumption and population blood pressure can now be understood as an artifact arising from the general failure of epidemiologic studies to take account of participants' systemic caffeine levels at the time of blood pressure measurement. Figure 5.1(a) shows that blood pressure in habitual caffeine consumers may be either increased, unchanged, or decreased, depending on the temporal relation between blood pressure measurement and caffeine ingestion, and Figure 5.1(b) shows that the hypotensive effects induced by caffeine abstinence persist and become more pronounced if overnight abstinence is extended into the following day. In this regard, it is interesting to note that in only one epidemiologic study conducted to date was a record taken of the time since caffeine was last consumed prior to blood pressure being measured. Shirlow et al. (1988) found that participants who reported consuming caffeine during the 3 hours prior to examination had significantly elevated blood pressure compared to those who had consumed no caffeine during the same period.

It therefore appears that the observed association between caffeine and blood pressure depends upon the distribution of caffeine consumers who happen to be caffeine-sated versus caffeine-withdrawn at the time of examination. In epidemiologic studies of caffeine and blood pressure, it is typical for participants to be asked to report the amount of caffeine they consume and for a single measurement of blood pressure to be taken. However, it is evident from the pattern of effects summarized in Figure 5.1 that the relationship between habitual caffeine use and blood pressure is complex. The relationship between caffeine and blood pressure depends on level of habitual usage *and* the time elapsed between the most recent intake of caffeine and the moment at which blood pressure is measured. Irrespective of habitual use, recent caffeine consumption will generally have a pressor effect (positive association). Conversely, in habitual consumers, blood pressure is likely to be unaffected after a relatively brief period of abstinence (null result), or decreased after a longer period (10 or more hours) of abstinence (inverse association).

Five of the seven epidemiologic studies of caffeine and blood pressure summarized in Table 5.1, including two based on the same cohort (Salvaggio et al., 1990, 1992), reported an inverse association between caffeine and blood pressure, and all five studies measured blood pressure after periods of abstinence capable of inducing reductions in blood pressure. Rather than indicating a protective effect (as has been suggested), the inverse association reported in these epidemiologic studies is consistent with caffeine having potentially damaging pressor effects during postingestion periods and hypotensive effects during periods of abstinence (as summarized in Figure 5.1). This phenomenon, whereby blood pressure in habitual consumers either increases or decreases, depending upon when the drug was last ingested, appears not to be unique to caffeine. A similar pattern has been identified for cigarette smoking and population blood pressure. Although smoking increases blood pressure acutely, epidemiologic studies have failed to show a sustained effect, apparently because in most studies, blood pressure measurements have been taken after the smokers had been abstinent from smoking for periods long enough to produce nicotine-withdrawal decreases in blood pressure (Pickering et al., 1991). Evidently, future epidemiologic studies of caffeine and blood pressure (and smoking and blood pressure) should adjust for systemic caffeine (nicotine) levels at the time of examination.

Caffeine, Stress, and Other Sources of Hemodynamic Reactivity

Reactivity to psychosocial "stress" has long been considered to be a possible causal factor in the development of cardiovascular disease, in general, and hypertension, in particular (Girdler et al., 1990; Manuck et al., 1990). Like caffeine, stress is ubiquitous. Moreover, caffeine consumption has been reported to increase during periods of heightened stress (Conway et al., 1981). Evidence that caffeine might exacerbate some of the harmful effects of stress was first reported by Henry and Stephens (1980) in a study in which rates of mortality and disease were monitored in mice living in large community cages. As conditions became more crowded and competitive, the incidence of cardiovascular and renal disease increased. Further increases in disease were observed when coffee was substituted for drinking water. In the first experimental study of caffeine and stress in humans, Lane (1983) found that the pressor effects of caffeine and stress (mental arithmetic) were additive. This initial study involved participants who were virtual nonusers of caffeine, and the findings were replicated in subsequent studies involving nonusers (Lane & Williams, 1985) and habitual consumers (Lane & Williams, 1987). Subsequent experimentation has repeatedly confirmed the additive nature of the pressor effects of caffeine and stress (Greenberg &

Shapiro, 1987; Greenstadt et al., 1988; James, 1990; Lane et al., 1990; Lovallo et al., 1989, 1991; Myers et al., 1989; Strickland et al., 1989), including stress encountered in the natural environment (France & Ditto, 1989, 1992; Lane et al., 1994; Pincomb et al., 1987).

Uncertainty has existed as to whether caffeine-induced pressor effects are due to cardiac stimulation of rate and/or contractility (leading to increased cardiac output) or vasoconstriction (leading to increased total peripheral resistance). Studies have suggested that the primary mechanism is likely to be increased vascular resistance (France & Ditto, 1988; Pincomb et al., 1988), and this is generally consistent with the evidence that many of the actions of caffeine are mediated by competitive blockade of endogenous adenosine. However, whereas caffeine increases vascular resistance when participants are at rest, it appears that during stress caffeine may stimulate both vascular *and* myocardial mechanisms (France & Ditto, 1992; Lovallo et al., 1991; Pincomb et al., 1991, 1993). Concern about the additive hemodynamic effects of caffeine and stress is heightened by the fact that these effects also appear to be additive to other sources of hemodynamic reactivity, including dispositional anxiety (James, 1990) and cigarette smoking (Freestone & Ramsay, 1982, 1983; Freestone et al., 1995; James & Richardson, 1991; Perkins, Sexton, Stiller, et al., 1994; Ray et al., 1986; Rose & Behm, 1991; Smits et al., 1993).

▓ Experimental Studies of Caffeine and Serum Cholesterol

The effect of caffeine on blood lipid levels has been an area of intense interest (Consensus Conference, 1985; Durrington et al., 1988) and intense controversy. Despite many apparently inconsistent findings, a consensus has recently emerged on how best to explain the relationship between coffee and cholesterol. Several early studies of the effects of caffeine on lipid metabolism indicated that coffee increases serum-free fatty acid levels in animals (Akinyanju & Yudkin, 1967; Bellet et al., 1968) and humans (Avogaro et al., 1973; Bellet et al., 1968; Oberman et al., 1975). These findings were of interest, because free fatty acids are related to other lipid fractions, especially those believed to be atherogenic (notably, cholesterol). Studies of caffeine, however, produced inconsistent results. Although significant cholesterolemic effects were observed for rabbits (Myasnikov, 1958) and rats (Fears, 1978), no effect was found for rhesus monkeys (Callahan et al., 1979) and humans (Naismith et al., 1970; Steinke, 1973). Then, in 1983, a strong association between coffee consumption and blood lipid levels was found in a large epidemiologic study conducted in the municipality of Tromsø in northern Norway (Thelle et al., 1983b). Due to the strength of the association, the study attracted considerable attention (Arab et al., 1983; Hofman et al., 1983; Kovar et al., 1983; Modest, 1983; Ockene et al., 1983; Roeckel, 1983; Shekelle et al., 1983; Stanton et al., 1978; Thelle et al., 1983a), and the Tromsø investigators subsequently sought to experimentally test the hypothesis that the two variables, coffee and cholesterol, may be causally linked (Arnesen et al., 1984).

A key feature of the epidemiologic study by Thelle et al. (1983b) was that the style of coffee said to be characteristically consumed by residents of the Tromsø region was described as being predominantly boiled. The intervention study was conducted over several weeks and compared the effects of boiled coffee (six or more cups per day) with abstinence from coffee in healthy volunteers. There was a significant increase in serum cholesterol levels during the period when coffee was consumed. Moreover, participants typically consumed the coffee without additives such as milk and sugar, so these factors did not explain the observed results. Thus, coffee was implicated, but there was a strong suspicion that the method of brewing may have been a critical factor. Accordingly, a second experiment was conducted in which boiled coffee, filtered coffee, and coffee abstinence were compared (Førde et al., 1985). In the boiled coffee condition, total serum cholesterol increased, whereas cholesterol levels decreased in the other conditions. At about the same time, a study conducted in the United Kingdom found that the consumption of six or more cups of instant coffee per day had no effect on serum cholesterol levels (Hill, 1985), thereby further implicating brewing method (boiling ground coffee beans) as the main factor responsible for the cholesterolemic effects observed in the Norwegian studies.

None of these studies, however, controlled for possible differences in the caffeine content of the beverages that were compared. That is, boiled coffee, in general, may have a higher caffeine concentration than either filtered or instant coffee, and it is conceivable that this difference could have been responsible for the enhanced cholesterolemic effects of boiled coffee. However, Bak and Grobbee (1989) compared boiled and filtered coffee beverages that had been prepared so as to contain comparable amounts of caffeine. Once again, boiled coffee was found to be cholesterolemic, whereas filtered coffee was not. Subsequent animal experimentation confirmed the results obtained with humans (Sanders & Sandaradura, 1992). Overall, then, the cumulative results are consistent. Unfiltered boiled coffee increases serum cholesterol levels (Arnesen et al., 1984; Aro et al., 1987; Bak & Grobbee, 1989; Førde et al., 1985), whereas filtered coffee has little or no such effect (Ahola et al., 1991; Aro et al., 1987; Bak & Grobbee, 1989; Bønaa et al., 1988; Førde et al., 1985; Fried et al., 1992; Rosmarin et al., 1990; Superko et al., 1991; van Dusseldorp et al., 1990, 1991). Consequently, attempts were made to try to identify the specific hypercholesterolemic compound present in unfiltered boiled coffee.

Zock et al. (1990) found that the lipid-enriched supernatant of boiled coffee had a marked cholesterol-raising effect in humans, and similar results have been reported for hamsters (Ratnayake et al., 1995). It was also found that the cholesterolemic compound in coffee can be removed by passing the beverage through a paper filter (Ahola et al., 1991; van Dusseldorp et al., 1991). Further investigation led to the identification of cafestol, and possibly also kahweol, as being the critical compounds (Heckers et al., 1994; Ratnayake et al., 1993; Weusten-Van der Wouw et al., 1994). Cafestol and kahweol are uncommon lipid compounds that are possibly unique to coffee (Folstrar, 1985), and their mechanism of action at the molecular level has yet to be elucidated. Ratnayake et al. (1993) compared the lipid content and composition of various styles of coffee brews prepared according to customary methods. Scandinavian-style boiled coffee contained 40 to 125 times more lipid than coffee passed through a filter paper. Filtered decaffeinated coffee appears to be relatively lipid-free (Wahrburg et al., 1994), and Italian coffee (prepared with a moka machine) may also be low in lipids (Sanguigni et al., 1995). Other major coffee styles, however, including Turkish/Greek-style, plunger (also known as French press or cafetière), and espresso all contain significant lipid fractions (Urgert et al., 1995).

▓ Experimental Studies of Caffeine and Cardiac Arrhythmia

Caffeine has long been suspected of having arrhythmogenic properties (Dobmeyer et al., 1983; Graboys & Lown, 1983), and the proscription of caffeine for individuals with irregular cardiac rhythm is a common medical practice (Graboys, 1989; Myers, 1988). However, cardiac arrhythmias are prevalent to varying degrees among healthy adults of all ages (Stamler et al., 1992), and ventricular extrasystoles (one of the more common arrhythmias) are believed to be predominantly harmless (Graboys, 1989; Graboys & Lown, 1983; Montague et al., 1983). Consequently, two key questions need to be considered: Is caffeine significantly arrhythmogenic (and not just believed to be)? If so, what implications does this have for cardiovascular health? Overall, there have been surprisingly few controlled investigations of the arrhythmogenic potential of caffeine. Although the first question has received some experimental attention, considerations of the second have been largely inferential.

Evidence for caffeine-induced arrhythmia in patients with cardiac disease has been reported in some studies (Dobmeyer et al., 1983; Polonovski et al., 1952; Sutherland et al., 1985), but not others (Chelsky et al., 1990; Gould et al., 1973, 1979; Graboys, 1989; Myers & Harris, 1990; Myers et al., 1987). Similarly, several studies involving healthy subjects have reported null results (Newcombe et al., 1988; Stamler et al., 1992; Sutherland et al., 1985), whereas one large study involving 7,252 men ages 37 to 75 years reported significant associations between caffeine consumption and frequency of extrasystoles observed during a 2-minute electrocardiogram (Prineas et al., 1980). Wennmalm and Wennmalm (1989) postulated a mechanism to explain how caffeine could cause clinically significant arrhythmogenic effects. However, considering the paucity of evidence in support of such effects, the proposed theoretical model may be somewhat premature. Overall, the prevailing opinion appears to be that moderate caffeine consumption poses no significant arrhythmogenic risk, even for people with ischemic heart disease or current ventricular ectopy. Nevertheless, commentators continue to caution that people with heart disease should avoid consuming "large" amounts of caffeine (Graboys, 1989; Myers, 1988). This would seem to be sound advice, considering the limited available evidence, and the fact that findings have been inconsistent.

SUMMARY

Various lines of evidence converge to suggest that, contrary to common belief, habitual caffeine consumers do *not* develop immunity to the pressor effects of the drug. Although comparatively modest, the blood pressure increases reported in recent studies (James, 1994b; Jeong & Dimsdale, 1990; Superko et al., 1994) are large enough to be clinically significant, especially in people who are already at risk for cardiovascular disease. Effects of this magnitude could contribute to errors in clinical diagnosis and undermine the benefits of antihypertensive medication. More important, because the population distribution of blood pressure in the "normal" range has a positive and essentially linear association with cardiovascular disease (MacMahon et al., 1990), any contribution by caffeine to population blood pressure levels threatens to contribute to the overall incidence of cardiovascular mortality and morbidity. Although caffeine-induced pressor effects are not constant (but depend on when caffeine was last consumed), current evidence indicates that habitual consumers experience elevations in blood pressure for substantial periods of every day that caffeine is ingested (James, 1994b; Jeong & Dimsdale, 1990; Superko et al., 1994). Among the factors determining the extent of benefit/harm arising from changes in population blood pressure levels are the size of the change in blood pressure, the duration of exposure to the factor responsible for the change, prevalence of exposure to the putative factor, and incidence of the pathological conditions to which elevated blood pressure contributes (e.g., coronary heart disease) (Collins et al., 1990).

Consideration of these factors suggests that the widespread use of caffeine probably contributes to population cardiovascular disease. Although the size of the reduction in population blood pressure that might accompany a reduction in caffeine use is likely to be modest in absolute terms, exposure to caffeine is generally long (virtually lifelong in the majority of consumers), the prevalence of exposure is very high (more than 80% in most countries), and the incidence of cardiovascular disease is high throughout the world. Recently, James (1997) has argued that if caffeine consumption had the effect of elevating average population blood pressure by 2 to 4 mm Hg (a reasonable inference considering the relevant experimental data; James, 1994b; Jeong & Dimsdale, 1990; Superko et al., 1994), and 80% of the population are assumed to be habitual consumers (Gilbert, 1984), extrapolation based on epidemiologic blood pressure data (MacMahon et al., 1990) suggests that population-wide cessation of caffeine use could lead to 9% to 14% less coronary heart disease and 17% to 24% less stroke. An additional adverse impact, due to increased serum cholesterol, is likely to be experienced in populations in which consumption of unfiltered coffee is widespread. Thus, the accumulated experimental and epidemiologic evidence indicates that caffeine-beverage consumption is a significant and preventible cardiovascular risk factor.

FURTHER READING

James, J. E. (1997). Caffeine and blood pressure: Habitual use is a preventable cardiovascular risk factor. *Lancet, 349,* 279-281.

Lane, J. D., Pieper, C. F., Barefoot, J. C., Williams, R. B., & Siegler, I. C. (1994). Caffeine and cholesterol: Interactions with hostility. *Psychosomatic Medicine, 56,* 260-266.

Lovallo, W. R., Pincomb, G. A., Sung, B. H., Everson, S. A., Passey, R. B., & Wilson, M. F. (1991). Hypertension risk and caffeine's effect on cardiovascular activity during mental stress in young men. *Health Psychology, 10,* 236-243.

Savitz, D. A., & Barron, A. E. (1989). Estimating and correcting for confounder misclassification. *American Journal of Epidemiology, 129,* 1062-1071.

Weusten-Van der Wouw, M. P., Katan, M. B., Viani, R., Huggett, A. C., Liardon, R., Lund-Larsen, P. G., Thelle, D. S., Ahola, I., Aro, A., Meyboom, S., & Beynen, A. G. (1994). Identity of the cholesterol-raising factor from boiled coffee and its effects on liver function enzymes. *Journal of Lipid Research, 35,* 721-733.

Caffeine and Cancer

Cancer is responsible for about 4 million deaths each year worldwide (Davis et al., 1990). In the developed countries, it is the second most common cause of death (after coronary heart disease), with about one in three people developing cancer during their lifetime (Renneker, 1988). Among the many environmental and lifestyle variables that are responsible for cancer in its many forms, diet is a major factor (Doll & Peto, 1981). Considering the near-universality of dietary caffeine, it is not surprising that the drug has come under suspicion as a possible cause of cancer.

Reminiscent of the preceding chapter on cardiovascular disease, research on caffeine and cancer can be divided into two broad categories of experimental and epidemiologic research. However, whereas there is an extensive experimental literature concerned with various indices of preclinical cardiovascular function in humans (e.g., blood pressure, cholesterol level, arrhythmia), few comparable indices are available for ethical experimentation on human carcinogens. Consequently, experimental research on the carcinogenic potential of caffeine has generally involved either in vitro study of lower organisms (e.g., bacteria and fungi) and mammalian (including human) cells in culture, or in vivo studies of intact nonhuman animals. The study of caffeine and cancer in intact humans has generally involved epidemiologic approaches.

■ Mutagenic Potential of Caffeine

Mutagens are chemical and/or environmental agents capable of inducing changes in cell DNA (the material responsible for the transmission of hereditary characteristics), and mutagenicity is one indication of carcinogenic potential. It has been firmly established that caffeine has mutagenic effects in lower organisms such as bacteria and fungi (Kihlman, 1977; Timson, 1977). However, these effects have generally only been observed at concentration levels far in excess of those that occur when humans consume caffeine. Mutagenic effects have been less consistently reported in cultured mammalian cells, and only then at caffeine concentrations that would be toxic, if not lethal, in humans (Kihlman & Andersson, 1987). Considering the relative rapidity with which caffeine is metabolized in mammals, the high concentrations needed to produce mutagenic effects are never likely to occur. Moreover, it appears that the occurrence of mutagenic effects in vivo is further mitigated by enzymes that are normally present in intact animals (Nehlig & Debry, 1994). Consequently, there is general agreement among reviewers (e.g., Aeschbacher, 1988; D'Ambrosio, 1994; IARC (International Agency for Research on Cancer), 1991; Kihlman & Andersson, 1987) that caffeine, as typically consumed, poses no *direct* mutagenic risk to humans.

Synergistic Mutagenicity

Although apparently having little human mutagenic potential in its own right, caffeine is capable of affecting the mutagenic action of a variety of other agents (IARC, 1991; Kihlman & Andersson, 1987). It has been shown, for example, that in mammalian cells, including human lymphocytes, caffeine may enhance cell transformation caused by X-rays, ultraviolet light, and a variety of chemical compounds (IARC, 1991; Nehlig & Debry, 1994). Conversely, caffeine has also been found to be capable of suppressing the action of some mutagenic agents in some cell lines. However, because the mechanisms responsible for these synergistic influences are not well understood, the particular influence, whether enhancing or inhibiting of mutagenicity, cannot be reliably predicted at present.

Inhibition of DNA repair is thought to be one mechanism by which caffeine may enhance the mutagenicity of other agents (Kihlman & Andersson, 1987). This is of particular interest in therapeutics. Because mutation often lessens cell viability, caffeine might act to increase the effectiveness of drugs used in cancer treatment. Indeed, growth of human tumor specimens has been found to be synergistically inhibited following treatment with combinations of anticancer agents and caffeine (Tomita & Tsuchiya, 1989). However, this same process also suggests the possibility that caffeine might enhance not only the primary therapeutic effect but also exacerbate untoward side effects of antitumor agents on nontumoric tissue. This concern has been tested empirically but was not confirmed (Sadzuka et al., 1993). It appears that caffeine may selectively enhance the effects of therapeutic drugs on tumor cells while having no effect on normal tissue (Sadzuka et al., 1995).

▣ Carcinogenic Potential of Caffeine

Several long-term studies suggest that caffeine has little or no carcinogenic potential in rodents. For example, Takayama and Kuwabara (1982) gave rats caffeine in solution estimated to be equivalent in human terms to about 40 to 70 cups of coffee daily. After 78 weeks of this regimen, the animals were given tap water for a further 26 weeks, while a control group received tap water without caffeine for 104 weeks. No differences in general condition or mortality were observed between experimental and control rats, and at 104 weeks, all surviving animals were sacrificed. Tumors were observed at a variety of sites (e.g., pituitary, mammary, uterus, thyroid, pancreas, skin, kidney), but they occurred with comparable frequency in experimental and control animals. Similar results were reported by the same investigators in studies of mice (Takayama et al., 1984), and by others in studies of rats (Mohr et al., 1984).

One focus of attention for in vivo studies has been the role of caffeine in the rate of breast cancer formation in rats, but unfortunately the results do not suggest a clear pattern of effects. Minton et al. (1983) reported that caffeine apparently hastened the development of breast tumors in rats fed a high-fat diet, whereas it delayed tumor development in rats fed a standard diet. Conversely, Welsch et al. (1983) found that caffeine administered in drinking water to rats prior to or during exposure to a known carcinogen had no significant effect on the incidence of breast tumors, whereas caffeine administered after exposure to the carcinogen increased the rate of tumor formation. Furthermore, using a different strain of rats and a different tumor-inducing method than was used by Minton et al. (1983) and Welsch et al. (1983), Petrek et al. (1985) found that caffeine inhibited rat breast cancer.

In summary, in vivo experiments involving laboratory animals have variously suggested that caffeine has no significant carcinogenic effect, that it may act as a carcinogen under particular circumstances, or that caffeine may have antitumoric properties. Overall, the prevailing opinion based on experimental evidence is that caffeine is unlikely to have carcinogenic effects in humans. However, it is not possible at present to assess the full implications of the laboratory findings, especially the many reports of synergistic inter-actions (both enhancing and inhibiting) in animals exposed to caffeine in combination with known carcinogens. There are many factors that may limit the generality of findings from animal experiments, including species-specific factors such as target tissue sensitivity, potential repair mechanisms at the molecular and cellular level, immune responses, and hormonal and enzymatic profiles (Würzner, 1988). Thus, although the experimental research suggests that exposure to caffeine alone is not a significant carcinogenic risk in humans, it remains unclear what risk exists when humans consume caffeine during periods of concomitant exposure to other dietary and environmental agents that are carcinogenic.

▤ Epidemiology of Caffeine and Cancer

Over the past three decades, there has been extensive investigation of the epidemiology of caffeine beverage consumption and cancer. Most of this research has been primarily concerned with coffee consumption, and to a much lesser extent, tea. Because comparatively few studies have examined caffeine specifically, the findings for coffee and tea consumption may be interpreted as being only indirectly suggestive of the carcinogenic potential of caffeine. Moreover, although most studies have been concerned with cancers located at one or a small number of specific sites, there has been some interest in examining associations between the consumption of caffeine beverages and overall cancer rates. For example, the responses of 10,064 participants in a hypertension detection program were also examined in relation to cancer rates (Martin et al., 1988). At the 4-year follow-up, exposure to caffeine was estimated on the basis of participants' reported consumption of coffee, tea, and caffeine-containing medications. No associations were found between caffeine consumption and mortality from cancer. Similarly, a 19-year follow-up of 1,910 men, ages 40 to 56 at the time of baseline examination, found no association between coffee consumption and incidence of cancers at all sites (LeGrady et al., 1987). However, cancer is not a single disease, and studies of specific sites indicate more complex associations than that suggested by examination of the relationship between caffeine consumption and overall cancer incidence.

Bladder Cancer

Following an initial report by Cole (1971) of a significant association between coffee consumption and cancer of the lower urinary tract (renal pelvis, ureter, bladder, and urethra), there has been considerable epidemiologic interest in coffee as a possible cause of bladder cancer. Notwithstanding many inconsistencies between studies, a substantial body of literature has accumulated to suggest a positive but weak association between coffee consumption and bladder cancer (IARC, 1991; James, 1991). Although reviewers have frequently expressed doubt as to whether this association is causal, it has been reported intermittently throughout the past two decades and has been observed in diverse populations around the world.

For example, in a recent case-control study involving 1,410 cases and controls resident in two different regions of northern Italy, a higher prevalence of coffee drinking was observed among cases than controls (D'Avanzo et al., 1992). Similar results were obtained in a cohort study involving 7,995 Japanese American men in Hawaii (Chyou et al., 1993). When followed up at 22 years, coffee consumption was found to be associated with an increased risk of bladder cancer. In these and the majority of previous studies in which a positive association was reported, adjustment was made for cigarette smoking and other potential confounders. Although it has been suggested that underadjustment due to misclassification of smoking might explain the positive findings, this seems unlikely (IARC, 1991). Indeed, evidence of an association between caffeine and bladder cancer was reported in a recent study in which nonsmoking participants were examined separately (Escolar-Pujolar et al., 1993). In addition, the association has been reported for both men and women, suggesting that occupational history is not likely to have been a serious confounding factor (IARC, 1991).

Although a dose-response relationship has been reported (Momas et al., 1994), the frequent absence of such a relationship has encouraged the belief that the association between coffee consumption and bladder cancer is not causal. However, considering the fact that the reported association has generally been weak, and that measurement of exposure to coffee has often been questionable, most epidemiologic studies probably did not have sufficient statistical power to detect a dose-response relationship even if one exists. On one hand, then, the available evidence is at least suggestive of a weak causal relationship between coffee consumption and bladder cancer. On the other hand, in a recent review of 35 case-control studies published over 20 years, the authors concluded that evidence of an increased risk of bladder cancer associated with coffee consumption may not be clinically significant (Viscoli et al., 1993). It therefore appears that the question remains open, and that further study is needed.

Kidney Cancer

Armstrong and Doll (1975) correlated incidence and/or mortality rates for a wide range of cancers in 32 countries and found a positive correlation between coffee consumption and cancer of the kidney. However, a subsequent case-control study by the same investigators (Armstrong et al., 1976) failed to confirm the association. Over the past two decades, the relationship between coffee and/or tea consumption and kidney cancer has been examined in fewer than 10 studies, and these have generally confirmed the absence of an association. One exception is a case-control study in which a significant association was observed for coffee drinking in women but not men (Asal et al., 1988).

Cancer of the Pancreas

Pancreatic cancer is one of the most rapidly fatal of human malignancies. Fewer than 10% of individuals are alive 1 year after diagnosis (Lyon et al., 1992; Zheng et al., 1993). Stocks (1970) examined age-adjusted death rates from cancers in relation to per capita consumption of cigarettes, solid fuel, tea, and coffee as measured by trade statistics in 20 countries and found a positive correlation between consumption of coffee and pancreatic cancer. However, it was not until a decade later that the possible involvement of coffee in the development of cancer of the pancreas became a matter of considerable public concern. This occurred following publication by MacMahon et al. (1981a) of a case-control study involving 369 patients with histologically confirmed cancer of the pancreas and 644 hospital patient controls. Intending primarily to investigate the role of smoking and alcohol in pancreatic cancer, the investigators found that coffee consumption was associated with an increased risk of the disease. The results also provided evidence of a dose-response relationship.

The MacMahon et al. (1981a) study prompted an immediate flurry of critical comment (Chalmers, 1981; Feinstein & Horwitz, 1982; Feinstein et al., 1981; Higgins et al.,1981; MacMahon et al., 1981b; Shedlofsky, 1981; Yakar, 1981), and a steady stream of further epidemiologic investigations followed. Some of these reported a positive correlation between coffee consumption and pancreatic cancer (e.g., Bernarde & Weiss, 1982; Cuckle & Kinlen, 1981), but most did not (e.g., Gold & Diener, 1981; Goldstein, 1982; Heuch et al., 1983; Kessler, 1981; La Vecchia, Ferrarioni, et al., 1989; La Vecchia et al., 1987; Nomura et al., 1981; Norell et al., 1986; Severson et al., 1982; Shibata et al., 1994; Stensvold & Jacobsen, 1994; Whittemore et al., 1983; Wynder et al., 1983; Zatonski et al., 1993).

In a review of the literature, MacMahon (1984) conceded that the original study (MacMahon et al., 1981a) contained a number of shortcomings, including methodological limitations in respect to the hospital-patient controls that had been used. In a subsequent study by the same group of investigators (Hsieh et al., 1986), 176 patients with histologically confirmed pancreatic cancer were compared with 273 controls composed primarily of patients with other cancers and benign tumors. The study made use of a revised questionnaire designed to elicit more detailed information on coffee consumption than had been obtained in most previous studies. In contrast to the earlier study, the results indicated a slightly increased risk only in relation to the heaviest coffee-consuming category (five or more cups per day) and no response-dependent relation. Hsieh et al. (1986) concluded that "if there is any association between coffee consumption and cancer of the pancreas, it is not as strong as our earlier data suggested" (p. 588). These findings are largely in agreement with those of the International Agency for Research on Cancer (IARC, 1991) which undertook a comprehensive review of the relevant research conducted prior to 1990. The IARC concluded that "the data are suggestive of a weak relationship between high levels of coffee consumption and the occurrence of pancreatic cancer" (p. 171) but cautioned that even this association could be due to bias or confounding.

Several recent studies have not supported the existence of even a modest positive correlation between coffee consumption and pancreatic cancer (Friedman & van den Eeden, 1993; Kalapothaki et al., 1993; Shibata et al., 1994; Zatonski et al., 1993; Zheng et al., 1993). One exception is a case-control study involving 149 cases and 363 controls conducted in the state of Utah, which has a disproportionately large population of Mormons (members of The Church of Jesus Christ of Latter-day Saints) and correspondingly fewer cigarette smokers and coffee drinkers than other areas of the United States (Lyon et al., 1992). In addition to showing an increased overall risk of pancreatic cancer for coffee drinkers, a dose-response relationship was found in both men and women and in cigarette smokers and nonsmokers. Although the particular characteristics of the population appear to have provided certain methodological advantages (e.g., a sufficient number of nonsmoking coffee drinkers to permit separate estimates to be made of the risk of coffee in smokers and nonsmokers), it is unclear to what extent the findings can be generalized to other populations. Moreover, a recent meta-analysis has added a new dimension by suggesting a U-shaped relationship such that small amounts of coffee might prevent pancreatic cancer, whereas large amounts might cause the disease (Nishi et al., 1996).

Benign Breast Disease

Considerable attention has been given to the possible involvement of coffee consumption in the development of fibrocystic breast disease. Although single and multiple benign (i.e., nonmalignant) cysts are fairly common, their presence is acknowledged as being a risk factor for the later development of breast cancer. Hence, initial reports of the involvement of caffeine in the development of benign breast disease (Minton et al., 1979a, 1979b) provoked widespread concern. Dramatic improvements were reported for fibrocystic breast disease in women who eliminated caffeine from their diet for periods of 1 to 6 months. The claims were subsequently repeated by the same investigators (Minton et al., 1981) and others (Brooks et al., 1981), although all the studies in question were largely uncontrolled and lacking in methodological rigor.

A number of subsequent intervention studies failed to substantiate the earlier claims (Allen & Froberg, 1987; Ernster et al., 1982; Heyden & Muhlbaier, 1984; Lubin et al., 1985; Mansel et al., 1982; Marshall et al., 1982; Schairer et al., 1987). Although not devoid of methodological short-comings (see James, 1991), the subsequent studies were generally better controlled and used more objective measurement criteria than the studies by Minton et al. (1979a, 1979b, 1981) and Brooks et al. (1981). Nevertheless, even these improved studies have not always been in agreement, with several reporting a modest increased incidence of the disease in association with caffeine consumption (Boyle et al., 1984; La Vecchia et al., 1985; Lawson et al., 1981; Odenheimer et al., 1984). Overall, there seems to be little objective support for the hypothesis that caffeine is causally related to benign breast disease. Whatever association there might be is likely to be slight and could well be the result of confounding.

Breast Cancer

As with benign breast disease, the epidemiologic evidence regarding caffeine and breast cancer is somewhat mixed. Several studies have reported a modest increased risk associated with caffeine consumption (La Vecchia et al., 1986; Lawson et al., 1981; Mansel et al., 1982; Rohan & McMichael, 1988), whereas several others found no association (Lubin et al., 1981, Rosenberg et al., 1985; Schairer et al., 1987). More recent studies, in particular, have tended to report no association between exposure to caffeine and increased risk of breast cancer (Ewertz, 1993; Folsom et al., 1993; McLaughlin et al., 1992; S. J. Smith et al., 1994).

Ovarian Cancer

Over the past 15 years, several studies have reported a significantly increased risk of ovarian cancer in coffee consumers (La Vecchia et al., 1984; Trichopoulos et al., 1981; Whittemore et al., 1988). A dose-dependent increased risk was reported in one case-control study of 247 women with histologically confirmed epithelial ovarian cancer and 494 hospital controls with acute conditions (La Vecchia et al., 1984). Conversely, several studies failed to find any significant association between caffeine consumption and ovarian cancer (Byers et al., 1983; Hartge et al., 1982; Polychronopoulou et al., 1993; Snowdon & Phillips, 1984). Inconsistent findings have even been reported by the same group of investigators for results obtained from the same case-control study. That is, although an initial analysis of 92 cases and 105 controls suggested a positive association between coffee consumption and ovarian cancer (Trichopoulos et al., 1981), the association was no longer evident following a subsequent analysis based on an expanded series of 150 cases and 250 controls (Trichopoulos et al., 1984; Tzonou et al., 1984). Overall, caffeine consumption does not appear to be a significant factor in the development of ovarian cancer.

Colorectal Cancer

Studies of caffeine consumption and cancer of the colon and/or rectum have yielded highly varied results. Some have reported no association between coffee consumption and increased risk of disease (Dales et al., 1979; Higginson, 1966; W. C. Lee et al., 1993; Nomura et al., 1986; Olsen & Kronborg, 1993); others have reported an increased risk (Slattery et al., 1990; Snowdon & Phillips, 1984); and still others have reported a reduced risk (Abu-Zeid et al., 1981; Baron et al., 1994; Centonze et al., 1994; Haenszel et al., 1973; Jacobsen et al., 1986; La Vecchia, Ferraroni, et al., 1989; La Vecchia et al., 1988). The frequency of reports of reduced risk (i.e., potential protective effect) has led to speculation about the possibility of compounds in coffee reducing the secretion of bile acids that promote colon carcinogenesis (Jacobsen & Thelle, 1987; La Vecchia, 1990). It appears, however, that any such protection is small at best.

Cancer of the Esophagus

Several studies have reported a significant association between esophageal cancer and the consumption of various caffeine beverages, including coffee (Llopis et al., 1992), tea (Brown et al., 1988; Ghadirian, 1987), and maté, as consumed in Argentina, Brazil, and Uruguay (De Stefani et al., 1990; Pintos et al., 1994; Victora et al., 1987). However, it has long been suspected that any involvement these beverages might have in the development of esophogeal cancer may not be due to caffeine or any other constituent, but rather the fact that in some parts of the world, caffeine beverages are routinely consumed at very high temperatures (Candreva et al., 1993).

Tea and Cancer Risk: Protective Effect?

Whether or not coffee was implicated as a cancer risk in the epidemiologic studies summarized in the preceding sections, tea consumption was often not considered, or yielded inconsistent associations with cancer incidence (IARC, 1991). In an early study, Stocks (1970) reported significant positive correlations between per capita tea consumption in 20 countries and age-adjusted deaths from cancers of the lung, larynx, and breast in women and the intestine (except the rectum) in both sexes. Tea consumption was also found to be inversely associated with uterine cancer and leukaemia in women, and stomach cancer in both sexes. More recently, two prospective studies of tea and cancer produced inconsistent findings. One study, involving Japanese American men in Hawaii, found a positive association with rectal cancer and an inverse association with prostate cancer (Heilbrun al., 1986). In the second study, conducted in London, significant positive associations were reported for deaths from cancer of the stomach, lung, and kidney (Kinlen et al., 1988). However, in a recent case-control study conducted in northern Italy, no significant associations were found between tea consumption and incidence of cancers at any of 17 different sites in the body (La Vecchia et al., 1992). Similarly negative results were obtained in a recent Dutch study of four major cancer sites (Goldbohm et al., 1996).

Over the past 5 years, there has been a marked increase in interest in tea and cancer risk. In contrast to the tenor of much preceding work, a major focus of the more recent research has been to assess the anticarcinogenic properties of tea. Green tea has attracted particular attention, although it appears that the general findings may also apply to black tea (Shi et al., 1994; Shiraki et al., 1994; Wang et al., 1994). As stated in Chapter 1, green tea, prepared in a manner that avoids oxidation of polyphenols, is favored throughout much of Asia, whereas fermented (i.e., oxidized) black tea is generally favored in the West.

Many studies involving laboratory rodents have shown that green tea preparations possess significant preventive properties against tumors induced by exposure to chemical carcinogens and solar radiation (Bu-Abbas et al., 1994a, 1994b; Mukhtar et al., 1992, 1994; Yang & Wang, 1993). These studies, which have included both caffeinated and decaffeinated preparations, indicate that the protective effects are due to the polyphenols in tea. The laboratory findings are consistent with a recent study of 3,380 female practitioners of *chanoyu*, the Japanese tea ceremony, which found that the practice was associated with a decreased incidence of fatal diseases including cancer. In light of such promising findings, it has been suggested that existing differences in the antimutagenic properties between tea varieties could provide the basis for selective breeding to enhance the protective action of tea (Apostolides & Weisburger, 1995). Nevertheless, tea-induced protective properties have yet to be demonstrated consistently in humans, and until this is achieved, it would be prudent to regard the recent laboratory findings as promising but in need of further confirmatory study in humans.

SUMMARY

Apart from the recent pronounced interest in the possible anticarcinogenic effects of tea, the direction of recent research and the findings that have resulted are broadly consistent with the general conclusions of previous major reviews (IARC, 1991; James, 1991). Whereas numerous studies of cultured cells in vitro have demonstrated the mutagenic potential of caffeine, in vivo studies of intact animals have suggested variously that caffeine is not a carcinogen, that it is carcinogenic under some conditions, and that it is antitumoric under other conditions. Although there is doubt about the relevance of the in vitro and in vivo findings to lifelong human exposure to caffeine, the weight of opinion is that the experimental evidence suggests that the drug is not a significant carcinogen in humans.

Unfortunately, the relevant human literature, consisting mainly of epidemiologic studies of the association between coffee consumption and cancer, contains too many inconsistencies to permit firm conclusions. Poor and inconsistent measurement of coffee usage is probably a major factor responsible for the inconsistent findings. Although most studies attempted to control for a variety of potential confounders (e.g., smoking, age, gender, diet, etc.), reported associations could be due to uncontrolled extraneous influences. Although the evidence remains equivocal for *all* of specific sites of cancer considered here, trends exist to suggest a possible weak causal association between coffee consumption in both bladder and pancreatic cancer and a possible weak protective action against colon cancer. If the observed trends are indicative of real effects, these could be due to constituents in coffee other than caffeine.

Promising results of anticarcinogenic actions have recently been obtained in laboratory studies of tea. Polyphenols, naturally present in tea, have been identified as being responsible for the observed effects. However, further study is needed to clarify whether the human consumption of tea confers benefits similar to those observed in the laboratory studies.

FURTHER READING

IARC Working Group. (1991). *IARC monographs on the evaluation of carcinogenic risks to humans. Coffee, tea, maté, methylxanthines, and methylglyoxal* (Vol. 51). Lyon, France: International Agency for Research on Cancer.

Kihlman, B. A., & Andersson, H. C. (1987). Effects of caffeine on chromosomes in cells of higher eukaryotic organisms. *Reviews on Environmental Health, 7,* 279-382.

MacMahon, B. (1984). Coffee and cancer of the pancreas: A review. In B. MacMahon & T. Sugimura (Eds.), *Banbury Report 17: Coffee and health* (pp. 109-117). New York: Cold Spring Harbor Laboratory.

Viscoli, C. M., Lachs, M. S., & Horwitz, R. I. (1993). Bladder cancer and coffee drinking: A summary of case-control research. *Lancet, 341,* 1432-1437.

Yang, C. S. & Wang, Z.-Y. (1993). Tea and cancer. *Journal of the National Cancer Institute, 85,* 1038-1049.

7

Caffeine, Pregnancy, and Perinatal Health

■

■ ■ The fact that most people consume caffeine beverages for most of their
■ ■ lives means that conception, pregnancy, and birth typically occur
against a background of caffeine use. In 1980, the U.S. Food and Drug
Administration (FDA) issued a warning advising pregnant women to restrict,
or eliminate, coffee consumption. One aim of the present chapter is to
consider the appropriateness of this warning in light of the overall evidence,
especially that which has accumulated since the warning was issued.

■ Maternal Use of Caffeine

It is not uncommon for women to spontaneously reduce their caffeine
intake during pregnancy (Aldridge et al., 1981). This self-initiated reduction
in consumption is consistent with pregnancy-induced changes in caffeine
pharmacokinetics, whereby the elimination rate of the drug reduces progressively during the course of pregnancy. Aldridge et al. (1981) found that

although the rate of caffeine clearance in the first trimester of pregnancy is comparable to the nonpregnant state, the rate slows to one half and then to less than one third of the nonpregnant rate during the second and third trimesters, respectively. Specifically, these authors reported an increase in caffeine half-life from a mean of about 5 hours in the first trimester to 18 hours in the 38th week of pregnancy. A number of studies have reported similar changes (Brazier et al., 1983; Christensen et al., 1981; Kling & Christensen, 1979; Knutti et al., 1982; Neims et al., 1979; Parsons & Pelletier, 1982), which appear to be the result of the altered hormonal milieu induced by pregnancy. The reduced rate of caffeine elimination means that caffeine plasma levels will be substantially increased, if drug intake remains unchanged. As such, it appears that the self-initiated reduction in caffeine consumption that sometimes accompanies pregnancy serves to maintain relative stability of plasma caffeine levels before, during, and after pregnancy.

Notwithstanding spontaneous reductions in overall intake, most women continue to consume some caffeine while pregnant. One study found that 73% of 1,510 mothers reported that they continued to consume coffee or tea throughout pregnancy (Kurppa et al., 1983), whereas another reported that 95% of a sample of 150 mothers consumed caffeine *at some time* during pregnancy (Horning et al., 1975). These indications of widespread caffeine use during pregnancy are supported by studies of the blood of newborns, the majority of whom have significant plasma caffeine concentrations (Brazier & Salle, 1981; Dumas et al., 1982; Parsons et al., 1976; Van't Hoff, 1982).

Pharmacology of Caffeine in the Fetus and Neonate

Although caffeine ingested by the mother is distributed across the placenta (Goldstein & Warren, 1962; Horning et al., 1975; Kimmel et al., 1984; Van't Hoff, 1982), the fetus is unable to metabolize the drug because the enzyme system that is needed to do so is not developed until later in life (Aldridge et al., 1979; Aranda, Collinge, et al., 1979; Aranda & Turmen, 1979; Gorodischer & Karplus, 1982; Haley, 1983; Horning et al., 1973; Kurppa et al., 1983; Parsons & Neims, 1981; Pearlman et al., 1989; Riechert et al., 1981). Notwithstanding marked differences between individuals, the average elimination half-life of caffeine at birth appears to be about 100 hours (Aldridge et al., 1979). This rate decreases progressively to approximate the adult rate of 5 hours by about 8 months (Aldridge et al., 1979), although complete maturation of the different pathways of caffeine metabolism does not occur before 1 year of age (Carrier et al., 1988). Thus, the developing fetus is dependent on the mother to metabolize the drug.

Caffeine is sometimes used therapeutically in the treatment of neonatal apnea, a condition characterized by cessation of spontaneous breathing. The clinical use of caffeine in this context (see Chapter 8) has provided important opportunities for examining the possible toxic effects of caffeine in newborns, and by implication, the likely effects of caffeine on the fetus during the later stages of pregnancy. Although it is evident that apneic infants sometimes show signs of psychomotor agitation when treated with caffeine (Banner & Czajka, 1980; Kulkarni & Dorand, 1979), few appear to be markedly distressed despite the fact that the clinical doses used are substantially higher than the levels ever likely to be experienced in utero (barring a caffeine overdose by the mother). Although this suggests that the fetus may be fairly robust to the systemic levels associated with typical patterns of maternal caffeine consumption, two important qualifications are needed. First, neonatal responses to caffeine may be indicative of fetal response during the later stages of pregnancy, but are likely to be less generalizable to earlier stages. Second, experience derived from the clinical use of caffeine may be relevant only to an understanding of the acute toxic effects of the drug. Conversely, fetal exposure to caffeine in utero is generally chronic, because usage of the drug is typically habitual.

▧ Morphological Abnormalities

The warning issued by the FDA in 1980, cautioning pregnant women against the use of coffee, was in response to evidence of caffeine-induced teratogenic effects in rodents. *Teratology* is the study of the causes and effects of congenital abnormalities, and there is an extensive literature on caffeine-induced teratogenic effects in laboratory animals. A much smaller literature has examined the possible involvement of caffeine in human congenital abnormalities, and the predominant approach in these studies has been epidemiologic rather than experimental. Furthermore, much of the animal and human research has been concerned with gross morphological abnormalities (i.e., "frank" teratogenicity), and the findings of this research are considered in the present section. However, teratology also includes the study of more subtle developmental and behavioral anomalies caused by prenatal events (Coyle et al., 1976), and these effects are considered later in this chapter.

Animal Experimental Studies

Many experimental studies of rodents (mice, rats, rabbits) have demonstrated caffeine-induced fetal abnormalities, most often including cleft palate, ectrodactyly (absence of part or all of one or more fingers or toes), and skeletal malformations (Collins et al., 1983; Driscoll et al., 1990; Elmazar et al., 1981; Fujii et al., 1969; Nishimura & Nakai, 1960; Nolen, 1981, 1982; Palm et al., 1978; Smith et al., 1987; Terada & Nishimura, 1975). Typically, however, teratologic effects have been consistently observed only when comparatively large doses, in the order of 100 mg/kg of body weight and above, have been administered to the pregnant animals. Moreover, when administered continuously, or repeatedly as divided doses in a manner analogous to human consumption patterns, larger total doses have been required to induce malformations (Collins et al., 1983; Elmazar et al., 1982; Nolen, 1981, 1982; Palm et al., 1978; Thayer & Kensler, 1973). Even daily doses as high as 300 mg/kg, when divided, have been associated with few effects. Accordingly, it has been suggested that rather than being due to the direct action of caffeine, malformations induced by the large doses involved in animal research may be an indirect result of toxicity in the dams and associated reductions in food and water intake (Elmazar et al., 1981, 1982).

In rodents, morphological abnormalities are only infrequently observed in response to single doses less than 100 mg/kg of body weight, and possibly not at all in response to a dose of less than 50 mg/kg (Collins, 1979; Wilson & Scott, 1984). In general, larger total doses appear to be needed to induce teratologic effects when the drug is administered in divided doses or when it is consumed ad libitum throughout the day, although Elmazar et al. (1982) reported a low incidence of cleft palate among the offspring of mice administered as little as 50 mg/kg daily. Overall, then, in pregnant rodents, 50 mg/kg of body weight would appear to be the approximate maximum safe level, administered either as a single dose or daily.

Ignoring interspecies differences in caffeine metabolism, as well as other potentially confounding factors such as mode of administration and pattern of exposure, the figure of 50 mg/kg of body weight translates to about 35 cups of moderately strong coffee for a 70-kg human. Although it is virtually impossible to consume the caffeine equivalent of 35 cups of coffee at a single sitting (except by overdosing with caffeine-containing tablets), 35 cups per day represents a plausible (albeit unusually high) level of daily consumption. By this standard, it might be reasonable to conclude that moderate caffeine-beverage consumption by pregnant women poses little or no risk of morphological abnormalities to the fetus (e.g., Wilson & Scott, 1984). However, the question arises as to what would be an appropriate margin of safety for defining moderate use in humans. The usual safety standard employed by the FDA in relation to the human consumption of food additives is one hundredth the maximum safe level of exposure in animals (U.S. Food and Drug Administration, 1995). By this standard, the results of animal research would indicate that virtually any pattern of habitual caffeine-beverage consumption by a woman who is pregnant would put her unborn child at risk. That is, applying the FDA's usual standards, pregnant women should abstain from caffeine completely.

Human Epidemiologic Studies

Notwithstanding uncertainty concerning the adequacy of animal models for testing potential human teratogens (Thayer & Palm, 1975), the suggestion that morphological abnormalities are unlikely to be induced by caffeine at levels typical of human consumption concurs with most of the relevant epidemiologic evidence. Several studies failed to find any significant associations between coffee or caffeine consumption and teratologic effects (Furuhashi et al., 1985; Kurppa et al., 1983; Linn et al., 1982; McDonald et al., 1992a; Rosenberg et al., 1982). One exception to the predominantly null findings is a Belgian study in which mothers of 190 malformed infants reported a modestly higher level of coffee consumption than mothers of 162 normal infants (Borlée et al., 1978). Unfortunately, however, there appears to have been no attempt to control for the potentially confounding effects of nicotine and alcohol, even though usage of these substances was recorded. The investigators were rightly cautious in their interpretation of the data and in a subsequent publication acknowledged the need for replication studies (Lechat et al., 1980).

Although generally reassuring, the epidemiologic studies conducted to date are relatively few in number. Moreover, the reliability of the measurement of participants' exposure to caffeine is open to question in most of the studies. As such, the findings are, at best, tentative for the same reason that the findings of the epidemiologic research discussed in the preceding chapters on cardiovascular disease and cancer are also tentative. Moreover, it must be remembered that the studies considered in the present section were concerned with frank teratogenicity. Therefore, even though the evidence suggests little or no threat of gross defects, this does not preclude the possibility that caffeine may contribute to other less obvious anomalies of pregnancy and reproduction.

Pregnancy Outcome

The range of possible caffeine-induced adverse pregnancy outcomes is large, and any classification is necessarily arbitrary. The present section is concerned with the effects of maternal caffeine consumption on a variety of pregnancy outcomes, including fetal loss, fetal growth, and preterm delivery.

Fetal Loss

One early study of the association between caffeine consumption and pregnancy outcome attracted particular attention because of the alarming nature of the findings (Weathersbee & Lodge, 1977). The study involved a cross-sectional survey of 489 women who had experienced pregnancy in the recent past. For 16 pregnancies of women whose caffeine intake exceeded 600 mg per day, 8 were reported to have ended in spontaneous abortion in the first trimester, 5 ended in stillbirth, and 2 in premature delivery, leaving only 1 pregnancy reported to have been uncomplicated. However, several methodological shortcomings, including possible recall bias and inadequate control for cigarette smoking and alcohol consumption, cast serious doubts over the findings (James, 1991). Notwithstanding these doubts and the fact that some subsequent studies failed to find a significant association between caffeine consumption and fetal loss (Linn et al., 1982; Mills et al., 1993; Watkinson & Fried, 1985), the majority of published results do in fact support the existence of an association between increased incidence of spontaneous abortion in association with increased maternal use of caffeine (Al-Ansary & Babay, 1994; Armstrong et al., 1992; Fenster et al., 1991b; Furuhashi et al., 1985; Infante-Rivard et al., 1993; Srisuphan & Bracken, 1986). In one recent case-control study, the relative risk of fetal loss (medically confirmed spontaneous abortion or fetal death), after adjustment for potential confounders, was estimated to be 1.22 for each 100 mg of caffeine (about one cup of coffee) consumed daily during pregnancy (Infante-Rivard et al., 1993).

One potential criticism of case-control studies, such as that reported by Infante-Rivard et al. (1993), is that the positive findings might be due to confounding arising from pregnancy-induced nausea. As mentioned above, pregnant women often spontaneously reduce their intake of caffeine, and it has been suggested that this temporary apparent "loss of taste" may be due to the nausea often experienced during the early months of pregnancy (Meyer et al., 1994). Because nausea is less frequent in pregnancies that miscarry than those that go to term, the association between fetal loss and higher caffeine intake could be the result of reduced caffeine consumption in women who experience nausea during the course of a successful pregnancy (Stein & Susser, 1991). However, the nausea hypothesis was not supported by a recent empirical study of caffeine and fetal loss that took account of occurrence of nausea during pregnancy (Fenster et al., 1991b).

In a recent overview of the findings on caffeine and pregnancy outcome, Eskenazi (1993) concluded that the weight of evidence indicated that "high levels of caffeine" are potentially harmful. For reasons stated below, it may not be wise to suppose that a useful distinction can be made between so-called "moderate" and "high" levels of caffeine consumption. It will be argued that if the evidence indicates that caffeine exposure within the usual range of consumption levels is harmful, then any habitual use should be regarded with suspicion. Moreover, Eskenazi equated "high" intake with an amount greater than 300 mg per day (the approximate equivalent of three cups of coffee per day), which even among pregnant women is not so unusual (Dlugosz & Bracken, 1992).

Fetal Growth

Caffeine fed to rodents during pregnancy has often been reported as resulting in fetuses of lower weight (e.g., Fujii & Nishimura, 1972; Gilbert & Pistey, 1973; Thayer & Kensler, 1973). Whereas deleterious effects on the growth and development of animals have been observed consistently for consumption levels in the order of 70 mg/kg or more per day, Dunlop and Court (1981) found that as little as 10 mg/kg of dietary caffeine given throughout gestation and lactation in rats produced significant growth reductions in offspring. Moreover, Pollard et al. (1987) found that caffeine administered daily to rats during pregnancy not only caused significant reductions in fetal and postnatal growth but a second litter not exposed to caffeine was also smaller at birth than control animals.

In respect to fetal growth, there is reasonably good agreement between the results of animal experiments and human epidemiologic studies spanning a period of more than 20 years, suggesting that caffeine consumed during pregnancy contributes to lower birth weight. Although several studies conducted during the 1970s and 1980s reported no association between maternal caffeine consumption and birth weight (Barr et al., 1984; Fried & O'Connell, 1987; Linn et al., 1982), the majority of studies reported that increased consumption was associated with lower birth weight (Caan & Goldhaber, 1989; Hogue, 1981; Martin & Bracken, 1987; Mau & Netter, 1974; van den Berg, 1977; Watkinson & Fried, 1985). In the mid-1980s, when James and Paull (1985) reviewed this field, it was concluded that the evidence on maternal caffeine consumption and birth weight was suggestive of a possible adverse influence of caffeine on intrauterine growth. In a subsequent review of the same field, the evidence implicating caffeine as a factor contributing to lower birth weight was found to have strengthened (James, 1991). Research conducted since 1990 has generally confirmed the trend identified in these earlier reviews. That is, the evidence implicating caffeine as a factor in lower birth weight has continued to strengthen.

Of ten epidemiologic studies published since 1990, seven reported a significant inverse association between caffeine consumed during pregnancy and birth weight (Fenster et al., 1991a; Fortier et al., 1993; Larroque et al., 1993a; McDonald et al., 1992b; Olsen et al., 1991; Peacock et al., 1991; Spinillo et al., 1994), while three studies reported no association (Larroque et al., 1993a; Mills et al., 1993; Shu et al., 1995). The persistence of inconsistencies in the findings is not easily explained. Differences between studies with respect to control of confounders does not appear to account for the differences in results. All studies included adjustment for cigarette smoking and a variety of other potential confounders. Alternatively, some if not all of the null findings could be the result of insufficient statistical power (leading to Type II error) due to misclassification of the exposure variable (caffeine ingestion), small number of cases, and insufficient variation in caffeine consumption among participants. Interestingly, in a commentary on their own investigation, the authors of one of the studies that yielded null results concluded that the overall epidemiologic evidence does indeed suggest that a "trend" exists between caffeine use and lower birth weight, and that "very heavy" use should be avoided during pregnancy (Larroque et al., 1993b).

In a recent study, Petridou et al. (1992) have argued that they may have identified the biological mechanism by which caffeine interferes with intra-uterine growth. In an earlier study, the same investigators found that estrogen levels during pregnancy were inversely correlated with cigarette smoking and birth weight (Petridou et al., 1990). This result suggests that smoking may contribute to lower estrogen levels, which may in turn have unfavorable effects on intrauterine growth. In their more recent study, the authors reported an inverse correlation between estrogen levels and coffee consumption in 141 pregnant women (Petridou et al., 1992). The implication that caffeine and cigarette smoking may interfere with intrauterine growth through a common biological mechanism (i.e., circulating estrogen levels) is consistent with the finding that the respective effects of caffeine and smoking on birth weight appear to be independent and additive (Spinillo et al., 1994).

Having now reviewed the literature on caffeine and reproduction on three separate occasions over a 10-year period, the present author believes that the evidence suggesting an involvement of caffeine in intrauterine growth retardation has not only become more consistent, it has also strengthened to an extent that it can no longer be ignored. Beginning with an initial tentative suggestion of causal involvement (James & Paull, 1985), the evidence has become inexorably stronger (James, 1991) and is now of sufficient strength to justify concerted public action. In brief, two decades of accumulated epidemiologic evidence is strongly indicative of a causal relationship between caffeine use during pregnancy and lower birth weight.

Preterm Delivery

Of 11 epidemiologic studies on the association between caffeine consumption during pregnancy and preterm delivery, three reported a significant positive association between caffeine use and risk of preterm delivery (Olsen et al., 1991; Weathersbee et al., 1977; Williams et al., 1992), whereas eight reported no association (Berkowitz et al., 1982; Fenster et al., 1991a; Fortier et al., 1993; Linn et al., 1982; McDonald et al., 1992b; Pastore & Savitz, 1995; van den Berg, 1977; Watkinson & Fried, 1985). The most recent of these studies was a case- control investigation of 408 cases of preterm infants (gestation period less than 37 weeks) and 490 full-term, normal-weight controls (Pastore & Savitz, 1995). Telephone interviews with participants assessed the consumption of caffeine from coffee, tea, and soft drinks. Consistent with the findings of most previous studies, no significant association was found between caffeine consumption and preterm delivery.

Fertility

Delayed Conception

The literature on caffeine and female fertility is not extensive, but interest in the question of whether caffeine may contribute to subfecundity (delayed conception) appears to be growing. Whereas several studies have reported an inverse association suggestive of an adverse effect of caffeine consumption on pregnancy rates (Christianson et al., 1989; Grodstein et al., 1993; Hatch & Bracken, 1993; Wilcox et al., 1988; Williams et al., 1990), some studies obtained little or no such evidence (Florack et al., 1994; Joesoef et al., 1990; Olsen, 1991). In one recent study, Grodstein et al. (1993) investigated participants' self-reported caffeine use in relation to four specific disorders of infertility, ovulatory failure, tubal disease, endometriosis, and idiopathic (unknown cause) infertility. The investigators reasoned that because of the multifactorial etiology of infertility, it is important to know whether caffeine contributes to particular fertility disorders and not others. This knowledge might also help to better understand the causative mechanisms, if caffeine is implicated as a risk factor for infertility. The study involved 1,050 women who had been unable to conceive and to deliver a liveborn child after 12 months of unprotected sexual intercourse, and 3,833 controls consisting of women who had recently given birth. A positive association was found between caffeine consumption and infertility due to tubal disease and endometriosis, but not ovulatory failure or idiopathic infertility.

Sperm Motility

Whereas caffeine may be a risk factor for female infertility, there is considerable interest in caffeine as a possible enhancer of male fertility. Once ingested, caffeine distributes rapidly into the prostatic and seminal vesicular secretions that contribute to the formation of the ejaculate (Beach et al., 1984; Goldstein & Warren, 1962). In semen, caffeine reaches concentrations almost identical to those observed concurrently in blood, and the half-life of caffeine in blood appears to be almost identical to that in semen (Beach et al., 1984). Considering the presence of caffeine in semen, the suggestion that the drug may affect male fertility (either positively or adversely) by influencing sperm quality is certainly plausible.

It was suggested more than two decades ago that caffeine might be useful clinically, because of its apparent ability to stimulate human sperm motility (Garbers et al., 1971). Subsequent extensive research has shown that the drug does stimulate sperm motility, and that it does so in a dose-dependent manner (Aitken et al., 1983; Barkay et al., 1977; Burge, 1973; Imoedehme et al., 1992; Moussa, 1983; Ruzich et al., 1987; Stachecki et al., 1994; Traub et al., 1982). However, there have been conflicting reports on the clinical utility of this action. Harrison (1978) found that semen samples treated with caffeine in an artificial insemination program did not lead to improved rates of fertilization. Following further examination, he and his colleagues concluded that despite increases in sperm motility, fertilization rates were not improved because the spermatozoa were damaged by caffeine (Harrison et al., 1980a, 1980b). Conflicting results, however, were obtained by Barkay et al. (1984), who reported improved pregnancy rates when spermatozoa were pretreated with caffeine. More recently, Imoedehme et al. (1992) reported results similar to those of Harrison (1978) and concluded that the clinical utility of the drug as a treatment of infertility was limited by the caffeine concentration levels required to achieve increases in sperm motility. On one hand, caffeine concentration levels need to be high to achieve significant improvements in sperm motility. On the other hand, the high concentration levels required appear to cause morphological damage to the spermatozoa, thereby impeding fertilizing ability and embryo development (Imoedehme et al., 1992; Scott & Smith, 1995).

Behavioral Effects of Maternal Caffeine Use

While there is an extensive literature on caffeine as a behavioral teratogen in rodents, there have been relatively few human studies. This is surprising, because animal models have demonstrated a wide range of fetal and postnatal neurochemical and behavioral effects of caffeine. Maternal and postnatal exposure to caffeine in rats has been found to produce long-lasting, and possibly permanent, biochemical changes in various regions of the rat brain

(Nakamoto et al., 1991; Yazdani et al., 1990). These effects appear to interact with nutritional status, being more pronounced in animals that have been protein malnourished (Nakamoto et al., 1989; Yazdani et al., 1987). Chronic prenatal caffeine exposure has also been shown to have a variety of behavioral effects in rodents, including impaired learning and decreased motor activity (Ajarem & Ahmad, 1991; Hughes & Beveridge, 1991; Yoshino et al., 1994; Zimmerberg et al., 1991). Similarly, maternal exposure to caffeine has been found to affect infant monkey behavior, including altered learning patterns and altered patterns of feeding (Gilbert & Rice, 1994).

In a prospective study representing one of the few relevant human investigations, no association between maternal caffeine use and behavioral effects was evident in children assessed at age 8 months (Streissguth et al., 1980). However, retrospective interviews with the mothers of 173 neonates indicated that caffeine consumption during pregnancy was related to poorer neuromuscular development and poorer reflex function (Jacobson et al., 1984). Interestingly, caffeine use *prior* to pregnancy was also assessed, and was found to be related to shorter gestation, poorer orientation, elevated arousal, and increased irritability, even after adjusting for level of caffeine consumption during pregnancy. In addition, salivary caffeine level in healthy neonates ages 24 to 48 hours was found to be associated with increased lability and less consolability (Emory et al., 1988). A recent prospective study examined the relationship between maternal caffeine use and intrauterine fetal behavior during the third trimester of pregnancy (Devoe et al., 1993). Using ultrasound, the fetuses of "high" caffeine-consuming mothers were found to have significantly higher levels of arousal than the fetuses of "low" caffeine-consuming mothers. However, it should be noted that, at the present time, it is not known what these behavioral differences might mean for subsequent emotional and behavioral development. Overall, reports of caffeine-induced pre- and postnatal behavioral effects in humans have been too few in number to suggest firm conclusions. However, the results that have been reported would seem to justify further studies of caffeine as a potential behavioral teratogen.

Caffeine Withdrawal

Given that most women consume caffeine during pregnancy, most newborns experience abrupt withdrawal of caffeine at the time of birth. Clinical studies have reported evidence of a caffeine-withdrawal syndrome, involving irritability, poor sleeping patterns, and vomiting, similar to neonatal narcotic abstinence syndrome (McGowan et al., 1988; Thomas, 1988). A recent study by Hadeed and Siegel (1993) used a double-blind protocol to compare two groups of infants, one having no history of maternal drug use other than caffeine (caffeine group) and a control group having no history of maternal drug use at all. Compared to the controls, the caffeine group was found to have significantly increased frequency of irregular heart beat and respiration and increased fine tremors as measured by a protocol previously used for assessment of narcotic withdrawal. These symptoms are probably the result of an overproduction of endogenous adenosine due to upregulation of adenosine receptors induced by months of intrauterine exposure to caffeine.

The question of caffeine withdrawal in newborns needs to be considered in the context of possible postnatal exposure to caffeine contained in breast milk. On one hand, caffeine consumed in milk could help to moderate the effects of caffeine withdrawal following birth. On the other hand, it is conceivable that further problems could be created, either by the direct action of caffeine on the infant, or in the form of delayed withdrawal symptoms that might occur between feeding occasions or when the infant is subsequently weaned. However, several investigators have suggested that the amount of caffeine ingested by breast-fed infants is generally very small and may be inconsequential (Bailey et al., 1982; Berlin et al., 1984; Blanchard et al., 1992; Hildebrandt et al., 1983). On a more speculative note, James (1991) has suggested that caffeine withdrawal could be a factor in neonatal apnea and sudden infant death syndrome (SIDS). In light of the respirogenic properties of caffeine, the drug could interfere with the development of respiratory homeostasis, which might be further undermined by caffeine withdrawal at birth. Recently, Tye et al. (1993) found that prenatal exposure to caffeine induced a developmental shift in rats, which caused lifelong alterations in breathing function with an apparent increased risk of apnea and SIDS in the exposed animals.

▧ Dental Health

Studies with mice suggest that caffeine exposure in early life may impair the development of sound teeth (Falster et al., 1992; Hashimoto et al., 1992; Nakamoto et al., 1993). In one study, lactating dams with suckling pups were fed 2 mg/100g of caffeine as part of their diet (Nakamoto et al., 1993). Exposure to caffeine commenced at the birth of the pups and continued for 22 days, at which point the pups were weaned and remained caffeine-free thereafter. When sacrificed at 50 days of age, the pups were found to have a significant increase in caries due to their early exposure to caffeine. These findings could have important implications for human dental health because most breast-feeding mothers consume caffeine daily, and caffeine-containing soft drinks are consumed in large quantities by children. However, replication studies involving other animal species are needed, as are appropriate human studies.

▒ Interactions With Other Teratogenic Agents

One consequence of the fact that most pregnant women consume caffeine daily is that any exposure to other potential behavioral and environmental teratogens is very likely to coincide with exposure to caffeine, thereby giving rise to the possibility of adverse interactions. Studies with rats have shown that the embryotoxic potential of caffeine is sometimes enhanced when administered concurrently with other drugs. For example, Ritter et al. (1982) found that caffeine and acetazolamide (a diuretic agent) had little effect when administered alone to pregnant rats, whereas marked embryotoxicity was evident when the two drugs were co-administered. Henderson and Schenker (1984) found that ethanol reduced fetal weight in rats, and that the effect was exacerbated when ethanol and caffeine were administered concurrently.

Unfortunately, there have been relatively few human studies of interactions arising from maternal use of multiple drugs involving caffeine. McDonald et al. (1992b) reported that the adverse effect of coffee consumption on birth weight was greater for women who consumed alcohol than for alcohol abstainers. Similarly, caffeine and cigarette smoking have been reported as having an adverse interaction on birth weight (Beaulac-Baillargeon & Desrosiers, 1987), although more recent evidence suggests that the effect of each is independent and additive rather than interactive (Petridou et al., 1992; Spinillo et al., 1994). Considering the ubiquity of caffeine, there is a great need for comprehensive study of whether caffeine potentiates, and/or is potentiated by, other harmful agents to which women may be exposed during pregnancy.

Should Pregnant Women Avoid Caffeine?

Considering the various risks described in the present chapter, the 1980 FDA warning advising pregnant women not to consume coffee seems highly appropriate, although not necessarily for the reasons stated at the time the warning was introduced. The main concern at that time was that maternal caffeine use might lead to increased risk of congenital abnormalities. Subsequent research, however, has drawn attention to other concerns, especially the contribution of caffeine to lower birth weight and its possible involvement in spontaneous abortion. Indeed, the available evidence suggests the need to strengthen the warning by making a clearer statement advising pregnant women to abstain completely from caffeine beverages (coffee, tea, caffeine soft drinks) and caffeine-containing medications. Complete avoidance of chocolate is probably not necessary, because the caffeine contained in chocolate products is generally very much less than that contained in caffeine beverages (Zoumas et al., 1980). Because the U.S. government appears to be alone in formally warning against caffeine use during pregnancy, it is important that steps be taken to have the warning promulgated worldwide.

Moderate Versus Heavy Caffeine Use During Pregnancy

Avoidance of "heavy" use of caffeine during pregnancy, as distinct from abstinence, is a recommendation which seems to be appearing in the literature with increased frequency (e.g., Eskenazi, 1993; Fortier et al., 1993; Infante-Rivard et al., 1993; Larroque et al., 1993b; Shiono & Klebanoff, 1993). However, the present author believes that a partial prohibition is neither logical nor sensible for two very different reasons. First, the existence of a safety threshold in respect to caffeine consumed during pregnancy does not seem particularly plausible from a biological standpoint, nor is it supported by the empirical evidence. Dose-response relationships have been demonstrated frequently in animal studies (e.g., Gilbert & Rice, 1994; Pollard et al., 1987), and not infrequently in studies involving humans (e.g., Fortier et al., 1993; Infante-Rivard et al., 1993). Many of the studies in which effects were observed for higher but not lower levels of consumption are questionable in terms of the statistical power required to detect effects across the spectrum of consumption levels. Measurement imprecision, inexact adjustment for confounders (including possible overadjustment), and small sample size are among many common shortcomings in the epidemiologic research on caffeine and pregnancy, all of which reduce statistical power. Thus, although heavy caffeine use may entail greater risk than moderate use, it does not follow that the latter is free of risk.

Second, advising against heavy use is likely to be less successful as a public health endeavor than advising abstinence, especially when the existing data do not permit a clear specification of the relevant cutoff for heavy use. It is important to remember that there are no positive benefits to be derived from caffeine ingestion during pregnancy, only potential risks. Virtual abstinence can be achieved by avoiding caffeine beverages (e.g., by switching to caffeine-free alternatives) and refraining from the use of caffeine-containing medications. In light of the available evidence, abstinence from caffeine during pregnancy is certainly appropriate. Furthermore, abstinence represents a simpler, and probably more effective, public health message than advice that warns only against heavy or excessive use.

SUMMARY

Whereas earlier research on the implications of caffeine consumption during pregnancy tended to be focused primarily on gross morphological abnormalities, later research has drawn attention to more subtle indicators of pregnancy outcome and fetal development. Regarding the occurrence of congenital morphological abnormalities, the available evidence suggests that maternal caffeine use is unlikely to be a significant causal factor. However, the fact that caffeine exposure during pregnancy has been well-established as a cause of congenital abnormalities in rodents (albeit when the dose is relatively large) should serve as a warning against complacency over the possibility of such effects in humans. Moreover, maternal caffeine use has been directly implicated as a causal factor in other adverse reproductive outcomes. In particular, there is strong evidence that caffeine consumed during pregnancy contributes to lower birth weight and moderate support for the suggestion that caffeine may increase the risk of spontaneous abortion.

Despite consistent evidence that caffeine stimulates sperm motility, the suggestion that caffeine might have clinical utility in the treatment of male infertility has not received strong empirical support. Indeed, the overall evidence suggests that caffeine might well have detrimental effects on fertility in both men and women. While there is strong evidence of a range of caffeine-induced fetal and postnatal neurochemical and behavioral effects in animals, there have been too few relevant studies to permit any firm conclusions regarding effects of this kind in humans. There is, however, good evidence that newborns may sometimes experience distress due to caffeine withdrawal, suggestive evidence that exposure to caffeine during early life could impair subsequent dental health, and some evidence that caffeine may exacerbate the adverse effects of other teratogenic agents to which pregnant women could be exposed. These various risks provide strong grounds for recommending total abstinence from caffeine beverages and caffeine-containing medications during pregnancy. Considering the widespread availability and use of caffeine, there is an urgent need for public health initiatives to be undertaken worldwide to discourage caffeine consumption during pregnancy.

FURTHER READING

Dlugosz, L., & Bracken, M. B. (1992). Reproductive effects of caffeine: A review and theoretical analysis. *Epidemiology Reviews, 14,* 83-100.

Fortier, I., Marcoux, S., & Beaulac-Baillargeon, L. (1993). Relation of caffeine intake during pregnancy to intrauterine growth retardation and preterm birth. *American Journal of Epidemiology, 137,* 931-940.

Imoedehme, D. A., Sigue, A. B., Pacpaco, E. L., Pacpaco, E. L., & Olazo, A. B. (1992). The effect of caffeine on the ability of spermatozoa to fertilize mature human oocytes. *Journal of Assisted Reproduction Genetics, 9,* 155-160.

Infante-Rivard, C., Fernandez, A., Gauthier, R., David, M., & Rivard, G. E. (1993). Fetal loss associated with caffeine intake before and during pregnancy. *Journal of the American Medical Association, 270,* 2940-2943.

Larroque, B., Kaminski, M., Lelong, N., Subtil, D., & Dehaene, P. (1993). Effects on birth weight of alcohol and caffeine consumption during pregnancy. *American Journal of Epidemiology, 137,* 941-950.

Beneficial Uses of Caffeine

■

■ ■ Whereas much of this book is concerned with the harm that may accrue
■ ■ from habitual exposure to caffeine, the present chapter describes a
number of possible benefits of the drug. As mentioned in previous chapters,
many of the diverse actions of caffeine are assumed to be due to antagonism
of adenosine. The involvement of two major classes of adenosine receptors
(A_1 and A_2) helps to explain the range of central and peripheral actions of
caffeine which are, or may be, beneficial.

■ Therapeutic Applications

Neonatal Apnea

The most successful therapeutic application of caffeine has been its use
in the treatment of neonatal apnea (cessation of spontaneous breathing), a
relatively common condition in premature babies. As mentioned in Chapter
2, methylxanthines stimulate respiration, and this property has led to caffeine

and theophylline being used therapeutically. Kuzemko and Paala (1973) were the first to report the use of theophylline to treat apneic infants, and caffeine was soon used for the same purpose (Aranda et al., 1977). The initial good results reported by Aranda et al. (1977) were confirmed by others (Koppe et al., 1979; Murat et al., 1981), and subsequent research sought to clarify the dosage levels of greatest therapeutic benefit (Aranda, Beharry, et al., 1983; Aranda, Cook, et al., 1979; Aranda, Turmen, et al., 1983; Turmen et al., 1981).

There were some initial concerns regarding possible side effects (e.g., tachycardia, central nervous system overarousal) (Banner & Czajka, 1980; Kulkarni & Dorand, 1979), but such effects appear to have occurred primarily in association with amounts considerably larger than the usual recommended dose of 10 mg/kg (Anwar et al., 1986; Flood, 1989; Gunn et al., 1979; Howell et al., 1981; Noerr, 1989). The consistently good therapeutic results with caffeine have encouraged its use in the prevention of apnea associated with anesthesia and surgery in premature infants (Welborn et al., 1988; Welborn & Greenspun, 1994), with treatment being adminis- tered either orally or intravenously. Recently, attention has been given to the development of preparations that enable the drug to be absorbed through the skin (Amato et al., 1992; Barrett & Rutter, 1994; Touitou et al., 1994).

From the time of its initial use in the treatment of neonatal apnea, caffeine was recognized as possessing potential advantages over theophylline. In particular, the exceptionally long neonatal half-life of caffeine (Aranda, Collinge, et al., 1979; Gorodischer & Karplus, 1982; Parsons & Neims, 1981) suggested the advantages of ease of administration (i.e., once or twice per day) and less fluctuation in plasma concentration (Aranda & Turmen, 1979). In addition, whereas the major pathway in theophylline metabolism in adults involves oxidative reactions (demethylation and oxidation), the predominant pathway in the newborn infant includes methylation to produce caffeine (Aranda, Cook, et al., 1979; Boutroy et al., 1979; Brazier et al., 1981; Gorodischer & Karplus, 1982; Lönnerholm et al., 1983). That is, caffeine is a major biotransformation product of theophylline metabolism in neonates. Indeed, it appears that some of the pharmacological effects ob- served during theophylline therapy for apnea may actually be due to caffeine (Aranda, Louridas, et al., 1979; Bory et al., 1979). Overall, there appears to be growing support for the use of caffeine as the drug of choice for the initial treatment of apnea of prematurity (Bairam et al., 1987; Brouard et al., 1985; Davis et al., 1987; Pearlman et al., 1989; Scanlon et al., 1992), although some investigators recommend the use of caffeine only in cases of persistent apnea unresponsive to theophylline (Harrison, 1992).

Pain

Caffeine has long been included in popular analgesic preparations in combination with known analgesic drugs such as aspirin (acetylsalicylic acid) and paracetamol (acetaminophen). Although the practice was, and continues to be, widespread, the therapeutic value of caffeine was essentially unknown for many years. The main evidence in support of caffeine as an analgesic adjuvant is contained in a review of empirical data compiled from clinical trials sponsored by a major pharmaceutical company (Laska et al., 1984). Most of the participants were postpartum patients, with various gynecologic and obstetric postoperative pain. When administered without caffeine, a 40% larger dose of analgesic was needed to achieve the same amount of pain relief as when caffeine was also administered. The review by Laska et al. (1984) led to a resurgence of interest in the role of caffeine as an analgesic adjuvant (Beaver, 1984; Sawynok & Yaksh, 1993), and corroborative studies have since been published (e.g., Forbes et al., 1990, 1991; Schachtel et al., 1991). Nevertheless, the number of independent empirical trials continues to be disappointingly low, and the mechanism of action remains poorly characterized (Castañeda-Hernández et al., 1994; Iqbal et al., 1995). Similarly, more needs to be learned about the specific analgesic-caffeine combinations that are most potent and the pain characteristics (e.g., intensity, site, nature of any underlying pathology, acute versus chronic) most responsive to analgesics that contain caffeine.

Headache. Cerebral blood flow studies have shown that caffeine acts as a vasoconstrictor on cerebral blood vessels (Cameron et al., 1990; Mathew & Wilson, 1985, 1990). As such, the use of caffeine in some headache-relieving formations appears to have a rational basis. Caffeine also appears to increase the absorption of ergotamine, a common migraine treatment, when given orally or as a suppository (Rall, 1990b). With regard to headache relief, caffeine has been found to be an effective analgesic adjuvant (Koch et al., 1994; Migliardi et al., 1994) and may even be partially effective when ingested alone (Ward et al., 1991). However, the use of caffeine in headache treatment is not without problems. As discussed in earlier chapters, abrupt cessation of caffeine consumption is liable to produce a host of dysphoric withdrawal symptoms, including headache (e.g., Silverman et al., 1992). Consequently, the use of caffeine in the relief of headache, or as a analgesic adjuvant, may itself induce headache when medication ceases. Indeed, when used to excess, caffeine may even be a direct cause of headache. A study of 54 patients with chronic headache attributed to abuse of multiple compound analgesics found that in 100% of cases, caffeine was contained in at least one of the compounds regularly used by the patients (Baumgartner et al., 1989).

Withdrawal headache associated with surgical procedures. It is relatively common for *postdural puncture headache* to be experienced following lumbar puncture for diagnostic purposes or following spinal anesthesia (Morewood, 1993). Reduced cerebrospinal fluid pressure due to leakage causes dilation of the intracranial veins. Because caffeine has a vasoconstrictive effect on the cerebral vasculature, it was tried and found to be effective (Sechzer & Abel, 1978). Although subsequent studies have confirmed the efficacy of caffeine in treating postdural puncture headache (Ford et al., 1989; Jarvis et al., 1986; Morewood, 1993; Sechzer, 1979), it is possible that the headaches are not due entirely to lumbar puncture, but also to caffeine withdrawal. This speculation is supported by the fact that *perioperative caffeine-withdrawal headache* is also commonly experienced in the general surgical context, due to the requirement that patients fast prior to anesthesia. For habitual caffeine consumers, this entails abrupt cessation of caffeine intake, which may lead to withdrawal headache (Fennelly et al., 1991; Galletly et al., 1989; Nikolajsen et al., 1994). Considering the many millions of surgical operations performed every year, perioperative caffeine-withdrawal headache is a problem of substantial proportions. Fortunately, prophylactic administration of caffeine appears to provide a simple and effective remedy (Hampl et al., 1995; Weber et al., 1993). Thus, although the overall evidence suggests that caffeine possesses modest general pain-relieving potential when used as an analgesic adjuvant, it has unequivocal analgesic potency when used to relieve caffeine-withdrawal headache.

Obesity

Obesity is a risk factor for hypertension, coronary heart disease, stroke, and non-insulin dependent diabetes mellitus. Because the balance between caloric intake and expenditure is a key determinant of body weight, weight-loss efforts typically aim to effect a negative energy balance by decreasing the former (through dietary control) and/or increasing the latter (through exercise management). Although caffeine has no nutritional value, it does have lipolytic and thermogenic actions (i.e., increases metabolic rate and energy expenditure). Known for over a century (Reichert, 1890), caffeine's thermogenic properties have been well-established empirically in both animals (Bukowiecki et al., 1983; Dulloo et al., 1994) and humans (Acheson et al., 1980; Astrup et al., 1990; Dulloo et al., 1989; Jung et al., 1981; Poehlman et al., 1989). Although there is some evidence to suggest that caffeine-induced thermogenic effects may be more pronounced in lean than in obese persons (Bracco et al., 1995; Dulloo et al., 1989), there is considerable interest in the therapeutic potential of caffeine as a pharmacological weight-loss adjuvant. Interest has centered, in particular, on the ability of caffeine to potentiate the thermogenic effect of ephedrine.

Ephedrine is a well-known sympathomimetic, with both anorectic and thermogenic properties. Several recent studies have examined the therapeutic efficacy of caffeine-ephedrine mixtures and have reported that weight loss following combined use of the drugs is greater than placebo and greater than either drug alone (Astrup & Toubro, 1993; Astrup et al., 1991, 1992; Breum et al., 1994; Daly et al., 1993; Dulloo et al., 1992; Toubro et al., 1993a, 1993b; Yoshida et al., 1994). However, the findings have not been universally positive, with at least one study reporting no difference between caffeine-ephedrine and placebo (Buemann et al., 1994). Generally, the side effects of treatment have been reported to be minimal, although some skepticism may be warranted in light of the claim that no clinically relevant withdrawal symptoms were observed among a group of obese patients following abrupt cessation of treatment involving the consumption of 600 mg of caffeine (with 20 mg ephedrine) per day (Toubro et al., 1993a). As discussed in earlier chapters, there is abundant evidence that abrupt cessation of caffeine frequently produces dysphoric effects, which can be pronounced in some consumers.

To date, the reported effects of caffeine-ephedrine treatment for obesity have been modest, whether with or without dietary restriction. Losses appear to be no greater than those typically reported for existing nonpharmacological behavioral treatments. Regarding exercise-induced weight loss, there is conflicting evidence as to whether caffeine enhances caloric expenditure during exercise (Donelly & McNaughton, 1992; Engels & Haymes, 1992). Considering the available evidence, it would seem useful to examine the efficacy of caffeine-ephedrine treatment combined with rigorous behavioral intervention incorporating dietary and exercise management. General use of caffeine-ephedrine treatment for obesity does not appear to be warranted at this time.

Postprandial and Orthostatic Hypotension

Elderly persons and patients with autonomic failure sometimes experience postprandial (after meals) reductions in blood pressure, which may cause angina pectoris, dizziness, syncope, and falls. Knowledge of the pressor effects of caffeine (see Chapter 5) has led to the drug being used to counter postprandial hypotension. Although positive treatment effects were obtained in several studies (Heseltine et al., 1991; Lenders et al., 1988; Nakajima et al., 1992; Onrot et al., 1985), others have reported few or no benefits (Jansen & Lipsitz, 1995; Lipsitz et al., 1994). In addition, caffeine pretreatment was found to have no effect on food-associated reductions in blood pressure experienced by patients requiring hemodialysis (Barakat et al., 1993).

One investigator has recommended that caffeine be used in the clinical management of elderly patients with orthostatic (or postural) hypotension, especially those inclined to experience hypotension when first getting out of bed in the morning (Tonkin, 1995). The specific recommendation was that the equivalent of two to three cups of coffee be consumed with breakfast and lunch, and for caffeine to be avoided for the rest of the day. However, because this regimen involves daily abstinence from caffeine for periods approximating 16 to 18 hours, it is arguable that early-morning orthostatic hypotension is more likely to be exacerbated than relieved. As discussed in Chapter 5, abstinence in excess of 12 to 14 hours produces hypotensive effects in habitual caffeine consumers. Consequently, patients with orthostatic hypotension who adopt a regimen involving consumption during the morning, followed by afternoon and evening abstinence, are likely to experience caffeine-induced hypotensive effects additional to the hypotension they already experience when getting out of bed in the morning.

Asthma

Epidemiologic studies have reported an inverse association between caffeine consumption and the prevalence of asthma (Pagano et al., 1988; Schwartz & Weiss, 1992). In addition, as discussed above, caffeine is employed as a respiratory stimulant in the treatment of neonatal apnea. Moreover, several studies have indicated that caffeine in relatively large amounts (equivalent to several cups of coffee) may improve a variety of indices of respiratory function and protect against bronchoconstriction (Becker et al., 1984; Duffy & Phillips, 1991; Kivity et al., 1990). It is less clear, however, whether amounts that approximate those typically consumed in caffeine beverages affect respiratory function (Colacone et al., 1990; Henderson et al., 1993). In any event, whereas the related methylxanthine theophylline is widely used in the clinical management of asthma, empirical evidence does not appear to support the use of caffeine for this purpose.

Electroconvulsive Therapy

Electroconvulsive therapy (ECT) is sometimes used in the treatment of severe depression and other serious psychiatric disorders. It is generally accepted among proponents of the procedure that seizure duration is an index of seizure adequacy, which in turn is predictive of therapeutic efficacy (Fink, 1994). Sometimes, however, seizure duration declines with successive ECT inductions, thereby diminishing the putative benefits of treatment. Although seizure length can be increased by increasing the intensity of the electrical current (until the maximum setting on the ECT device is reached), it has been found that increased seizure length can be achieved without increasing the current by pretreating patients with caffeine (Acevedo & Smith, 1988; Coffey et al., 1987, 1990; Hinkle et al., 1987; Kelsey & Grossberg, 1995; Shapira et al., 1987). It has also been claimed that the use of caffeine increases the antidepressant effect of treatment, thereby reducing the number of inductions and ameliorating some of the adverse cognitive effects (e.g., memory deficits; Calev, 1994). However, although the fact that caffeine lengthens seizure duration has not been denied, the claimed improvements in treatment outcome have been questioned (McCall et al., 1993; Rosenquist et al., 1994).

Hyperactivity

Of the limited amount of research that has been conducted on the effects of caffeine in children, one short-lived focus of attention was children diagnosed as hyperactive. It was suggested that caffeine might serve as a useful substitute for the stimulant drugs sometimes prescribed for hyperactivity (Schackenberg, 1973). However, with one exception (Harvey & Marsh,

1978), replication studies have reported no beneficial effects attributable to caffeine (Conners, 1975; Gross, 1975; Huestos et al., 1975; Kupietz & Winsberg, 1977).

Diagnostic Applications

Liver Function

Owing to its pharmacokinetic properties, caffeine is suitable for quantifying liver function (Burg, 1975; Ziebell & Shaw-Stiffel, 1995). It is rapidly and completely absorbed after oral ingestion, is distributed throughout the total body water, and undergoes virtually complete biotransformation in the healthy liver, with minimal renal elimination. Caffeine has been found to be particularly useful as a diagnostic probe for identifying persons with alcoholic liver disease, in whom the drug shows a markedly diminished rate of elimination (Joeres et al., 1993; Lewis & Rector, 1992; Statland & Demas, 1980). In addition, the half-life of caffeine has been found to be significantly correlated with clinical and biochemical measurements of severity of liver disease in children being assessed for liver transplantation (Baker et al., 1995). The drug has also been suggested for use as a probe in testing children for cystic fibrosis, which appears to selectively alter liver enzyme activities (Hamelin et al., 1994; Parker et al., 1994). Compromised caffeine metabolism has been observed by measurement of caffeine clearance in blood (Desmond et al., 1980; Holstege et al., 1989; Joeres et al., 1993) and saliva (Jost et al., 1987; Lewis & Rector, 1992) and by measurement of demethylation products in breath (Renner et al., 1984). However, several factors have been suggested as possibly limiting the usefulness of caffeine as a probe for early liver disease, including the effect of cigarette smoking on clearance rate (Joeres et al., 1988; Lane, 1988), the effects of various pharmaceutical drugs (Broughton & Rogers, 1981; Joeres et al., 1987; Tarrus et al., 1987), and possible confounding due to caffeine ingestion from sources other than the diagnostic dose (Marchesini et al., 1988).

Acetylator Phenotyping

Regulation of drug metabolism is a major hereditary determinant of individual differences in the pharmacokinetics of numerous drugs, including caffeine. *Acetylation* is an important pathway of drug metabolism, and several studies have examined caffeine as a probe for determining acetylator phenotype (Carrillo & Benitez, 1994; Cribb et al., 1994; Dobrocky et al., 1994; El-Yazigi et al., 1989; Evans et al., 1989; Fuhr & Rost, 1994; McQuilkin et al., 1995). Poor acetylators have been found to derive less benefit from some therapeutic drugs and to be at greater risk of certain cancers (Vistisen et al., 1992). Slow acetylation has also been reported as being more evident in AIDS patients with acute illness than in healthy controls (B. L. Lee et al., 1993).

Malignant Hyperthermia

Malignant hyperthermia is a rare inherited condition characterized by a susceptibility to halogenated anesthetics, in which afflicted people experience elevated body temperature, skeletal muscle rigidity, circulatory failure, and possible death (Denborough & Lovell, 1960). It has been found that skeletal muscle fibers from people with the susceptibility show an accentuated level of contracture in vitro in response to caffeine and halothane (Britt et al., 1982; Figarella-Branger et al., 1993; Fletcher et al., 1989; Heiman-Patterson et al., 1988; Kalow et al., 1970; Krivosic-Horber et al., 1988; Ørding, 1988; Shomer et al., 1994). This peculiar sensitivity is such that the current standard diagnostic test for malignant hyperthermia susceptibility is the caffeine and halothane contracture test (Johnson & Edleman, 1992; Kaus & Rockoff, 1994). Although highly sensitive, the test has been reported as yielding a small number of false negatives (Isaacs & Badenhorst, 1993). Caffeine contracture testing has also been used as a diagnostic probe for neuroleptic malignant syndrome, a complication of neuroleptic drug therapy, that is characterized by several clinical features common to malignant hyperthermia (Araki et al., 1988). It had been hypothesized that people susceptible to malignant hyperthermia may have a heightened sensitivity to caffeine, and therefore should avoid the drug, but the hypothesis was not confirmed when tested empirically (Flewellen & Nelson, 1983).

Athletic Performance

Caffeine has long been regarded as having ergogenic properties, and for this reason, it has attracted considerable attention as a possible doping agent in competitive sport. Shortly before the 1984 Olympic Games, caffeine was added to the list of banned substances by the International Olympic Committee (IOC). The drug had previously been banned, but the ban was removed in 1971. Under the current ruling, athletes must not exceed a urinary caffeine concentration of 12 µg/ml, which is purported to allow for the consumption of up to 500 to 600 mg of caffeine (four to seven cups of coffee) within 1 to 2 hours. It is assumed that anyone exceeding this urinary caffeine concentration level must have been using the drug for the express purpose of assisting performance. It has been found that "social" intake of caffeine beverages is generally unlikely to result in the IOC limit being exceeded (Van der Merwe et al., 1988), and urinary caffeine concentrations below the IOC limit have been obtained in athletes who have consumed more than 600 mg before exercising (Graham & Spriet, 1991; Van Soeren et al., 1993). To date, only one athlete, an Australian at the 1988 Seoul Olympics, has been disqualified from Olympic competition for exceeding the caffeine limit. However, because rate of caffeine metabolism varies substantially, it appears that some individuals could exceed the IOC limit despite having only consumed amounts that are within the "normal" consumption range for the population (Birkett & Miners, 1991).

Physical Endurance

There is considerable evidence that caffeine can enhance endurance during prolonged exercise, such as is involved in distance cross-country skiing, cycling, and running (Berglund & Hemmingsson, 1982; Costill et al., 1978; Falk et al., 1990; Graham & Spriet, 1991; Lindinger et al., 1993; Spriet et al., 1992). Typically, the drug is taken about 60 minutes before commencing exercise involving sustained activity at 75% to 80% of maximal oxygen uptake (VO_2 max). Effects are more likely to be observed at relatively high caffeine doses (e.g., 8 to 10 mg/kg of body weight, the equivalent of six to eight cups of coffee), although null results have been reported even at these high doses (e.g., Alves et al., 1995). It is believed that the ergogenic properties of caffeine are due to the action of the drug in stimulating epinephrine secretion, either by acting on the central nervous system or by direct stimulation of the adrenal medulla. This, in turn, stimulates adipose tissue lipolysis leading to increased free fatty acid levels in the blood and glycogen sparing (Costill et al., 1978; Essig et al., 1980). In practical terms, the typical caffeine-induced effect has been described as large enough to "separate the fastest and slowest of a field of elite athletes in many competitions" (Graham et al., 1994, p. 132).

Consistent with the glycogen-sparing account given by Costill and his colleagues (Costill et al., 1978; Essig et al., 1980), caffeine has been found to increase epinephrine response during exercise (e.g., Anderson & Hickey, 1994). The process, however, appears to be influenced by caffeine-consumer status, with habitual consumers showing a diminished epinephrine response to the drug during exercise (Bangsbo et al., 1992; Van Soeren et al., 1993). This may explain the apparent absence of an ergogenic effect among habitual consumers (Tarnopolsky et al., 1989). Notwithstanding the supportive evidence, it is believed that glycogen sparing provides only a partial explanation of the reported ergogenic effects of caffeine. Indeed, apart from other possible physiological mechanisms (Graham et al., 1994), it remains an open question as to whether observed improvements in performance are due, at least in part, to the indirect effects of caffeine-induced improvements in mood (Calhoun, 1971).

Power and Strength

Numerous animal studies involving high caffeine doses have reported increased force development in isolated skeletal muscle preparations (Dodd et al., 1993). However, with some exceptions (e.g., Anselme et al., 1992), caffeine has generally not been found to have a beneficial effect on human muscular performance during high-intensity, short-term physical exertion such as is involved in sprinting, power lifting, and throwing (Kendrick et al., 1994; Lopes et al., 1983; Tarnopolsky, 1993; Williams et al., 1988). Williams et al. (1987) speculated that caffeine may change motor unit recruitment and discharge characteristics during sustained voluntary muscular contractions, thereby increasing the force of maximal voluntary contraction and/or delaying the onset or rate of fatigue. However, the same authors found that maximal handgrip strength was not significantly improved after caffeine, nor did caffeine improve endurance capacity during voluntary isometric handgrip exercise. Thus, Williams et al. (1987) concluded that although caffeine may have ergogenic effects for some activities, it does not appear to improve performance on activities requiring strength and/or short-term endurance.

Caffeine as an Ergogenic Dosing Agent

Several authors have advocated the use of caffeine as an ergogenic aid and have suggested that athletes might benefit from abstaining from the drug for several days preceding a sporting event, thereby obtaining maximum benefit on the day of competition. However, abstaining only on the days that precede a sporting event will put the athlete at risk of experiencing adverse withdrawal effects (e.g., headache, sleepiness, impaired concentration), which could undermine final precompetition preparation. Moreover, it has been suggested that caffeine withdrawal may affect lipolysis in such a way as to interfere with the putative mechanism responsible for the drug's ergogenic properties (Hetzler et al., 1994). Consequently, if there is a benefit to be derived from caffeine, athletes would be better advised to remain caffeine-free between events and to ingest about 500 mg of the drug about 60 minutes prior to an event.

However, advocacy of caffeine as an ergogenic aid in competitive sport raises important ethical questions. Attempting to devise a doping regimen that works without breaching the IOC limit may be legal, but is it ethical? Graham et al. (1994) have stated their belief that either the IOC restriction on caffeine should be removed or caffeine use by elite competitors should be banned altogether. One of the problems these authors identified with the current situation is that experimentation with caffeine may lead to it functioning as a "gateway drug" that encourages young athletes to experiment further with stimulants, steroids, and other doping agents. Moreover, caffeine use in general may not be conducive to elite performance. It has been suggested that habitual caffeine consumption may have an *ergolytic* (energy impairing) effect on athletic performance for some people (Williams, 1992), due to daytime sleepiness caused by caffeine-induced chronic impairment of sleep quality (Eichner, 1993; Regestein, 1989).

SUMMARY

The major areas of human function and dysfunction for which caffeine-induced benefits have been sought are summarized in Table 8.1. It is interesting to note that for each of the demonstrated successful applications

Table 8.1   Possible Beneficial Uses of Caffeine

Condition	Benefits
Therapeutic Applications	
Neonatal apnea	Yes
Pain	
General	Likely
Headache	Likely
Obesity	Unlikely
Hypotension	
Postprandial	Unlikely
Orthostatic	No
Asthma	No
Electroconvulsive therapy (ECT)	Yes
Hyperactivity	No
Diagnostic Applications	
Liver function	Yes
Acetylator phenotyping	Yes
Malignant hyperthermia	Yes
Athletic Performance	
Physical endurance	Yes
Power and strength	No

summarized in Table 8.1, including treatment (neonatal apnea, analgesic adjuvant, withdrawal headache; adjunctive use in ECT), diagnostic testing (liver function, acetylator phenotyping, and malignant hyperthermia), and athletic performance (enhancement of physical endurance), the drug has been found to be effective only when used acutely. When used chronically, beneficial effects appear to be diminished (e.g., the potential to enhance physical endurance appears to decline with repeated use). The only apparent exception to this rule is the chronic application of caffeine as an analgesic adjuvant for pain and headache. However, as discussed above, chronic use of caffeine in the treatment of pain is ill-advised, because the main symptom of physical dependence on caffeine is pain in the form of withdrawal-induced headache. That is, Table 8.1 shows that there are several therapeutic and diagnostic areas for which caffeine has important applications, but none involves chronic use of the drug. Indeed, as has been seen throughout this book, habitual (i.e., chronic) use of caffeine involves only adverse outcomes.

FURTHER READING

Bracco, D., Ferrarra, J. M., Arnaud, M. J., Jequier, E., & Schutz, Y. (1995). Effects of caffeine on energy metabolism, heart rate, and methylxanthine metabolism in lean and obese women. *American Journal of Physiology, 269*, E671-E678.

Graham, T. E., Rush, W. E., & van Soeren, M. H. (1994). Caffeine and exercise: Metabolism and performance. *Canadian Journal of Applied Physiology, 19*, 111-138.

Laska, E. M., Sunshine, A., Mueller, F., Elvers, W. B., Siegel, C., & Rubin, A. (1984). Caffeine as an analgesic adjuvant. *Journal of the American Medical Association, 251*, 1711-1718.

Welborn, L. G., & Greenspun, J. C. (1994). Anesthesia and apnea: Perioperative considerations in the former preterm infant. *Pediatric Clinics of North America, 41*, 181-198.

Ziebell, J., & Shaw-Stiffel, T. (1995). Update on the use of metabolic probes to quantify liver function: Caffeine versus lidocaine. *Digestive Diseases, 13*, 239-250.

Overview

Is Caffeine a Drug of Abuse?

Two key questions about caffeine were asked in Chapter 2: Why is it so popular? What are the consequences of habitual use? The intervening chapters have addressed the second question in some detail, whereas discussion of the first has been much more sparing. This, the final chapter, attempts to draw together the disparate biobehavioral threads of the preceding chapters in order to summarize what is known about the consequences of habitual caffeine consumption and to address more directly, if somewhat tentatively, the reasons for the continued widespread use of the drug. The overview of effects and the discussion of reasons for caffeine use provide the foundation for considering, in the final passages of the book, two additional key questions: Is there a safe level of caffeine consumption? Is caffeine a drug of abuse?

Brief Overview of the Biobehavioral Effects of Caffeine

The relentless growth in the worldwide consumption of caffeine is such that its use has become almost universal (Chapter 1). Although the acute actions of the drug are largely benign, the cumulative biobehavioral effects may be very significant, considering the multiplying factors that are involved, including daily exposure, the lifetime of the individual, and the large majority of the population.

Much is known about the human pharmacology of the drug, its absorption, distribution, and metabolism (Chapter 2). There is also good understanding of the principal mechanism of action, namely, antagonism of endogenous adenosine. Through this mechanism, caffeine influences a pervasive array of basic and essential bodily functions and processes. If consumed in amounts greatly in excess of usual dietary levels, the effects can be dangerous, even fatal. At ordinary dietary levels, however, the acute effects of caffeine are usually subtle and go largely unnoticed by the consumer. Even so, occasional acute adverse effects may occur. For example, dysphoria may be experienced in association with intermittent periods of abstinence, and caffeine may interact adversely with other drugs.

Despite extensive investigation, the common belief that caffeine enhances psychomotor and cognitive performance remains largely unsubstantiated (Chapter 3). Whatever effects the drug may have are almost certainly too slight to be of much practical importance. The psychoactive action of caffeine is usually experienced as little more than a subtle enhancement of mood. In the absence of prior exposure, the psychoactive, discriminative stimulus, and reinforcing properties of caffeine are weak. In the habitual consumer, however, these properties may be markedly potentiated by abstinence, even that which is brief (e.g., the overnight abstinence typical of most habitual consumption).

The inclusion of several caffeine-associated clinical syndromes in *DSM-IV* (1994) has been important in drawing attention to the potential of caffeine to undermine psychological well-being (Chapter 4), but further work is needed. The syndrome of caffeine withdrawal (physical dependence) has strong empirical support, and there is evidence that caffeine may interfere with sleep and exacerbate existing anxiety problems. However, there is little direct support for *caffeine intoxication,* the main caffeine-associated clinical syndrome described in *DSM-IV.* In exceptional circumstances (e.g., extreme fatigue, use of other psychoactive substances), caffeine in unusually large amounts may contribute to psychotic-like transient hallucinations and delusions. Unfortunately, there has been a general absence of attention to the effects of caffeine on psychological well-being in children.

Caffeine is known to produce acute increases in blood pressure, but concern over these effects has been dampened by the long-held belief that tolerance develops with habitual use of the drug (Chapter 5). Contrary to the tolerance hypothesis, several lines of evidence converge to show that habitual consumers are *not* immune to caffeine-induced increases in blood pressure. Extrapolation based on population blood pressure data suggests that caffeine could account for about 12% of deaths from coronary heart disease and 20% of deaths from stroke.

The extensive literature on the association between caffeine consumption and cancer contains too many inconsistencies to permit firm conclusions (Chapter 6). Of the many cancer sites that have been considered, a weak causal association may exist for bladder cancer and pancreatic cancer, and a possible weak protective action may exist in relation to colon cancer. If the observed associations are indeed causal, they could be due to constituents in coffee other than caffeine.

Although maternal exposure to relatively large amounts of caffeine causes congenital abnormalities in rodents, the available evidence indicates that maternal caffeine use during pregnancy is not likely to be a cause of congenital morphological abnormalities in humans (Chapter 7). However, evidence from animal studies suggests that caffeine could exacerbate adverse effects on fetal health arising from other agents (e.g., alcohol, medications) to which pregnant women might be exposed. In addition, there is evidence that newborns may experience distress due to caffeine withdrawal associated with intrauterine exposure to the drug. More importantly, there is strong evidence that caffeine consumed during pregnancy contributes to lower birth weight and moderate support for the suggestion that caffeine may increase the risk of spontaneous abortion. Overall, the evidence indicates that there is an urgent need for health authorities to advocate total abstinence from caffeine during pregnancy.

Notwithstanding these various harmful effects of caffeine, the drug has also been found to have a number of beneficial uses (Chapter 8). Its main therapeutic applications are as a respiratory stimulant in the treatment of neonatal apnea, as an analgesic adjuvant, and as pretreatment to enhance the putative benefits of ECT. In addition, caffeine has reliable diagnostic applications as a probe for liver function, acetylator phenotyping, and malignant hyperthermia. Furthermore, there has been considerable interest in caffeine as a possible ergogenic aid to athletic performance. It appears that caffeine can enhance activities that demand physical endurance, but not those involving intense bursts of power and strength. However, in virtually all instances, beneficial effects are associated with short-term use of the drug. Despite possibly being the most intensively researched constituent of the human diet, caffeine has no demonstrated biobehavioral benefits when consumed habitually.

■ Why Is Caffeine So Popular?

It is evident from the preceding brief overview, and the more detailed treatment contained in previous chapters, that the habitual consumption of caffeine has a variety of harmful effects and no obvious benefits. Why, then, does caffeine continue to be so popular? This enigmatic question has only rarely been broached in a serious manner. In one such analysis, Rogers and Richardson (1993) suggested that liking for the sensory qualities of caffeine beverages may be acquired as a result of association with mood changes following ingestion, and that liking may be strengthened by the development of physical dependence.

Acquired taste or liking is probably one component of a broader constellation of influences that transform initial use into a sustained habit. Figure 9.1 summarizes what appear to be the main biobehavioral determinants of *initial* individual use of caffeine, and subsequent *habitual* use. It is hypothesized that the behavior of ingesting caffeine beverages is influenced by particular antecedent conditions (discriminative stimuli) and consequences (reinforcers). Caffeine beverages are ubiquitous and form part of the discriminative stimulus array encountered by most people daily. Caffeine consumption is also an integral aspect of much social intercourse. As such, a host of discriminative stimuli (situational and cognitive/social) that set the occasion for initial use, which is likely to be reinforced by various subtle consequences, both psychopharmacological (e.g., slight enhancement of mood) and social (e.g., approval for engagement in reciprocal social behavior).

Repeated use, however, produces changes in physiology (in particular, upregulation of adenosine receptors), thereby creating a new set of discriminative stimuli to be added to those that encouraged initial use. These new psychopharmacological stimuli are associated with plasma caffeine levels. Low levels signal the onset of aversive withdrawal effects (e.g., sleepiness, impaired concentration, headache) and set the occasion for caffeine ingestion, which is reinforced by cessation or avoidance of withdrawal effects. In time, an increased array of situational variables, including meals, snacks, time of day, and work and social settings also come to acquire discriminative stimulus properties, which set the occasion for caffeine ingestion. In addition to being reinforced by cessation of aversive withdrawal effects, caffeine consumption in this expanded range of situations is likely to be reinforced by a host of pleasurable subjective states associated with such activities as ingestion of food and taking rest breaks, as well as being socially reinforced

Phase of Use	Main Discriminative Stimuli	Behavior	Main Reinforcers
Initial	Situational: ready availability of caffeine beverages; social settings ("Here, have a cup of coffee")	Caffeine beverage purchase/ preparation/ingestion; acceptance of offer of beverage	Psychopharmacological: pleasant sensory effects; slight increase in arousal, subtle enhancement of mood
	Cognitive/social: curiosity; sociability		Social: approval/participation
Habitual	Psychopharmacological: depleted plasma caffeine levels, **onset of withdrawal effects** (sleepiness, impaired concentration, headache)	Established pattern of consumption: **intermittent daytime use followed by** overnight abstinence	Psychopharmacological: **cessation of withdrawal effects**, pronounced restoration of arousal, attentiveness, and mood
	Situational: meals, snacks, time of day, work setting, social settings		Situational: paired with rest breaks, food, and so on
	Cognitive/social: sociability		Social: approval/participation

Figure 9.1. Schematic summary of the principal biobehavioral influences that encourage initial individual use of caffeine and subsequent habitual use.

NOTE: Bold text highlights the key "motivational" variable underlying individual habitual consumption of caffeine.

by others with whom these activities, including caffeine consumption, are shared.

▩ Caffeine and the Public

By focusing on the individual, Figure 9.1 provides a partial representation of the determinants of caffeine use. It is important, also, to take account of the wider social environment within which individual behavior occurs. Figure 9.2 provides a schematic summary of the hypothesized principal societal influences that encourage caffeine consumption by individuals and ultimately the general public.

Attitudes and Beliefs

Caffeine, when considered in the context of possible harmful effects, appears to be an emotive subject. The depth of feeling sometimes elicited is evident in the comments of investigators surprised at the reaction to their research on caffeine. For example, trying to explain why so much public attention was given to his research on coffee and pancreatic cancer (see Chapter 6), MacMahon (1984) suggested that it was because the work seemed to be interpreted as "an attack on another American institution" (p. 109). In a similar vein, Thelle (1988) lamented that his research on the hypercholesterolemic properties of coffee (see Chapter 5) exposed him to "flak from all corners" (p. 223). Moreover, beliefs about the effects of caffeine have been found to be related to consumer status (Page, 1987). Habitual consumers, it seems, are inclined to believe that caffeine beverages give people more energy, help them to relax, help them to feel better, and are refreshing. Conversely, people who consume caffeine infrequently are apparently more likely to believe that caffeine beverages are habit-forming, make people more irritable, nervous/anxious, and jittery, and may result in ulcers, headache, kidney/bladder damage, upset stomach, high blood pressure, and cancer. Thus, beliefs about caffeine and its effects are highly variable, and not necessarily well-informed.

The Caffeine Lobby[1]

As mentioned in Chapter 1, coffee consumption declined substantially from the early 1960s to the early 1980s (Masterson, 1983). Although there

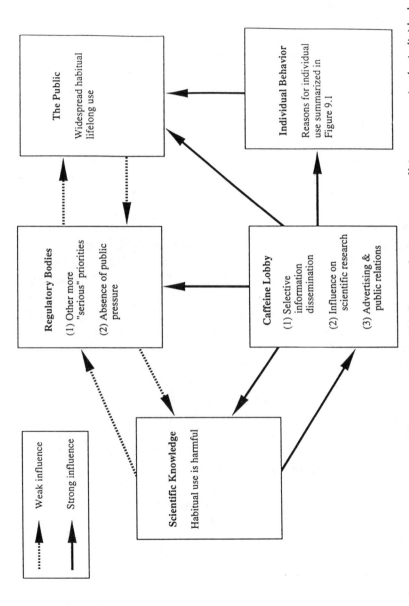

Figure 9.2. Schematic summary of the principal societal influences that encourage caffeine consumption by individuals and the public.

153

has been little objective investigation of the causes of the decline, there is a belief within the coffee industry that public awareness of harmful effects was at least partly responsible (Heuman, 1994a, 1994b; Richards, 1994). In this context, it is important to recognize that the production, distribution, and sale of caffeine products are multinational, multibillion-dollar enterprises, and that people responsible for the success of these enterprises are unlikely to remain indifferent to threats of a commercial nature. Indeed, by the 1980s, the caffeine industry had developed internationally coordinated strategies to counter the perceived commercial damage caused by scientific evidence of caffeine-induced harm.

Following passage by the U.S. Congress of new laws on foods and drugs in 1958, a list was compiled of some hundreds of additives, including caffeine, that were generally recognized as safe (GRAS). Subsequent revisions of GRAS compounds conducted by the U.S. Food and Drug Administration (FDA) threatened removal of caffeine from the list. The caffeine industry countered this threat by supporting a range of activities sponsored by a variety of bodies, including the International Life Sciences Institute (ILSI). Although this organization and others like it (e.g., the International Food Information Council, the Institute of Scientific Information on Coffee) have the superficial appearance of associations of dispassionate scholars, they have been created by the caffeine industry to serve commercial interests. For example, in the early 1980s, ILSI coordinated a major response to a proposal by the FDA to regulate caffeine. ILSI's success may be measured in part by the fact that caffeine has retained its GRAS classification.

Since the early 1980s, the caffeine industry has sponsored a variety of "scientific" activities, including meetings and publications that have served to disseminate selective interpretations of the empirical findings. Typically, these activities have portrayed caffeine as an enjoyable, benign, and even beneficial substance (e.g., Barone & Grice, 1990, 1994; Dews et al., 1994). The information is transmitted to the public arena by way of information updates to industry bodies and press releases to international media networks. Besides influencing the dissemination of information, the caffeine industry has also sought to influence the course of scientific research by being a sponsor of research (e.g., the Physiological Effects of Coffee Research Fund). In this way, industry can directly encourage research that is neutral or beneficial to its commercial interests, while discouraging research that casts caffeine in an unfavorable light. Considering the competitive nature of research funding, selective industry support represents a serious threat to research being conducted in the interests of the general public as distinct from more narrow commercial interests.

Attempts by industry to influence the dissemination of information and the direction of scientific research are not unique to the caffeine industry. The same key tactics have long been employed by the tobacco industry (e.g., Warner, 1991). It is well-documented that tobacco manufacturers, motivated to maximize profits, have committed considerable resources to counter public awareness of scientific evidence of the hazards of smoking (e.g., Houston, 1991; Samuels & Glantz, 1991). The tobacco industry policy of supporting research through industry bodies such as the Council for Tobacco Research was described by one U.S. senator as "a stroke of ingenuity" (Neuberger, 1963), because of the strategy's success in obfuscating the true impact of tobacco on health. For decades, the mere act of supporting research gave credibility to industry claims of concern for the public interest. More importantly, by advertising its support for research, the tobacco industry succeeded in creating doubt in the general community about the severity of the hazards of smoking when no such doubts existed in the scientific community (Warner, 1991). Like the tobacco industry before it, the caffeine industry has discovered that the allocation of funds for research that is essentially health neutral represents a good investment in public relations, while also promoting confusion about potential hazards.

Recent Caffeine Consumption Trends

Industry strategies for countering the adverse commercial impact of scientific evidence of caffeine-induced harmful effects have been in operation for at least 15 years. Although objective analyses of causes and effects would be very difficult to conduct in this area, industry sources apparently believe that efforts to counter public concern about the hazards of caffeine have been successful and that this success in changing public perceptions has resulted in increased business (Heuman, 1994a, 1994b; Richards, 1994). As mentioned in Chapter 1, in the late 1980s, the industry experienced a halt to the preceding many years of declining coffee consumption, with increased sales of coffee and tea being achieved over several successive years, at least in the United States. According to authoritative industry insiders, these improvements in sales are attributable to the industry's campaign to counter scientific evidence of caffeine-induced adverse effects on human health (Heuman, 1994a; Richards, 1994).

Perhaps encouraged by success in subverting evidence of hazards, unfounded claims of positive benefits arising from caffeine use are now commonplace in industry literature. A plethora of "fact" sheets, available from coffee and tea associations around the world, proclaim the benefits of caffeine products. This propaganda is used to respond to queries from the public and to brief news media. Alert to tobacco industry experience arising out of public awareness of the hazards of smoking, the caffeine industry has taken action which, in its own words, is designed "to counter evidence that coffee is harmful" (Lee, 1993, p. 6). Motivated by concern over loss of profits arising from public awareness of the hazards of caffeine, industry sources have sought to manipulate both the dissemination of scientific knowledge and the direction of scientific research. In turn, by undermining the integrity of the scientific process, the caffeine industry has had some success in subverting the public interest.

The Individual in Society

Again, in reference to cigarette smoking, it has been said that public awareness of scientific evidence of the hazards of cigarette smoking was a decisive factor in tobacco use being identified as a social problem requiring regulatory controls (Troyer & Markle, 1984). As such, the scientific community can claim to have had a major role in events leading to the introduction of public policies aimed at limiting tobacco use (e.g., mandatory health warnings on packaging, restrictions and bans on cigarette advertising, no-smoking zones). The number of people worldwide who consume caffeine daily is far greater than the number who smoke, and the cumulative impact of caffeine on population health could be comparable to that of cigarette smoking. However, recognition of caffeine consumption as a social problem will depend on whether caffeine beverages are understood by the general public to have been identified by the scientific community as harmful to health.

Unlike the caffeine industry, which is well-organized to protect its commercial interests, the scientists upon whom the public interest depends remain poorly organized regarding caffeine and its effects. Consequently, the influence that the scientific community has on the regulatory bodies responsible for public health is represented as being comparatively weak in the hypothetical model summarized in Figure 9.2. In contrast to the countless cancer societies, heart foundations, and other public and private consumer organizations actively engaged in trying to reduce the prevalence of smoking, there is virtually no organized discouragement of the use of caffeine (with the minor exceptions of the proscription on caffeine imposed by some religious minorities, the FDA caution about caffeine use during pregnancy, and the ban by the IOC on the consumption of large amounts prior to Olympic competition). In the absence of concerted scientific input, regulatory bodies have other priorities all too likely to take precedence over caffeine. Conversely, the caffeine lobby is an active consumer of scientific information and is quick to exploit scientific findings in the marketplace. In addition, as suggested in Figure 9.2, this well-organized lobby group has a history of directly trying to influence the activities of the scientific community (e.g., selective information dissemination, selective support for research), regulatory bodies (e.g., ILSI's selective input to FDA review processes), the individual (e.g., advertising), and the public (e.g., public relations activities).

▒ Is There a Safe Level of Caffeine Consumption?

The evidence reviewed in the preceding chapters and summarized above supports the conclusion that habitual caffeine consumption is harmful. In particular, at ordinary levels of habitual use, caffeine is a probable cardiovascular risk factor, poses a threat to fetal growth, interacts adversely with common therapeutic drugs, and produces dysphoric effects after brief abstinence. Consequently, it is reasonable to ask whether there is a safe level of caffeine consumption. The appropriate answer to this question appears to be that there is *no safe level.* Even the equivalent of one cup of coffee produces modest increases in blood pressure lasting 2 to 3 hours. Habitual use may diminish but does not remove this effect. Experienced over a lifetime, these daily elevations in blood pressure probably contribute to cardiovascular disease. Any exposure to caffeine during pregnancy exposes the fetus to a dose equivalent to that received by the mother, with probable harmful effects in a proportion of pregnancies. Caffeine has adverse interactive effects with some therapeutic drugs, but interactions with the majority of therapeutic drugs currently in use have not been studied. Habitual use produces physical dependence, even at low levels of intake. Against this background, it seems reasonable to conclude that the drug should be avoided altogether, because it has *no nutritional value, is demonstrably harmful, and has no demonstrated benefits.*

▨ Conclusion: Caffeine Is a Drug of Abuse

The addiction literature is replete with definitions and distinctions, some of which are considered in Chapter 4. There is, however, no universally accepted definition of *abuse*. The American Psychiatric Association (1994) does not regard caffeine as a drug of abuse, nor does it regard nicotine as such. Indeed, of the long list of named substances in *DSM-IV* (1994), only caffeine and nicotine are excluded from being regarded as drugs of abuse, a position that is inconsistent with their known biobehavioral actions relative to other drugs.

Repeated use of caffeine produces physical dependence. This feature is shared by all prototypic drugs of abuse (e.g., alcohol, cocaine, heroin) and appears to be the key motivational factor responsible for continued use (see Figure 9.1). Furthermore, the term *abuse*, when used in the context of drug use, has wide currency in the general community and carries the straightforward connotation of being "harmful to health." The evidence reviewed in this book indicates that habitual use of caffeine is harmful. As such, habitual caffeine use appears to involve the two key sets of processes and outcomes encompassed by the term *abuse*. That is, habitual caffeine use involves both physical dependence and potential harm to health.

Thus, in response to the question posed by the title of this chapter, it seems reasonable to conclude in the affirmative. Caffeine *is* a drug of abuse, because (a) habitual use leads to the development of physical dependence, and (b) habitual use is potentially harmful to health. Although commercial interests have sought either to conceal or to sanitize the facts, the available evidence indicates that widespread cessation of caffeine consumption would lead to substantial reductions in population levels of avoidable death and disease.

▨ NOTE

1. This section is based in part on a previously published article (James, 1994a) and associated correspondence (Golding, 1995; James, 1995a, 1995b; Smith, 1995).

References

Abe, Y., Umemura, S., Sugimoto, K., Hirawa, N., Kato, Y., Yokoyama, N., Yokoyama, T., Iwai, J., & Ishii, M. (1995). Effect of green tea rich in gamma-aminobutyric acid on blood pressure of Dahl salt-sensitive rats. *American Journal of Hypertension, 8,* 74-79.

Abernethy, D. R., & Todd, E. L. (1985). Impairment of caffeine clearance by chronic use of low-dose oestrogen-containing oral contraceptives. *European Journal of Clinical Pharmacology, 28,* 425-428.

Abu-Zeid, H. A., Choi, N. W., & Hsu, P. H. (1981). Factors associated with risk of cancer of the colon and rectum. *American Journal of Epidemiology, 114,* 442.

Acevedo, A. G., & Smith, J. K. (1988). Adverse reaction to use of caffeine in ECT [Letter to the editor]. *American Journal of Psychiatry, 145,* 529-530.

Acheson, K. J., Zahorska-Markiewica, B., Pittet, P., Aantharaman, K., & Jequier, E. (1980). Caffeine and coffee: Their influence on metabolic rate and substrate utilization in normal weight and obese individuals. *American Journal of Clinical Nutrition, 33,* 989-997.

Aeschbacher, H. U. (1988). *Mutagenicity of coffee.* London: Elsevier Applied Science.

Ahola, I., Jauhiainen, M., & Aro, A. (1991). The hypocholestrolemic factor in boiled coffee is retained by a paper filter. *Journal of Internal Medicine, 230,* 293-297.

Aitken, R. J., Best, F., Richardson, D. W., Schats, R., & Simm, G. (1983). Influence of caffeine on movement characteristics, fertilizing capacity, and ability to penetrate cervical mucus of human spermatozoa. *Journal of Reproduction and Fertility, 67,* 19-27.

Ajarem, J. S., & Ahmad, M. (1991). Behavioral and biochemical consequences of perinatal exposure of mice to instant coffee: A correlative evaluation. *Pharmacology Biochemistry and Behavior, 40,* 847-852.

Akinyanju, P., & Yudkin, J. (1967). Effect of coffee and tea on serum lipids in the rat. *Nature, 214,* 426.

Al-Ansary, L. A., & Babay, Z. A. (1994). Risk factors for spontaneous abortion: A preliminary study on Saudi women. *Journal of the Royal Society of Health, 114,* 188-193.

Alder, H. F., Burkhardt, W. L., Ivy, A. C., & Atkinson, A. J. (1950). Effect of various drugs on psychomotor performance at ground level and simulated altitudes of 18,000 feet in a low pressure chamber. *Journal of Aviation Medicine, 21,* 221-236.

159

Aldridge, A., Aranda, J. V., & Neims, M. D. (1979). Caffeine metabolism in the newborn. *Clinical Pharmacology and Therapeutics, 25,* 447-453.

Aldridge, A., Bailey, J., & Neims, A. H. (1981). The disposition of caffeine during and after pregnancy. *Seminars in Perinatology, 5,* 310-314.

Alkaysi, H. N., Shiekh Salem, M., & El-Sayed, Y. M. (1988). High perofrmance liquid chromatographic analysis of caffeine concentrations in plasma and saliva. *Journal of Clinical Pharmacy and Therapeutics, 13,* 109-115.

Allen, S. S., & Froberg, D. G. (1987). The effect of decreased caffeine consumption on benign proliferative breast disease: A randomized clinical trial. *Surgery, 101,* 720-730.

Alstott, R. L., Miller, A. J., & Forney, R. B. (1972). Report of a human fatality due to caffeine. *Journal of Forensic Sciences, 14,* 135-137.

Alves, M. N., Ferrari-Auarek, W. M., Pinto, K. M., Sa, K. R., Viveiros, J. P., Pereira, H. A., Ribeiro, A. M., & Rodrigues, L. O. (1995). Effects of caffeine and tryptophan on rectal temperature, metabolism, total exercise time, rate of perceived exertion, and heart rate. *Brazilian Journal of Medical and Biological Research, 28,* 705-709.

Amato, M., Huppi, P., Isenschmid, M., & Schneider, H. (1992). Developmental aspects of percutaneous caffeine absorption in premature infants. *American Journal of Perinatology, 9,* 431-434.

American Psychiatric Association. (1987). *Diagnostic and statistical manual of mental disorders* (3rd ed., rev.). Washington, DC: Author.

American Psychiatric Association. (1994). *Diagnostic and statistical manual of mental disorders* (4th ed.). Washington, DC: Author.

Anderson, D. E., & Hickey, M. S. (1994). Effects of caffeine on the metabolic and catecholamine responses to exercise in 5 and 28 degrees C. *Medicine and Science in Sports and Exercise, 26,* 453-458.

Anderson, K. J., & Revelle, W. (1982). Impulsivity, caffeine, and proofreading: A test of the Easterbrook Hypothesis. *Journal of Experimental Psychology: Human Perception and Performance, 8,* 614-624.

Anderson, K. J., & Revelle, W. (1983). The interactive effects of caffeine, impulsivity, and task demands on a visual search task. *Personality and Individual Differences, 4,* 127-134.

Anderson, K. J., & Revelle, W. (1994). Impulsivity and time of day: Is rate of change in arousal a function of impulsivity? *Journal of Personality and Social Psychology, 67,* 334-344.

Ando, K. (1975). Profile of drug effects on temporally spaced responding in rats. *Pharmacology, Biochemistry, and Behavior, 3,* 833-841.

Anselme, F., Collomp, K., Mercier, B., Ahmaidi, S., & Prefaut, C. (1992). Caffeine increases maximal anaerobic power and blood lactate concentration. *European Journal of Applied Physiology, 65,* 188-191.

Anwar, M., Mondestin, H., Mojica, N., Novo, R., Graff, M., Hiatt, M., & Hegyi, T. (1986). Effect of caffeine on pneumogram and apnoea of infancy. *Archives of Disease in Childhood, 61,* 891-895.

Apfeldorf, W. T., & Shear, M. K. (1993). Caffeine potentiation of taste in panic-disorder patients. *Biological Psychiatry, 33,* 217-219.

Apostolides, Z., & Weisburger, J. H. (1995). Screening of tea clones for inhibition of PhIP mutagenicity. *Mutation Research, 326,* 219-225.

Arab, L., Kohlmeier, M., Schlierf, G., & Schettler, G. (1983). Coffee and cholesterol [Letter to the editor]. *New England Journal of Medicine, 309,* 1250.

Araki, M., Takagi, A., Higuchi, I., & Sugita, H. (1988). Neuroleptic malignant syndrome: Caffeine contracture of single muscle fibers and muscle pathology. *Neurology, 38,* 297-301.

Aranda, J. V., Beharry, K., & Kinlough, L. (1983). Ontogeny of caffeine biotransformation in humans. *Clinical Pharmacology and Therapeutics, 33,* 244.

Aranda, J. V., Collinge, J. M., Zinman, R., & Watters, G. (1979). Maturation of caffeine elimination in infancy. *Archives of Disease in Childhood, 54,* 946-949.

Aranda, J. V., Cook, C. E., Gorman, W., Collinge, J. M., Loughnan, P. M., Outerbridge, E. W., Aldridge, A., & Neims, A. H. (1979). Pharmacokinetic profile of caffeine in the premature newborn infant with apnea. *Journal of Pediatrics, 94,* 663-668.

Aranda, J. V., Gorman, W., Bergsteinsson, H., & Gunn, T. (1977). Efficacy of caffeine in the treatment of apnea in the low-birth-weight infant. *Journal of Pediatrics, 90,* 467-472.

Aranda, J. V., Louridas, A. T., Vitullo, B. B., Thom, P., Aldridge, A., & Haber, R. (1979). Metabolism of theophylline to caffeine in human fetal liver. *Science, 206,* 1319-1321.

Aranda, J. V., Sitar, D. S., Parsons, W. D., Loughnan, P. M., & Neims, A. H. (1976). Pharmacokinetic aspects of theophylline in premature newborns. *New England Journal of Medicine, 295,* 413-416.

Aranda, J. V., & Turmen, T. (1979). Methylxanthines in apnea of prematurity. In L. F. Soyka (Ed.), *Clinics in perinatology: Symposium on pharmacology* (Vol. 6, No. 1, pp. 87-108). Philadelphia: W. B. Saunders.

Aranda, J. V., Turmen, T., Davis, J., Trippenbach, T., Grondin, D., Zinman, R., & Watters, G. (1983). Effect of caffeine on control of breathing in infantile apnea. *Journal of Pediatrics, 103,* 975-978.

Archimandritis, A., Sipsas, N., Tryphonos, M., Tsirantonaki, M., & Tjivras, M. (1995). Significance of various factors in patients with functional dyspepsia and peptic ulcer disease in Greece: A comparative prospective study. *Annales de Médecine Interne, 146,* 299-303.

Armstrong, B., & Doll, R. (1975). Environmental factors and cancer incidence and mortality in different countries, with special reference to dietary practices. *International Journal of Cancer, 15,* 617.

Armstrong, B., Garrod, A., & Doll, R. (1976). A retrospective study of renal cancer with special reference to coffee and animal protein consumption. *British Journal of Cancer, 33,* 127.

Armstrong, B. G., McDonald, A. D., & Sloan, M. (1992). Cigarette, alcohol, and coffee consumption and spontaneous abortion. *American Journal of Public Health, 82,* 85-87.

Arnaud, M. J. (1987). The pharmacology of caffeine. *Progress in Drug Research, 31,* 273-313.

Arnesen, E., Førde, O. H., & Thelle, D. S. (1984). Coffee and serum cholesterol. *British Medical Journal, 288,* 1960.

Arnold, M. E., Petros, T. V., Beckwith, B. E., Coons, G., & Gorman, N. (1987). The effects of caffeine, impulsivity, and sex on memory for word lists. *Physiology and Behavior, 41,* 25-30.

Aro, A., Tuomilehto, J., Kostiainen, E., Uusitalo, U., & Pietinen, P. (1987). Boiled coffee increases serum low density lipoprotein concentration. *Metabolism, 36,* 1027-1030.

Asal, N. R., Geyer, J. R., Risser, D. R., Lee, E. T., Kadamani, S., & Cherng, N. (1988). Risk factors in renal cell carcinoma: II. Medical history, occupation, multivariate analysis, and conclusions. *Cancer Detection and Prevention, 13,* 263-279.

Astrup, A., & Toubro, S. (1993). Thermogenic, metabolic, and cardiovascular responses to ephedrine and caffeine in man. *International Journal of Obesity and Related Metabolic Disorders, 17*(Suppl. 1), S41-S43.

Astrup, A., Toubro, S., Cannon, S., Hein, P., Breum, L., & Madsen, J. (1990). Caffeine: A double-blind, placebo-controlled study of its thermogenic, metabolic, and cardiovascular effects in healthy volunteers. *American Journal of Clinical Nutrition, 51,* 759-767.

Astrup, A., Toubro, S., Cannon, S., Hein, P., & Madsen, J. (1991). Thermogenic synergism between ephedrine and caffeine in healthy volunteers: A double-blind, placebo-controlled study. *Metabolism, 40,* 323-329.

Astrup, A., Toubro, S., Christensen, N. J., & Quaade, F. (1992). Pharmacology of thermogenic drugs. *American Journal of Clinical Nutrition, 55* (Suppl. 1), 246S-248S.

Avogaro, P., Capri, C., Pais, M., & Cazzolato, G. (1973). Plasma and urine cortisol behavior and fat mobilization in man after coffee ingestion. *Israel Journal of Medical Sciences, 9,* 114-119.

Ayers, J., Ruff, C. F., & Templer, D. I. (1976). Alcoholism, cigarette smoking, coffee drinking, and extraversion. *Journal of Studies on Alcohol, 37,* 983-985.

Bailey, D. N., Weibert, R. T., Naylor, A. J., & Shaw, R. F. (1982). A study of salicylate and caffeine excretion in the breast milk of two nursing mothers. *Journal of Analytical Toxicology, 6,* 64-68.

Bairam, A., Boutroy, M. J., Badonnel, Y., & Vert, P. (1987). Theophylline versus caffeine: Comparative effects in treatment of idiopathic apnea in the preterm infant. *Journal of Pediatrics, 110,* 636-639.

Bak, A. A., & Grobbee, D. E. (1989). The effect on serum cholesterol levels of coffee brewed by filtering or boiling. *New England Journal of Medicine, 321,* 1432-1437.

Bak, A. A., & Grobbee, D. E. (1990). A randomized study on coffee and blood pressure. *Journal of Human Hypertension, 4,* 259-264.

Baker, A., Girling, A., Worthington, D., Ballantine, N., Smith, S., Tarlow, M., & Kelly, D. (1995). The prognostic significance of caffeine half-life in saliva in children with chronic liver disease. *Journal of Pediatric Gastroenterology and Nutrition, 20,* 196-201.

Baker, W. J., & Theologus, G. C. (1972). Effects of caffeine on visual monitoring. *Journal of Applied Psychology, 56,* 422-427.

Balogh, A., Klinger, G., Henschel, L., Borner, A., Vollanth, R., & Kuhnz, W. (1995). Influence of ethinylestradiol-containing combination oral contraceptives with gestodene or levonorgestrel on caffeine elimination. *European Journal of Clinical Pharmacology, 48,* 161-166.

Bangsbo, J., Jacobsen, K., Nordberg, N., Christensen, N. J., & Graham, T. (1992). Acute and habitual caffeine ingestion and metabolic responses to steady-state exercise [published erratum appears in J Appl Physiol 1992 Aug;73(2):following table of contents]. *Journal of Applied Physiology, 72,* 1297-1303.

Banner, W., & Czajka, P. A. (1980). Acute caffeine overdose in the neonate. *American Journal of Diseases of Children, 134,* 495-498.

Barakat, M. M., Nawab, Z. M., Yu, A. W., Lau, A. H., Ing, T. S., & Daugirdas, J. T. (1993). Hemodynamic effects of intradialytic food ingestion and the effects of caffeine. *Journal of the American Society of Nephrology, 3,* 1813-1818.

Barger-Lux, M .J., Heaney, R. P., & Stegman, M. R. (1990). Effects of moderate caffeine intake on the calcium economy of premenopausal women. *American Journal of Clinical Nutrition, 52,* 722-725.

Barkay, J., Bartoor, B., & Ben-Ezra, S. (1984). The influence of in vitro caffeine treatment on human sperm morphology and fertilizing capacity. *Fertility and Sterility, 41,* 913-917.

Barkay, J., Zuckerman, H., Sklan, D., & Gordon, S. (1977). Effects of caffeine on increasing the motility of frozen human sperms. *Fertility and Sterility, 28,* 175-177.

Barmack, J. E. (1940). The time of administration and some effects of 2 Grs. of alkaloid caffeine. *Journal of Experimental Psychology, 27,* 690-698.

Baron, J. A., Gerhardsson-de-Verdier, M., & Ekbom, A. (1994). Coffee, tea, tobacco, and cancer of the large bowel. *Cancer Epidemiology, Biomarkers and Prevention, 3,* 565-570.

Barone, J. J., & Grice, H. C. (1990). Sixth International caffeine workshop, Hong Kong. *Food and Chemical Toxicology, 28,* 279-283.

Barone, J. J., & Grice, H. C. (1994). Seventh International Caffeine Workshop, Santorini, Greece 13-17 June 1993. *Food and Chemical Toxicology, 32,* 65-77.

Barone, J. J., & Roberts, H. (1984). *Human consumption of caffeine.* Berlin: Springer-Verlag.

Barr, H. M., Streissguth, A. P., Martin, D. C., & Horst, T. E. (1981). *Methodological issues in assessment of caffeine intake: A method for quantifying consumption and a test-retest reliability study.* New York: Raven Press.

Barr, H. M., Streissguth, A. P., Martin, D. C., & Horst, T. E. (1984). Infant size at 8 months of age: Relationship to maternal use of alcohol, nicotine, and caffeine during pregnancy. *Pediatrics, 74,* 336-341.

Barrett, D. A., & Rutter, N. (1994). Transdermal delivery and the premature neonate. *Critical Reviews in Therapeutic Drug Carrier Systems, 11,* 1-30.

Barrett-Connor, E., Chang, J. C., & Edelstein, S. L. (1994). Coffee-associated osteoporosis offset by daily milk consumption: The Rancho Bernardo study. *Journal of the American Medical Association, 271,* 280-283.

Bättig, J., & Buzzi, R. (1986). Effect of coffee on the speed of subject-paced information processing. *Neuropsychobiology, 16,* 126-130.

Bättig, K., & Welzl, H. (1993). Psychopharmacological profile of caffeine. In S. Garattini (Ed.), *Caffeine, coffee, and health* (pp. 213-253). New York: Raven Press.

Baumgartner, C., Wessely, P., Bingol, C., Maly, J., & Holzner, F. (1989). Long-term prognosis of analgesic withdrawal in patients with drug-induced headaches. *Headache, 29,* 510-514.

Beach, C. A., Bianchine, J. R., & Gerber, N. (1984). The excretion of caffeine in the semen of man: Pharmacokinetics and comparison of the concentrations in blood and semen. *Journal of Clinical Pharmacology, 24,* 120-126.

Beaulac-Baillargeon, L., & Desrosiers, C. (1987). Caffeine-cigarette interaction on fetal growth. *American Journal of Obstetrics and Gynecology, 157,* 1236-1240.

Beaver, W. T. (1984). Caffeine revisited [Editorial]. *Journal of the American Medical Association, 251,* 1732-1733.

Becker, A. B., Simons, K. J., Gillespie, C. A., & Simons, F. E. R. (1984). The bronchodilator effects and pharmacokinetics of caffeine in asthma. *New England Journal of Medicine, 310,* 743-746.

Belland, K. M., & Bissell, C. (1994). A subjective study of fatigue during Navy flight operations over southern Iraq: Operation Southern Watch. *Aviation, Space, and Environmental Medicine, 65,* 557-561.

Bellet, S., Kershbaum, A., & Finck, E. M. (1968). Response of free fatty acids to coffee and caffeine. *Metabolism, 17,* 702-707.

Bellet, S., Kostis, J., Roman, L., & De Castro, O. (1969). Effect of coffee ingestion on adrenocortical secretion in young men and dogs. *Metabolism, 18,* 1007-1012.

Bellet, S., Roman, L., Decastro, O., Evin-Kim, K., & Kershbaum, A. (1969). Effect of coffee ingestion on catecholamine release. *Metabolism, 18,* 288-291.

Benowitz, N. L., Jacob, P., Mayan, H., & Denaro, C. (1995). Sympathomimetic effects of paraxanthine and caffeine in humans. *Clinical Pharmacology and Therapeutics, 58,* 684-691.

Benowitz, N. L., Osterloh, J., Goldschl, N., Kaysen, G., Pond, S., & Forhan, S. (1982). Massive catecholamine release from caffeine poisoning. *Journal of the American Medical Association, 248,* 1097-1098.

Berger, J., & Wynder, E. L. (1994). The correlation of epidemiological variables. *Journal of Clinical Epidemiology, 47,* 941-952.

Berglund, B., & Hemmingsson, P. (1982). Effects of caffeine ingestion on exercise performance at low and high altitudes in cross-country skiers. *International Journal of Sports Medicine, 3*, 234.

Berkowitz, G. S., Holford, T. R., & Berkowitz, R. L. (1982). Effects of cigarette smoking, alcohol, coffee, and tea consumption on preterm delivery. *Early Human Development, 7*, 239-250.

Berlin, C. M., Jr. (1981). Excretion of the methylxanthines in human milk. *Seminars in Perinatology, 5*, 389-394.

Berlin, C. M., Denson, A. M., Daniel, C. H., & Ward, R. M. (1984). Disposition of dietary caffeine in milk, saliva, and plasma of lactating women. *Pediatrics, 73*, 59-63.

Bernard, M. E., Dennehy, S., & Keefauver, L. W. (1981). Behavioral treatment of excessive coffee and tea drinking: A case study and partial replication. *Behavior Therapy, 12*, 543-548.

Bernarde, M. A., & Weiss, W. (1982). Coffee consumption and pancreatic cancer. *British Medical Journal, 284*, 400.

Berndt, B., Mensink, G. B., Kohlmeier, M., Kohlmeier, L., & Kottgen, E. (1993). Lipoprotein metabolism and coffee intake—who is at risk? *Zeitschrift für Ernahrungswissenschaft, 32*, 163-175.

Bernstein, E., & Diskant, B. M. (1982). Phenylpropanolamine: A potentially hazardous drug. *Annals of Emergency Medicine, 11*, 311-315.

Berthou, F., Ratanasavanh, D., Alix, D., Carlhant, D., Riche, C., & Guillouzo, A. (1988). Caffeine and theophylline metabolism in newborn and adult human hepatocytes: Comparison with adult rat hepatocytes. *Biochemical Pharmacology, 37*, 3691-3700.

Bertrand, C. A., Pomper, I., Hillman, G., Duffy, J. C., & Michell, I. (1978). No relation between coffee and blood pressure. *New England Journal of Medicine, 299*, 315-316.

Biaggioni, I., Olafsson, B., Robertson, R. M., Hollister, A. S., & Robertson, D. (1987). Cardiovascular and respiratory effects of adenosine in conscious man. *Circulation Research, 61*, 779-786.

Biaggioni, I., Onrot, J., Hollister, A. S., & Robertson, D. (1986). Cardiovascular effects of adenosine infusion in man and their modulation by dipyridamol. *Life Sciences, 39*, 2229-2236.

Biaggioni, I., Paul, S., Puckett, A., & Arzubiaga, C. (1991). Caffeine and theophylline as adenosine receptor antagonists in humans. *Journal of Pharmacology and Experimental Therapeutics, 258*, 588-593.

Birkett, D. J., & Miners, J. O. (1991). Caffeine renal clearance and urine caffeine concentrations during steady state dosing: Implications for monitoring caffeine intake during sports events. *British Journal of Clinical Pharmacology, 31*, 405-408.

Birkett, N. J., & Logan, A. G. (1988). Caffeine-containing beverages and the prevalence of hypertension. *Journal of Hypertension (Suppl. 6)*, S620-S622.

Bittner, A. C. J., Carter, R. C., Kennedy, R. S., Harbeson, M. M., & Krouse, M. (1986). Performance evaluation tests for environmental research (PETER): Evaluation of 114 measures. *Perceptual and Motor Skills, 63*, 683-708.

Blanchard, J., & Sawers, S. J. A. (1983a). Comparative pharmacokinetics of caffeine in young and elderly men. *Journal of Pharmacokinetics and Biopharmaceutics, 11*, 109.

Blanchard, J., & Sawers, S. J. A. (1983b). Relationship between urine flow-rate and renal clearance of caffeine in man. *Journal of Clinical Pharmacology, 23*, 134-138.

Blanchard, J., Weber, C. W., & Shearer, L. E. (1992). Methylxanthine levels in breast milk of lactating women of different ethnic and socioeconomic classes. *Biopharmaceutics and Drug Disposition, 13*, 187-196.

Blount, J. P., & Cox, W. M. (1985). Perception of caffeine and its effects: Laboratory and everyday abilities. *Perception and Psychophysics, 38,* 55-62.

Bønaa, K., Arnesen, E., Thelle, D. S., & Førde, O. H. (1988). Coffee and cholesterol: Is it all in the brewing? The Tromsø study. *British Medical Journal, 297,* 1103-1104.

Bonati, M., & Garattini, S. (1984). *Interspecies comparison of caffeine disposition.* Berlin: Springer-Verlag.

Bonati, M., Latini, R., Galletti, F., Young, J. F., Tognoni, G., & Garattini, S. (1982). Caffeine disposition after oral doses. *Clinical Pharmacology and Therapeutics, 32,* 98-106.

Bonnet, M. H., & Arand, D. L. (1992). Caffeine use as a model of acute and chronic insomnia. *Sleep, 15,* 526-536.

Bonnet, M. H., & Arand, D. L. (1994a). Impact of naps and caffeine on extended nocturnal performance. *Physiology and Behavior, 56,* 103-109.

Bonnet, M. H., & Arand, D. L. (1994b). The use of prophylactic naps and caffeine to maintain performance during a continuous operation. *Ergonomics, 37,* 1009-1020.

Bonnet, M. H., & Webb, W. B. (1979). The return to sleep. *Biological Psychology, 8,* 225-233.

Borcherding, S. M., Stevens, R., Nicholas, R. A., Corley, C. R., & Self, T. (1996). Quinolones: A practical review of clinical uses, dosing considerations, and drug interactions. *Journal of Family Practice, 42,* 69-78.

Borlée, I., Lechat, M. F., Bouckaert, A., & Misson, C. (1978). Le café, facteur de risque pendant la grossesse? [Coffee, risk factor during pregnancy?]. *Louvain Médical, 97,* 279-284.

Bory, C., Baltassat, P., Porthault, M., Bethenod, M., Frederich, A., & Aranda, J. V. (1979). Metabolism of theophylline to caffeine in premature newborn infants. *Journal of Pediatrics, 94,* 988-993.

Boston Collaborative Drug Surveillance Program. (1972). Coffee drinking and acute myocardial infarction. *Lancet, 2,* 1278-1283.

Boulenger, J.-P., Patel, J., & Marangos, P. J. (1982). Effects of caffeine and theophylline on adenosine and benzodiazepine receptors in human brain. *Neuroscience Letters, 30,* 161-166.

Boulenger, J.-P., Uhde, T. W., Wolff, E. A., III, & Post, R. M. (1984). Increased sensitivity to caffeine in patients with panic disorders. *Archives of General Psychiatry, 41,* 1067-1071.

Boutroy, M. J., Vert, P., Royer, R., Monin, P., & Royer-Morrot, M. J. (1979). Caffeine: A metabolite of theophylline during the treatment of apnea in the premature infant. *Journal of Pediatrics, 94,* 663-668.

Bowyer, P. A., Humphreys, M. S., & Revelle, W. (1983). Arousal and recognition memory: The effects of impulsivity, caffeine, and time on task. *Personality and Individual Differences, 4,* 41-49.

Boyle, C. A., Berkowitz, G. S., LiVolsi, V. A., Ort, S., Merino, M. J., White, C., & Kelsey, J. L. (1984). Caffeine consumption and fibrocystic breast diesase: A case-control epidemiologic study. *Journal of the National Cancer Institute, 72,* 1015-1019.

Bracco, D., Ferrarra, J. M., Arnaud, M. J., Jequier, E., & Schutz, Y. (1995). Effects of caffeine on energy metabolism, heart rate, and methylxanthine metabolism in lean and obese women. *American Journal of Physiology, 269,* E671-E678.

Brazer, S. R., Onken, J. E., Dalton, C. B., Smith, J. W., & Schiffman, S. S. (1995). Effect of different coffees on esophageal acid contact time and symptoms in coffee-sensitive subjects. *Physiology and Behavior, 57,* 563-567.

Brazier, J. L., Ritter, J., Berland, M., Khenfer, D., & Faucan, G. (1983). Pharmacokinetics of caffeine during and after pregnancy. *Developmental Pharmacology and Therapeutics, 6,* 313.

Brazier, J. L., & Salle, B. (1981). Conversion of theophylline to caffeine by the human fetus. *Seminars in Perinatology, 5*, 315-320.

Brazier, J. L., Salle, B., Desage, M., & Renaud, H. (1981). In vivo N-methylation of theophylline to caffeine in premature infants: Studies with use of stable isotopes. *Developmental Pharmacology and Therapeutics, 2*, 137-144.

Breier, A., Charney, D. S., & Heninger, G. R. (1986). Agoraphobia with panic attacks. Development, diagnostic stability, and course of illness. *Archives of General Psychiatry, 43*, 1029-1036.

Breum, L., Pedersen, J. K., Ahlstrom, F., & Frimodt-Moller, J. (1994). Comparison of an ephedrine/caffeine combination and dexfenfluramine in the treatment of obesity: A double-blind multi-centre trial in general practice. *International Journal of Obesity and Related Metabolic Disorders, 18*, 99-103.

Brezinová, V. (1975). Two types of insomnia: Too much waking or not enough sleep. *British Journal of Psychiatry, 126*, 439-445.

Bridge, N. (1893). Coffee-drinking as a frequent cause of disease. *Transactions of the Association of American Physicians, 8*, 281-288.

Britt, B. A., Frodis, W., Scott, E., Clements, M.-J., & Endrenyi, L. (1982). Comparison of the caffeine skinned fibre tension (CSFT) test with the caffeine-halothane contracture (CHC) test in the diagnosis of malignant hyperthermia. *Canadian Anaesthetists Society Journal, 29*, 550-562.

Brooks, P. G., Gart, S., Heldfond, A. J., Margolin, M. L., & Allen, A. S. (1981). Measuring the effect of caffeine restriction on fibrocystic breast disease: The role of graphic stress telethermometry as an objective monitor of disease. *Journal of Reproductive Medicine, 26*, 279-282.

Brouard, C., Moriette, G., Murat, I., Flouvat, B., Pajot, N., Walti, H., de Gamarra, E., & Relier, J.-P. (1985). Comparative efficacy of theophylline and caffeine in the treatment of idiopathic apnoea in premature infants. *American Journal of Diseases in Childhood, 139*, 698-700.

Broughton, L. J., & Rogers, H. J. (1981). Decreased systemic clearance of caffeine due to cimetidine. *British Journal of Clinical Pharmacology, 12*, 155-159.

Broughton, R., & Roberts, J. (1985). A survey of subjective sleep measures and performance in working adults. *Sleep Research, 14*, 89.

Brown, C. A., Bolton-Smith, C., Woodward, M., & Tunstall-Pedoe, H. (1993). Coffee and tea consumption and the prevalence of coronary heart disease in men and women: Results from the Scottish Heart Health Study. *Journal of Epidemiology and Community Health, 47*, 171-175.

Brown, L. M., Blot, W. J., Schuman, S. H., Smith, V. M., Ershow, A. G., Marks, R. D., & Fraumeni, J. F., Jr. (1988). Environmental factors and high risk of esophageal cancer among men in coastal South Carolina. *Journal of the National Cancer Institute, 80*, 1620-1625.

Bruce, M., Scott, N., Lader, M., & Marks, V. (1986). The psychopharmacological and electrophysiological effects of single doses of caffeine in healthy human subjects. *British Journal of Clinical Pharmacology, 22*, 81-87.

Bruce, M., Scott, N., Shine, P., & Lader, M. (1991). Caffeine withdrawal: A contrast of withdrawal symptoms in normal subjects who have abstained from caffeine for 24 hours and for 7 days. *Journal of Psychopharmacology, 5*, 129-134.

Bryant, J. (1981). Suicide by ingestion of caffeine—Letter to the editor. *Archives of Pathology and Laboratory Medicine, 105*, 685-686.

Bu-Abbas, A., Clifford, M. N., Walker, R., & Ioannides, C. (1994a). Marked antimutagenic potential of aqueous green tea extracts: Mechanism of action. *Mutagenesis, 9,* 325-331.

Bu-Abbas, A., Clifford, M. N., Walker, R., & Ioannides, C. (1994b). Selective induction of rat hepatic CYP1 and CYP4 proteins and of peroxisomal proliferation by green tea. *Carcinogenesis, 15,* 2575-2579.

Buemann, B., Marckmann, P., Christensen, N. J., & Astrup, A. (1994). The effect of ephedrine plus caffeine on plasma lipids and lipoproteins during a 4.2 MJ/day diet. *International Journal of Obesity and Related Metabolic Disorders, 18,* 329-332.

Bukowiecki, L. J., Lupien, J., Follea, N., & Jahjah, L. (1983). Effects of sucrose, caffeine and cola beverages on obesity, cold resistance, and adipose tissue cellularity. *American Journal of Physiology, 244,* R500-R507.

Bunker, M. L., & McWilliams, M. (1979). Caffeine content of common beverages. *Journal of the American Dietetic Association, 74,* 28-32.

Bunker, V. W. (1994). The role of nutrition in osteoporosis. *British Journal of Biomedical Science, 51,* 228-240.

Burg, A. W. (1975). Physiological disposition of caffeine. *Drug Metabolism Reviews, 4,* 199-228.

Burge, R. G. (1973). Caffeine stimulation of ejaculated human spermatozoa. *Urology, 1,* 371.

Burghardt, W., Geist, D., Grün, M., Staib, A. H., & Wernze, H. (1982). *Does caffeine influence the sympathoadrenal-system, renin-angiotensin-aldosterone-system and blood pressure?* London: Academic Press.

Burgio, K. L., Matthews, K. A., & Engel, B. T. (1991). Prevalence, incidence, and correlates of urinary incontinence in healthy, middle-aged women. *Journal of Urology, 146,* 1255-1259.

Burke, V., Beilin, L. J., German, R., Grosskopf, S., Ritchie, J., Puddey, I. B., & Rogers, P. (1992). Association of lifestyle and personality characteristics with blood pressure and hypertension: A cross-sectional study in the elderly. *Journal of Clinical Epidemiology, 45,* 1061-1070.

Bush, A., Busst, C. M., Clarke, B., & Barnes, P. J. (1989). Effect of infused adenosine on cardiac output and systemic resistance in normal subjects. *British Journal of Clinical Pharmacology, 27,* 165-171.

Byers, T., Marshall, J., Graham, S., Mettlin, C., & Swanson, M. (1983). A case-control study of dietary and nondietary factors in ovarian cancer. *Journal of the National Cancer Institute, 71,* 681-686.

Caan, B. J., & Goldhaber, M. K. (1989). Caffeinated beverages and low birthweight: A case-control study. *American Journal of Public Health, 79,* 1299-1300.

Caballero, T., García-Ara, C., Pascual, C., Diaz-Pena, J. M., & Ojeda, A. (1993). Urticaria induced by caffeine. *Journal of Investigational Allergology and Clinical Immunology, 3,* 160-162.

Calev, A. (1994). Neuropsychology and ECT: Past and future research trends. *Psychopharmacology Bulletin, 30,* 461-469.

Calhoun, W. H. (1971). *Central nervous system stimulants.* New York: Academic Press.

Callahan, M. M., Robertson, R. S., Arnaud, M. J., Branfman, A. R., McComish, M. F., & Yesair, D. W. (1982). Human metabolism of [1-methyl-14C] and [2-14C] caffeine after oral administration. *Drug Metabolism and Disposition, 10,* 417-423.

Callahan, M. M., Robertson. R. S., Branfman, A. R., McComish, M. F., & Yesair, D. W. (1983). Comparison of caffeine metabolism in three nonsmoking populations after oral administration of radiolabelled caffeine. *Drug Metabolism and Disposition, 11,* 211-217.

Callahan, M. M., Rohovsky, M. W., Robertson, R. S., & Yesair, D. W. (1979). The effect of coffee consumption on plasma lipids, lipoproteins, and the development of aortic atherosclerosis in rhesus monkeys fed an atherogenic diet. *American Journal of Clinical Nutrition, 32,* 834.

Cameron, O. G., Modell, J. G., & Hariharan, M. (1990). Caffeine and human cerebral blood flow: A positron emission tomography study. *Life Sciences, 47,* 1141-1146.

Cameron, P., & Boehmer, J. (1982). And coffee too. *International Journal of Addictions, 17,* 569-574.

Campbell, M. E., Spielberg, S. P., & Kalow, W. (1987). A urinary metabolite ratio that reflects systemic caffeine clearance. *Clinical Pharmacology and Therapeutics, 42,* 157-165.

Candreva, E. C., Keszenman, D. J., Barrios, E., Gelos, U., & Nunes, E. (1993). Mutagenicity induced by hyperthermia, hot maté infusion, and hot caffeine in *Saccharomyces cerevisiae. Cancer Research, 53,* 5750-5753.

Carbó, M., Segura, J., De la Torre, R., Badenas, J. M., & Camí, J. (1989). Effect of quinolones on caffeine disposition. *Clinical Pharmacology and Therapeutics, 45,* 234-240.

Carmody, T. P., Brischetto, C. S., Matarazzo, J. D., O'Donnell, R. P., & Connor, W. E. (1985). Co-occurrent use of cigarettes, alcohol, and coffee in healthy, community-living men and women. *Health Psychology, 4,* 323-335.

Carpenter, J. A. (1959). The effect of caffeine and alcohol on simple visual reaction time. *Journal of Comparative and Physiological Psychology, 52,* 491-496.

Carrier, O., Pons, G., Rey, E., Richard, M. O., Moran, C., Badoual, J., & Olive, G. (1988). Maturation of caffeine metabolic pathways in infancy. *Clinical Pharmacology and Therapeutics, 44,* 145-151.

Carrillo, J. A., & Benitez, J. (1994). Caffeine metabolism in a healthy Spanish population: N-acetylator phenotype and oxidation pathways. *Clinical Pharmacology and Therapeutics, 55,* 293-304.

Carroll, M. E., Hagen, E. W., Asencio, M., & Brauer, L. H. (1989). Behavioral dependence on caffeine and phencyclidine in rhesus monkeys: Interactive effects. *Pharmacology, Biochemistry, and Behavior, 31,* 927-932.

Carson, C. A., Caggiula, A. W., Meilahn, E. N., Matthews, K. A., & Kuller, L. H. (1994). Coffee consumption: Relationship to blood lipids in middle-aged women. *International Journal of Epidemiology, 23,* 523-527.

Carson, C. A., Cauley, J. A., & Caggiula, A. W. (1993). Relation of caffeine intake to blood lipids in elderly women. *American Journal of Epidemiology, 138,* 94-100.

Carter, A. J., O'Connor, W. T., Carter, M. J., & Ungerstedt, U. (1995). Caffeine enhances acetylcholine release in the hippocampus in vivo by a selective interaction with adenosine A1 receptors. *Journal of Pharmacology and Experimental Therapeutics, 273,* 637-642.

Casiglia, E., Bongiovì, S., Paleari, C. D., Petucco, S., Bono, M., Colangeli, G., Penzo, M., & Pessina, A. C. (1991). Haemodynamic effects of coffee and caffeine in normal volunteers: A placebo-controlled clinical study. *Journal of Internal Medicine, 229,* 501-504.

Casiglia, E., Paleari, C. D., Petucco, S., Bongiovi, S., Colangeli, G., Baccilieri, M. S., Pavan, L., Pernice, M., & Pessina, A. C. (1992). Haemodynamic effects of coffee and purified caffeine in normal volunteers: A placebo-controlled clinical study. *Journal of Human Hypertension, 6,* 95-99.

Castañeda-Hernández, G., Castillo-Mendez, M. S., Lopez-Munoz, F. J., Granados-Soto, V., & Flores-Murrieta, F. J. (1994). Potentiation by caffeine of the analgesic effect of aspirin in the pain-induced functional impairment model in the rat. *Canadian Journal of Physiology and Pharmacology, 72,* 1127-1131.

Cattell, R. B. (1930). The effects of alcohol and caffeine on intelligent and associate performance. *British Journal of Medical Psychology, 10,* 20-33.

Caughlin, L. J., & O'Halloran, R. L. (1993). An accidental death related to cocaine, co-caethylene, and caffeine. *Journal of Forensic Sciences, 38,* 1513-1515.

Cazeneuve, C., Pons, G., Rey, E., Treluyer, J. M., Cresteil, T., Thiroux, G., D'Athis, P., & Olive, G. (1994). Biotransformation of caffeine in human liver microsomes from foetuses, neonates, infants and adults. *British Journal of Clinical Pharmacology, 37,* 405-412.

Centonze, S., Boeing, H., Leoci, C., Guerra, V., & Misciagna, G. (1994). Dietary habits and colorectal cancer in a low-risk area: Results from a population-based case-control study in southern Italy. *Nutrition and Cancer, 21,* 233-246.

Chait, L. D., & Griffiths, R. R. (1983). Effects of caffeine on cigarette smoking and subjective response. *Clinical Pharmacology and Therapeutics, 34,* 612-622.

Chait, L. D., & Johanson, C. E. (1988). Discriminative stimulus effects of caffeine and benzphetamine in amphetamine-trained volunteers. *Psychopharmacology, 96,* 302-308.

Chalmers, T. C. (1981). Coffee and cancer of the pancreas. *New England Journal of Medicine, 304,* 1605.

Charney, D. S., Galloway, M. P., & Heninger, G. R. (1984). The effects of caffeine on plasma MHPG, subjective anxiety, autonomic symptoms, and blood pressure in healthy humans. *Life Sciences, 35,* 135-144.

Charney, D. S., Heninger, G. R., & Jalow, P. I. (1985). Increased anxiogenic effects of caffeine in panic disorders. *Archives of General Psychiatry, 42,* 233-243.

Chelsky, L. B., Cutler, J. E., Griffith, K., Kron, H., McClelland, J. H., & McAnulty, J. H. (1990). Caffeine and ventricular arrhythmias. An electrophysiological approach. *Journal of the American Medical Association, 264,* 2236-2240.

Cheney, R. H. (1935). Comparative effect of caffeine per se and a caffeine beverage (coffee) upon the reaction time in normal young adults. *Journal of Pharmacology, 53,* 304-313.

Cheney, R. H. (1936). Reaction time behavior after caffeine and coffee consumption. *Journal of Experimental Psychology, 19,* 357-369.

Cherek, D. R., Steinberg, J. L., & Brauchi, J. T. (1983). Effects of caffeine on human aggressive behavior. *Psychiatry Research, 8,* 137-145.

Cherek, D. R., Steinberg, J. L., & Brauchi, J. T. (1984). Regular or decaffeinated coffee and subsequent human aggressive behavior. *Psychiatry Research, 11,* 251-258.

Christensen, A. H., Gjorup, T., Andersen, I. B., & Matzen, P. (1994). Opinions in Denmark on the causes of peptic ulcer disease: A survey among Danish physicians and patients. *Scandinavian Journal of Gastroenterology, 29,* 305-308.

Christensen, H. D., Manion, C. V., & Kling, O. R. (1981). Caffeine kinetics during late pregnancy. In L. F. Soyka & G. P. Redmond (Eds.), *Drug metabolism of the immature infant* (pp. 163-181). New York: Raven Press.

Christensen, L., Miller, J., & Johnson, D. (1991). Efficacy of caffeine versus expectancy in altering caffeine-related symptoms. *Journal of General Psychology, 118,* 5-12.

Christianson, R. E., Oechsli, F. W., & van den Berg, B. J. (1989). Caffeinated beverages and decreased fertility. *Lancet, 1,* 378.

Chvasta, T. E., & Cooke, A. R. (1971). Absorption and emptying of caffeine from the human stomach. *Gastroenterology, 61,* 838-843.

Chyou, P. H., Nomura, A. M., & Stemmermann, G. N. (1993). A prospective study of diet, smoking, and lower urinary tract cancer. *Annals of Epidemiology, 3,* 211-216.

Clubley, M., Bye, C. E., Henson, T. A., Peck, A. W., & Riddington, C. S. (1979). Effects of caffeine and cyclizine alone and in combination on human performance, subjective effects, and EEG activity. *British Journal of Clinical Pharmacology, 7,* 157-163.

Clubley, M., Henson, T., Peck, A. W., & Riddington, C. (1977). Effects of caffeine and cyclizine alone and in combination on human performance an subjective ratings. *British Journal of Clinical Pharmacology, 4,* 652.

Coffey, C. E., Figiel, G. S., Weiner, R. D., & Saunders, W. B. (1990). Caffeine augmentation of ECT. *American Journal of Psychiatry, 147,* 579-585.

Coffey, C. E., Weiner, R. D., Hinkle, P. E., Cress, M., Daughtry, G., & Wilson, W. H. (1987). Augmentation of ECT seizures with caffeine. *Biological Psychiatry, 22,* 637-649.

Cohen, S., & Booth, G. H. (1975). Gastric acid secretion and lower-esophageal-sphincter pressure in response to coffee and caffeine. *New England Journal of Medicine, 293,* 897-899.

Colacone, A., Bertolo, L., Wolkove, N., Cohen, C., & Kreisman, H. (1990). Effect of caffeine on histamine bronchoprovocation in asthma. *Thorax, 45,* 630-632.

Cole, P. (1971). Coffee drinking and cancer of the lower urinary tract. *Lancet, 2,* 1335.

Collins, R., Peto, R., MacMahon, S., Herbert, P., Fiebach, N. H., Eberlein, K. A., Godwin, J., Qizilbash, N., Taylor, J. O., & Hennekens, C. H. (1990). Blood pressure, stroke, and coronary heart disease: Part 2, short-term reductions in blood pressure: overview of randomised drug trials in their epidemiological context. *Lancet, 335,* 827-838.

Collins, T. F. X. (1979). Review of reproduction and teratology studies of caffeine. *FDA By-Lines, 7,* 352-373.

Collins, T. F. X., Welsh, J. J., Black, T. N., & Ruggles, D. I. (1983). A study of the teratogenic potential of caffeine ingested in drinking water. *Food and Chemical Toxicology, 21,* 763-777.

Conners, C. K. (1975). A placebo-crossover study of caffeine treatment of hyperkinetic children. *International Journal of Mental Health, 4,* 132-143.

Conrad, K. A., Blanchard, J., & Trang, J. M. (1982). Cardiovascular effects of caffeine in elderly men. *Journal of the American Geriatrics Society, 30,* 267-272.

Consensus Conference. (1985). Lowering blood cholesterol to prevent heart disease. *Journal of the American Medical Association, 253,* 2080-2086.

Conway, T. L., Vickers, R. R., Jr., Ward, H. W., & Rahe, R. H. (1981). Occupational stress and variation in cigarette, coffee, and alcohol consumption. *Journal of Health and Social Behaviour, 22,* 155-165.

Cooper, C., Atkinson, E. J., Wahner, H. W., O'Fallon, W. M., Riggs, B. L., Judd, H. L., & Melton, L. J. (1992). Is caffeine consumption a risk factor for osteoporosis? *Journal of Bone and Mineral Research, 7,* 465-471.

Copeland, K. T., Checkoway, H., & McMichael, A. J. (1977). Bias due to misclassification in the estimation of relative risk. *American Journal of Epidemiology, 105,* 488-495.

Costill, D. L., Dalsky, G. P., & Fink, W. J. (1978). Effects of caffeine ingestion on metabolism and exercise performance. *Medicine and Science in Sports and Exercise, 10,* 155-158.

Couturier, E. G., Hering, R., & Steiner, T. J. (1992). Weekend attacks in migraine patients: Caused by caffeine withdrawal. *Cephalalgia, 12,* 99-100.

Coyle, I., Wagner, M. J., & Singer, G. (1976). Behavioral teratogenesis: A critical evaluation. *Pharmacology, Biochemistry, and Behavior, 4,* 191-200.

Craig, M. J., Humphrey, M. S., Rocklin, T., & Revelle, W. (1979). Impulsivity, neuroticism, and caffeine—Do they have an additive effect on arousal? *Journal of Research in Personality, 13,* 404-419.

Cribb, A. E., Isbrucker, R., Levatte, T., Tsui, B., Gillespie, C. T., & Renton, K. W. (1994). Acetylator phenotyping: The urinary caffeine metabolite ratio in slow acetylators correlates with a marker of systemic NAT1 activity. *Pharmacogenetics, 4,* 166-170.

Cuckle, H. S., & Kinlen, L. J. (1981). Coffee and cancer of the pancreas. *British Journal of Cancer, 44*, 760.

Cumming, R. G., & Klineberg, R. J. (1994a). Case-control study of risk factors for hip fractures in the elderly. *American Journal of Epidemiology, 139*, 493-503.

Cumming, R. G., & Klineberg, R. J. (1994b). A study of the reproducibility of long-term recall in the elderly. *Epidemiology, 5*, 116-119.

Cummings, S. R., Nevitt, M. C., Browner, W. S., Stone, K., Fox, K. M., Ensrud, K. E., Cauley, J., Black, D., & Vogt, T. M. (1995). Risk factors for hip fracture in white women: Study of Osteoporotic Fractures Research Group. *New England Journal of Medicine, 332*, 767-773.

Dales, L. G., Friedman, G. D., Ury, H. K., Grossman, S., & Williams, S. R. (1979). A case-control study of relationships of diet and other traits to colorectal cancer in American blacks. *American Journal of Epidemiology, 109*, 132-144.

Daly, J. W., Shi, D., Nikodijevic, O., & Jacobson, K. A. (1994). The role of adenosine receptors in the central action of caffeine. *Pharmacopsychoecologia, 7*, 201-213.

Daly, P. A., Krieger, D. R., Dulloo, A. G., Young, J. B., & Landsberg, L. (1993). Ephedrine, caffeine, and aspirin: Safety and efficacy for treatment of human obesity. *International Journal of Obesity, 17*(Suppl. 1), S73-S78.

D'Ambrosio, S. M. (1994). Evaluation of the genotoxity data on caffeine. *Regulatory Toxicology and Pharmacology, 19*, 243-281.

Daubresse, J. C., Luyckx, A., Demey-Ponsart, E., Franchimont, P., & Lefèbvre, P. (1973). Effects of coffee and caffeine on carbohydrate metabolism, free fatty acid, insulin, growth hormone, and cortisol plasma levels in man. *Acta Diabetologica Latina, 10*, 1069-1084.

D'Avanzo, B., La Vecchia, C., Franceschi, S., Negri, E., Talamini, R., & Buttino, I. (1992). Coffee consumption and bladder cancer risk. *European Journal of Cancer, 28A*, 1480-1484.

D'Avanzo, B., Santoro, L., Nobill, A., & La-Vecchia, C. (1993). Coffee consumption and serum cholesterol: GISSI-EFRIM Study Group. *Preventive Medicine, 22*, 219-224.

Davidson, R. A. (1991). Caffeine and novelty: Effects on electrodermal activity and performance. *Physiology and Behavior, 49*, 1169-1175.

Davis, D. L., Hoel, D., Fox, J., & Lopez, A. D. (1990). International trends in cancer mortality in France, West Germany, Italy, Japan, England and Wales, and the United States. *Annals of the New York Academy of Sciences, 609*, 5-48.

Davis, J. M., Spitzer, A. R., Stefano, J. L., Bhutani, V., & Fox, W. W. (1987). Use of caffeine in infants unresponsive to theophylline in apnea of prematurity. *Pediatric Pulmonology, 3*, 90-93.

Davis, T. R. K., Kensler, C. J., & Dews, P. B. (1973). Comparison of behavioral effects of nicotine, d-amphetimine, caffeine, and dimethylheptyl tetrahydrocannabinol in squirrel monkeys. *Psychopharmacologia, 32*, 51-65.

Dawber, T. R., Kannel, W. B., & Gordon, T. (1974). Coffee and cardiovascular disease: Observations from the Framingham study. *New England Journal of Medicine, 291*, 871-874.

Debas, H. T., Cohen, M. M., Holubisky, I. B., & Harrison, R. C. (1971). Caffeine-stimulated gastric acid and pepsin secretion: Dose-response studies. *Scandinavian Journal of Gastroenterology, 6*, 453-457.

Debrah, K., Haigh, R., Sherwin, R., Murphy, J., & Kerr, D. (1995). Effect of acute and chronic caffeine use on the cerebrovascular, cardiovascular, and hormonal responses to orthostasis in healthy volunteers. *Clinical Science, 89*, 475-480.

De Freitas, B., & Schwartz, G. (1979). Effects of caffeine in chronic psychiatric patients. *American Journal of Psychiatry, 136,* 1337-1338.

Dekker, D. K., Paley, M., Popkin, S. M., & Tepas, D. I. (1993). Locomotive engineers and their spouses: Coffee consumption, mood, and sleep reports. *Ergonomics, 36,* 233-238.

DeMet, E., Stein, M. K., Tran, C., Chicz-DeMet, A., Sandahl, C., & Nelson, J. (1989). Caffeine taste test for panic disorder: Adenosine receptor supersensitivity. *Psychiatry Research, 30,* 231-242.

Denaro, C. P., Brown, C. R., Jacob, P. I., & Benowitz, N. L. (1991). Effects of caffeine with repeated dosing. *European Journal of Clinical Pharmacology, 40,* 273-278.

Denborough, M. A., & Lovell, R. R. H. (1960). Anesthetic deaths in a family. *Lancet, 2,* 45.

Deng, J. F., Spyker, D. A., Rall, T. W., & Steward, O. (1983). Reduction in caffeine toxicity by acetaminophen. *Journal of Toxicology: Clinical Toxicology, 19,* 1031.

Derlet, R. W., Tseng, J. C., & Albertson, T. E. (1992). Potentiation of cocaine and d-amphetamine toxicity with caffeine. *American Journal of Emergency Medicine, 10,* 211-216.

Desmond, P. V., Patwardham, R. V., Johnson, R. F., & Schenker, S. (1980). Impaired elimination of caffeine in cirrhosis. *Digestive Diseases and Sciences, 25,* 193.

De Stefani, E., Muñoz, N., Esteve, J., Vasallo, A., & Victora, C. G. (1990). Maté drinking, alcohol, tobacco, diet, and esophageal cancer in Uruguay. *Cancer Research, 50,* 426-431.

Devoe, L. D., Murray, C., Youssif, A., & Arnaud, M. (1993). Maternal caffeine consumption and fetal behavior in normal third-trimester pregnancy. *American Journal of Obstetrics and Gynecology, 168,* 1105-1111.

Dews, P. B. (Ed.) (1994). *Behavioral effects of caffeine.* Berlin: Springer-Verlag.

De Zottir, R., Patussi, V., Fiorito, A. & Lareser, F. (1988). Sensitization to green coffee bean (GCB) and castor bean (CB) allergens among dock workers. *International Archives of Occupational and Environmental Health, 61,* 7-120.

Dimaio, V. J. M., & Garriott, J. C. (1974). Lethal caffeine poisoning in a child. *Forensic Science, 3,* 275-278.

Dimpfel, W., Schober, F., & Spuler, M. (1993). The influence of caffeine on human EEG under resting conditions and during mental loads. *Clinical Investigator, 71,* 197-207.

Dlugosz, L., & Bracken, M. B. (1992). Reproductive effects of caffeine: A review and theoretical analysis. *Epidemiology Reviews, 14,* 83-100.

Dobmeyer, D. J.; Stine, R. A., Leier, C. V., Greenber, A., & Schaal, S. F. (1983). The arrhythmogenic effects of caffeine in human beings. *New England Journal of Medicine, 308,* 814-816.

Dobrocky, P., Bennett, P. N., & Notarianni, L. J. (1994). Rapid method for the routine determination of caffeine and its metabolites by high-performance liquid chromatography. *Journal of Chromatography B: Biomedical Applications, 652,* 104-108.

Dodd, S. L., Brooks, E., Powers, S. K., & Tulley, R. (1991). The effects of caffeine on graded exercise performance in caffeine naive versus habituated subjects. *European Journal of Applied Physiology, 62,* 424-429.

Dodd, S. L., Herb, R. A., & Powers, S. K. (1993). Caffeine and exercise performance: An update. *Sports Medicine, 15,* 14-23.

Doll, R., & Peto, R. (1981). The causes of cancer: Quantitative estimates of avoidable risks of cancer in the United States today. *Journal of the National Cancer Institute, 66,* 1192-1203.

Donelly, K., & McNaughton, L. (1992). The effects of two levels of caffeine ingestion on excess postexercise oxygen consumption in untrained women. *European Journal of Applied Physiology, 65,* 459-463.

Dorfman, L. J., & Jarvik, M. E. (1970). Comparative stimulant and diuretic actions of caffeine and theobromine in man. *Clinical Pharmacology and Therapeutics, 11,* 869-872.

Dreisbach, R. H., & Pfeiffer, C. (1943). Caffeine withdrawal headache. *Journal of Laboratory and Clinical Medicine, 28,* 1212-1219.

Drewitt, P. N., Butterworth, K. R., Springall, C. D., & Moorhouse, S. R. (1993). Plasma levels of aluminium after tea ingestion in healthy volunteers. *Food and Chemical Toxicology, 31,* 19-23.

Driscoll, P. G., Joseph, F. J., & Nakamoto, T. (1990). Prenatal effects of maternal caffeine intake and dietary high protein on mandibular development in fetal rats. *British Journal of Nutrition, 63,* 285-292.

Druffel, A. (1988). The caffeine zone. *International UFO Reporter, 13,* 18-22.

Duffy, P., & Phillips, Y. Y. (1991). Caffeine consumption decreases the response to broncho-provocation challenge with dry gas hyperventilation. *Chest, 99,* 1374-1377.

Duggan, J. M., Dickeson, J. E., Tynan, P. F., Houghton, A., & Flynn, J. E. (1992). Aluminium beverage cans as a dietary source of aluminium. *Medical Journal of Australia, 156,* 604-605.

Dulloo, A. G., Geissler, C. A., Horton, T., Collins, A., & Miller, D. S. (1989). Normal caffeine consumption: Influence on thermogenesis and daily energy expenditure in lean and postobese human volunteers. *American Journal of Clinical Nutrition, 49,* 44-50.

Dulloo, A. G., Seydoux, J., & Girardier, L. (1992). Potentiation of the thermogenic antiobesity effects of ephedrine by dietary methylxanthines: Adenosine antagonism or phosphodi-esterase inhibition? *Metabolism, 41,* 1233-1241.

Dulloo, A. G., Seydoux, J., & Girardier, L. (1994). Paraxanthine (metabolite of caffeine) mimics caffeine's interaction with sympathetic control of thermogenesis. *American Journal of Physiology, 267,* E801-E804.

Dumas, M., Gouyon, J. B., Tenenbaum, D., Michiels, Y., Escousse, A., & Alison, M. (1982). Systematic determination of caffeine plasma concentrations at birth in preterm and full-term infants. *Developmental Pharmacology and Therapeutics, 4,* 182-186.

Dunlop, M., & Court, J. M. (1981). Effects of maternal caffeine ingestion on neonatal growth in rats. *Biology of the Neonate, 39,* 178-184.

Durrington, P. N., Ishola, M., Hunt, L., Arrol, S., & Bhatnagar, D. (1988). Apoliproteins (a), AI, and B and parental history in men with early onset ischaematic heart disease. *Lancet, 1,* 1070-1073.

Eaton, W. W., & McLeod, J. (1984). Consumption of coffee or tea and symptoms of anxiety. *Journal of Public Health, 74,* 66-68.

Eddy, N. B., & Downs, A. W. (1928). Tolerance and cross tolerance in the human subject to the diuretic effect of caffeine, theobromine, and theophylline. *Journal of Pharmacology and Experimental Therapeutics, 33,* 167-174.

Edelstein, B. A., Keaton-Brasted, C., & Burg, M. M. (1984). Effects of caffeine withdrawal on nocturnal enuresis, insomnia, and behavior restraints. *Journal of Consulting and Clinical Psychology, 52,* 857-862.

Eggertsen, R., Andreasson, A., Hedner, T., Karlberg, B. E., & Hansson, L. (1993). Effect of coffee on ambulatory blood pressure in patients with treated hypertension. *Journal of Internal Medicine, 233,* 351-355.

Eichner, E. R. (1993). Ergolytic drugs in medicine and sports. *American Journal of Medicine, 94,* 205-211.

Elkins, R. N., Rapoport, J. L., Zahn, T. P., Buchsbaum, M. S., Weingartner, H., Kopin, I. J., Langer, D., & Johnson, C. (1981). Acute effects of caffeine in normal prepubertal boys. *American Journal of Psychiatry, 138,* 178-183.

Elmazar, M. M. A., McElhatton, P. R., & Sullivan, F. M. (1981). Acute studies to investigate the mechanism of action of caffeine as a teratogen in mice. *Human Toxicology, 1,* 53-63.

Elmazar, M. M. A., McElhatton, P. R., & Sullivan, F. M. (1982). Studies on the teratogenic effects of different oral preparations of caffeine in mice. *Toxicology, 23,* 57-71.

Elseviers, M. M., & De Broe, M. E. (1994). Analgesic nephropathy in Belgium is related to the sales of particular analgesic mixtures. *Nephrology, Dialysis, Transplantation, 9,* 41-46.

El Shabrawy Ali, M., & Felimban, F. M. (1993). A study of the impact of Arabic coffee consumption on serum cholesterol. *Journal of the Royal Society of Health, 113,* 288-291.

El-Yazigi, A., Chaleby, K., & Martin, C. R. (1989). A simplified and rapid test for acetylator phenotyping by use of the peak height ratio of two urinary caffeine metabolites. *Clinical Chemistry, 35,* 848-851.

Emory, E. K., Konopka, S., Hronsky, S., Tuggey, R., & Davé, R. (1988). Salivary caffeine and neonatal behavior: Assay modification and functional significance. *Psychopharmacology, 94,* 64-68.

Engels, H. J., & Haymes, E. M. (1992). Effects of caffeine ingestion on metabolic responses to prolonged walking in sedentary males. *International Journal of Sport Nutrition, 2,* 386-396.

Erikson, G. C., Hager, L. B., Houseworth, C., Dungan, J., Petros, T., & Beckwith, B. E. (1985). The effects of caffeine on memory for word lists. *Physiology and Behavior, 35,* 47-51.

Ernster, V. L., Mason, L., Goodson, W. H., III, Sickles, S. T., Selvin, S., Dupuy, M. E., Hawkinson, J., & Hunt, T. K. (1982). Effects of caffeine-free diet on benign breast disease: A randomized trial. *Surgery, 91,* 263.

Escolar-Pujolar, A., González, C. A., López-Abente, G., Errezola, M., Izarzugaza, I., Nebot, M., & Riboli, E. (1993). Bladder cancer and coffee consumption in smokers and nonsmokers in Spain. *International Journal of Epidemiology, 22,* 38-44.

Eskenazi, B. (1993). Caffeine during pregnancy: Grounds for concern? [Editorial; comment]. *Journal of the American Medical Association, 270,* 2973-2974.

Essig, D., Costill, D. L., & van Handel, P. J. (1980). Effects of caffeine ingestion on utilization of muscle glycogen and lipid during leg ergometer cycling. *International Journal of Sports Medicine, 1,* 86-90.

Estler, C.-J. (1982). *Caffeine.* New York: Springer-Verlag.

Evans, S. M., Critchfield, T. S., & Griffiths, R. R. (1994). Caffeine reinforcement demonstrated in a majority of moderate caffeine users. *Behavioral Pharmacology, 5,* 231-238.

Evans, S. M., & Griffiths, R. R. (1991). Dose-related caffeine discrimination in normal volunteers: Individual differences in subjective effects and self-reported cues. *Behavioral Pharmacology, 2,* 345-356.

Evans, S. M., & Griffiths, R. R. (1992). Caffeine tolerance and choice in humans. *Psychopharmacology, 108,* 51-59.

Evans, W. E., Relling, M. V., Petros, W. P., Meyer, W. H., Mirro, J., Jr., & Crom, W. R. (1989). Dextromethorphan and caffeine as probes for simultaneous determination of debrisoquin-oxidation and N-acetylation phenotypes in children. *Clinical Pharmacology and Therapeutics, 45,* 568-573.

Ewertz, M. (1993). Breast cancer in Denmark. Incidence, risk factors, and characteristics of survival. *Acta Oncologia, 32,* 595-615.

Eysenck, H. J. (1967). *Biological basis of personality.* Springfield, IL: Charles C Thomas.

Fagan, D., Swift, C. G., & Tiplady, B. (1988). Effects of caffeine on vigilance and other performance tests in normal subjects. *Journal of Psychopharmacology, 2,* 19-25.

Fairweather-Tait, S. J., Piper, Z., Fatemi, S. J., & Moore, G. R. (1991). The effect of tea on iron and aluminium metabolism in the rat. *British Journal of Nutrition, 65,* 61-68.

Falk, B., Burstein, R., Rosenblum, J., Shapiro, Y., Zylber-Katz, E., & Bashan, N. (1990). Effects of caffeine ingestion on body fluid balance and thermoregulation during exercise. *Canadian Journal of Physiology and Pharmacology, 68,* 889-892.

Falk, J. L., & Lau, C. E. (1991). Synergism by caffeine and by cocaine of the motor control deficit produced by midazolam. *Pharmacology, Biochemistry, and Behavior, 39,* 525-529.

Falster, A. U., Hashimoto, K., Nakamoto, T., & Simmons, W. B. (1992). Physical examination of caffeine's effects on the enamel surface of first molar in newborn rats. *Archives of Oral Biology, 37,* 111-118.

Farago, A. (1968). Fatal accidental caffeine poisoning of a child. *Bulletin of the International Association of Forensic Toxicology, 5,* 203.

Fears, R. (1978). The hypercholesterolaemic effect of caffeine in rats fed on diets with and without supplementary cholesterol. *British Journal of Nutrition, 39,* 363-374.

Feinstein, A. R., & Horwitz, R. I. (1982). Double standards, scientific methods, and epidemiologic research. *New England Journal of Medicine, 307,* 1611-1617.

Feinstein, A. R., Horwitz, R. I., Spitzer, W. O., & Battista, R. N. (1981). Coffee and pancreatic cancer: The problems of etiologic science and epidemiologic case-control research. *Journal of the American Medical Association, 246,* 957.

Fennelly, M., Galletly, D. C., & Purdie, G. I. (1991). Is caffeine withdrawal the mechanism of postoperative headache? *Anesthesia and Analgesia, 72,* 449-453.

Fenster, L., Eskenazi, B., Windham, G. C., & Swan, S. H. (1991a). Caffeine consumption during pregnancy and fetal growth. *American Journal of Public Health, 81,* 458-461.

Fenster, L., Eskanazi, B., Windham, G. C., & Swan, S. H. (1991b). Caffeine consumption during pregnancy and spontaneous abortion. *Epidemiology, 2,* 168-174.

Ferré, S., Popoli, P., Giménez-Llort, L., Finnman, U. B., Martínez, E., Scotti-de-Carolis, A., & Fuxe, K. (1994). Postsynaptic antagonistic interaction between adenosine A1 and dopamine D1 receptors. *Neuroreport, 6,* 73-76.

Ferré, S., Schwarcz, R., Li, X. M., Snaprud, P., Ögren, S. O., & Fuxe, K. (1994). Chronic haloperidol treatment leads to an increase in the intramembrane interaction between adenosine A2 and dopamine D2 receptors in the neostriatum. *Psychopharmacology, 116,* 279-284.

Figarella-Branger, D., Kozak-Ribbens, G., Rodet, L., Aubert, M., Borsarelli, J., Cozzone, P. J., & Pellissier, J. F. (1993). Pathological findings in 165 patients explored for malignant hyperthermia susceptibility. *Neuromuscullar Disorders, 3,* 553-556.

File, S. E., Baldwin, H. A., Johnston, A. L., & Wilks, L. J. (1988). Behavioral effects of acute and chronic administration of caffeine in the rat. *Pharmacology, Biochemistry, and Behavior, 30,* 809-815.

File, S. E., Bond, A. J., & Lister, R. G. (1982). Interaction between effects of caffeine and lorazepam in performance tests and self-ratings. *Journal of Clinical Psychopharmacology, 2,* 102-106.

Fillmore, M., & Vogel-Sprott, M. (1992). Expected effect of caffeine on motor performance predicts the type of response to placebo. *Psychopharmacology, 106,* 209-214.

Fillmore, M. T., Mulvihill, L. E., & Vogel-Sprott, M. (1994). The expected drug and its expected effect interact to determine placebo responses to alcohol and caffeine. *Psychopharmacology, 115,* 383-388.

Findlay, J. W. A. (1983). The distribution of some commonly used drugs in human breast milk. *Drug Metabolism Reviews, 14,* 653-658.

Fine, B. J., Kobrick, J. L., Lieberman, H. R., Marlowe, B., Riley, R. H., & Tharion, W. J. (1994). Effects of caffeine or diphenhydramine on visual vigilance. *Psychopharmacology, 114,* 233-238.

Fink, M. (1994). Optimizing ECT. *Encephale, 20,* 297-302.

Finn, I. B., & Holtzman, S. G. (1987). Pharmacologic specificity of tolerance to caffeine-induced stimulation of locomotor activity. *Psychopharmacology, 93,* 428-434.

Flaten, T. P., & Ødegård, M. (1988). Tea, aluminium, and Alzheimer's disease [Letter to the editor]. *Food and Chemical Toxicology, 26,* 959-960.

Fletcher, J. E., Rosenberg, H., & Lizzo, F. H. (1989). Effects of droperidol, haloperidol, and ketamine on halothane, succinylcholine, and caffeine contractures: Implications for malignant hyperthermia. *Acta Anaesthesiologica Scandinavica, 33,* 187-192.

Flewellen, E. H., & Nelson, T. E. (1983). Is theophylline, aminophylline, or caffeine (methylxanthines) contraindicated in malignant hyperthermia susceptible patients. *Anesthesia and Analgesia, 62,* 115-118.

Fligner, C. L., & Opheim, K. E. (1988). Caffeine and its dimethylxanthine metabolites in two cases of caffeine overdose: A cause of falsely elevated theophylline concentrations in serum. *Journal of Analytical Toxicology, 12,* 339-343.

Flood, E. (1989). Caffeine citrate in the NICU. *Neonatal Network. Journal of Neonatal Nursing, 7,* 37-39, 27-30.

Florack, E. I., Zielhuis, G. A., & Rolland, R. (1994). Cigarette smoking, alcohol consumption, and caffeine intake and fecundability. *Preventive Medicine, 23,* 175-180.

Flory, C. D., & Gilbert, J. (1943). The effects of benzedrine sulphate and caffeine citrate on the efficiency of college students. *Journal of Applied Psychology, 27,* 121-134.

Folsom, A. R., McKenzie, D. R., Bisgard, K. M., Kushi, L. H., & Sellers, T. A. (1993). No association between caffeine intake and postmenopausal breast cancer incidence in the Iowa Women's Health Study. *American Journal of Epidemiology, 138,* 380-383.

Folstrar, P. (1985). Lipids. In R. J. Clarke & R. Macrae (Eds.), *Coffee: Vol. 1. Chemistry* (pp. 203-222). New York: Elsevier.

Forbes, J. A., Beaver, W. T., Jones, K. F., Kehm, C. J., Smith, W. K., Gongloff, C. M., Zeleznock, J. R., & Smith, J. W. (1991). Effect of caffeine on ibuprofen analgesia in postoperative oral surgery pain. *Clinical Pharmacology and Therapeutics, 49,* 674-684.

Forbes, J. A., Jones, K. F., Kehm, C. J., Smith, W. K., Gongloff, C. M., Zeleznock, J. R., Smith, J. W., Beaver, W. T., & Kroesen, M. (1990). Evaluation of aspirin, caffeine, and their combination in postoperative oral surgery pain. *Pharmacotherapy, 10,* 387-393.

Ford, C. D., Ford, D. C., & Koenigsberg, M. D. (1989). A simple treatment of post-lumbar-puncture headache. *Journal of Emergency Medicine, 7,* 29-31.

Førde, O. H., Knutsen, S. F., Arnesen, E., & Thelle, D. S. (1985). The Tromsø heart study: Coffee consumption and serum lipid concentrations in men with hypercholesterolaemia: A randomized intervention study. *British Medical Journal [Clinical Research], 290,* 893-895.

Foreman, N., Barraclough, S., Moore, C., Mehta, A., & Madon, M. (1989). High doses of caffeine impair performance of a numerical version of the Stroop task in men. *Pharmacology, Biochemistry, and Behavior, 32,* 399-403.

Forney, R. B., & Hughes, F. W. (1965). Effect of caffeine and alcohol on performance under stress of audiofeedback. *Quarterly Journal of Studies on Alcohol, 26,* 206-212.

Forrest, W. H., Bellville, J. W., & Brown, B. W. (1972). The interaction of caffeine and pentobarbital as a nighttime hypnotic. *Anesthesiology, 36,* 37-41.

Fortier, I., Marcoux, S., & Beaulac-Baillargeon, L. (1993). Relation of caffeine intake during pregnancy to intrauterine growth retardation and preterm birth. *American Journal of Epidemiology, 137,* 931-940.

Foxx, R. M. (1982). Behavioral treatment of caffeinism: A 40-month follow-up. *Behavior Therapist, 5,* 23-24.

Foxx, R. M., & Axelroth, E. (1983). Nicotine fading, self-monitoring, and cigarette fading to produce cigarette abstinence or controlled smoking. *Behaviour Research and Therapy, 21,* 17-27.

Foxx, R. M., & Brown, R. A. (1979). Nicotine fading and self-monitoring for cigarette abstinence or controlled smoking. *Journal of Applied Behavior Analysis, 2,* 111-125.

Foxx, R. M., & Rubinoff, A. (1979). Behavioral treatment of caffeinism: Reducing excessive coffee drinking. *Journal of Applied Behavior Analysis, 12,* 344-355.

France, C., & Ditto, B. (1988). Caffeine effects on several indices of cardiovascular activity at rest and during stress. *Journal of Behavioral Medicine, 11,* 473-482.

France, C., & Ditto, B. (1989). Cardiovascular responses to occupational stress and caffeine in telemarketing employees. *Psychosomatic Medicine, 51,* 145-151.

France, C., & Ditto, B. (1992). Cardiovascular responses to the combination of caffeine and mental arithmetic, cold pressor, and static exercise stressors. *Psychophysiology, 29,* 272-282.

Franchetti, P., Messini, L., Capellacci, L., Grifantini, M., Lucacchini, P., Martini, C. & Senatore, G. (1994). 8-Azaxanthine derivatives as antagonists of adenosine receptors. *Journal of Medicinal Chemistry, 37,* 2970-2975.

Franks, H. M., Hagedorn, H., Hensley, V. R., Hensley, W. J., & Starmer, G. A. (1975). The effect of caffeine on human performance, alone and in combination with ethanol. *Psychopharmacologia, 45,* 177-181.

Fraser, H. S., Dotson, O. Y., Howard, L., Grell, G. A. C., & Knight, F. (1983). Drug metabolizing capacity in Jamaican cigarette and marijuana smokers and nonsmokers. *West Indian Medical Journal, 32,* 207-211.

Fredholm, B. B. (1984). *Cardiovascular and renal actions of methylxanthines.* New York: Alan R. Liss.

Fredholm, B. B. (1985). On the mechanism of action of theophylline and caffeine. *Acta Medica Scandinavica, 217,* 149-153.

Fredholm, B. B. (1995). Adenosine, adenosine receptors, and the actions of caffeine [Astra Award Lecture]. *Pharmacology and Toxicology, 76,* 93-101.

Fredholm, B. B., & Sollevi, A. (1986). Cardiovascular effects of adenosine. *Clinical Physiology, 6,* 1-21.

Freestone, S., & Ramsay, L. E. (1982). Effect of coffee and cigarette smoking on the blood pressure of untreated and diuretic-treated hypertensive patients. *American Journal of Medicine, 73,* 348-353.

Freestone, S., & Ramsay, L. E. (1983). Effect of B-blockade on the pressor response to coffee plus smoking in patients with mild hypertension. *Drugs, 25*(Suppl. 2), 141-145.

Freestone, S., Yeo, W. W., & Ramsay, L. E. (1995). Effect of coffee and cigarette smoking on the blood pressure of patients with accelerated (malignant) hypertension. *Journal of Human Hypertension, 9,* 89-91.

Fried, P. A., & O'Connell, C. M. (1987). A comparison of the effects of prenatal exposure to tobacco, alcohol, cannabis, and caffeine on birth size and subsequent growth. *Neurotoxicology and Teratology, 9,* 79-85.

Fried, R. E., Levine, D. M., Kwiterovich, P. O., Diamond, E. L., Wilder, L. B., Moy, T. F., & Pearson, T. A. (1992). The effect of filtered-coffee consumption on plasma lipid levels: Results of a randomized clinical trial. *Journal of the American Medical Association, 267,* 811-815.

Friedman, G. D., & van den Eeden, S. K. (1993). Risk factors for pancreatic cancer: An exploratory study. *International Journal of Epidemiology, 22,* 30-37.

Fudin, R., & Nicastro, R. (1988). Can caffeine antagonize alcohol-induced performance decrements in humans? *Perceptual and Motor Skills, 67,* 375-391.

Fuhr, U., & Rost, K. L. (1994). Simple and reliable CYP1A2 phenotyping by the paraxanthine/caffeine ratio in plasma and in saliva. *Pharmacogenetics, 4,* 109-116.

Fujii, S., Inada, S., Yoshida, S., Kusanagi, C., Mima, K., & Natsumo, Y. (1972). Pharmacological studies on doping drugs for race horses: II. Caffeine. *Japanese Journal of Veterinary Science, 34,* 141.

Fujii, T., & Nishimura, H. (1972). Adverse effects of prolonged administration of caffeine on rat fetus. *Toxicology and Applied Pharmacology, 22,* 449-457.

Fujii, T., Sasaki, H., & Nishimura, H. (1969). Teratogenicity of caffeine in mice related to its mode of administration. *Japanese Journal of Pharmacology, 19,* 134-138.

Fuller, R. W., Maxwell, D. L., Conradson, T.-B., Dixon, C. M. S., & Barnes, P. J. (1987). Circulatory and respiratory effects of infused adenosine in conscious man. *British Journal of Clinical Pharmacology, 24,* 309-317.

Furlong, F. W. (1975). Possible psychiatric significance of excessive coffee consumption. *Canadian Psychiatric Association Journal, 20,* 577-583.

Furuhashi, N., Sato, S., Suzuki, M., Hiruta, M., Tanaka, M., & Takahashi, T. (1985). Effects of caffeine ingestion during pregnancy. *Gynecologic and Obstetric Investigation, 19,* 187-191.

Galletly, D. C., Fennelly, M., & Whitwam, J. G. (1989). Does caffeine withdrawal contribute to postanaesthetic morbidity? [Letter to the editor]. *Lancet, 1,* 1335.

Garbers, D. L., First, N. L., Sullivan, J. J., & Lardy, H. A. (1971). Stimulation and maintenance of ejaculated bovine spermatozoan respiration motility by caffeine. *Biology of Reproduction, 5,* 336-339.

Garrett, B. E., & Holtzman, S. G. (1994a). Caffeine cross-tolerance to selective dopamine D1 and D2 receptor agonists but not to their synergistic interaction. *European Journal of Pharmacology, 262,* 65-75.

Garrett, B. E., & Holtzman, S. G. (1994b). D1 and D2 dopamine receptor antagonists block caffeine-induced stimulation of locomotor activity in rats. *Pharmacology Biochemistry and Behavior, 47,* 89-94.

Garriott, J. C., Simmons, L. M., Poklis, A., & Mackell, M. A. (1985). Five cases of fatal overdose from caffeine-containing "look-alike" drugs. *Journal of Analytical Toxicology, 9,* 141-144.

Gartside, P. S., & Glueck, C. J. (1993). Relationship of dietary intake to hospital admission for coronary heart and vascular disease: The NHANES II National Probability Study. *Journal of the American College of Nutrition, 12,* 676-684.

Ghadirian, P. (1987). Thermal irritation and esophageal cancer in northern Iran. *Cancer, 60,* 1909-1914.

Ghoneim, M. M., Hinrichs, J. V., Chiang, C. K., & Loke, W. H. (1986). Pharmacokinetic and pharmacodynamic interactions between caffeine and diazepam. *Journal of Clinical Psychopharmacology, 6,* 75-80.

Gibbs, F. A., & Maltby, G. L. (1943). Effect on the electrical activity of the cortex of certain depressant and stimulant drugs—Barbiturates, morphine, caffeine, benzedrine, and adrenalin. *Journal of Pharmacology and Experimental Therapeutics, 78,* 1-10.

Gilbert, R. M. (1976). *Caffeine as a drug of abuse.* In R. J. Gibbins, Y. Israel, H. Kalant, R. E. Popham, W. Schnidt, & R. G. Smart (Eds.), *Research advances in alcohol and drug problems* (vol. 3, pp. 49-176). New York: John Wiley.

Gilbert, R. M. (1984). *Caffeine consumption.* New York: Alan R. Liss.

Gilbert, R. M., Marshman, J. A., Schwieder, M., & Berg, R. (1976). Caffeine content of beverages as consumed. *Canadian Medical Association Journal, 114,* 205-208.

Gilbert, R. M., & Pistey, W. R. (1973). Effect on the offspring of repeated caffeine administration to pregnant rats. *Journal of Reproduction and Fertility, 34,* 495-499.

Gilbert, S. G., & Rice, D. C. (1994). In utero caffeine exposure affects feeding pattern and variable ratio performance in infant monkeys. *Fundamental and Applied Toxicology, 22,* 41-50.

Gilliland, A. R., & Nelson, D. (1939). The effects of coffee on certain mental and physiological functions. *Journal of General Psychology, 21,* 339-348.

Gilliland, K. (1980). The interactive effect of intraversion-extraversion with caffeine induced arousal on verbal performance. *Journal of Research in Personality, 14,* 482-492.

Gilliland, K., & Andress, D. (1981). Ad lib caffeine consumption, symptoms of caffeinism, and academic performance. *American Journal of Psychiatry, 138,* 512-514.

Gilliland, K., & Bullock, W. (1984). *Caffeine: A potential drug of abuse.* New York: Haworth.

Girdler, S. S., Turner, J. R., Sherwood, A., & Light, K. C. (1990). Gender differences in blood pressure control during a variety of behavioral stressors. *Psychosomatic Medicine, 52,* 571-591.

Gold, E. B., & Diener, M. (1981). A case-control study of pancreatic cancer. *The American Journal of Epidemiology, 114,* 442-443.

Goldberg, S. R., Prada, J. A., & Katz, J. L. (1985). Stereoselective behavioral effects of N6-phenylisopropyl-adenosine and antagonism by caffeine. *Psychopharmacology, 87,* 272-277.

Goldbohm, R. A., Hertog, M. G., Brants, H. A., van-Poppel, G., & van-den-Brandt, P. A. (1996). Consumption of black tea and cancer risk: A prospective cohort study. *Journal of the National Cancer Institute, 88,* 93-100.

Golding, J. (1995). Caffeine, health, and commercial interests. *Addiction, 90,* 988-999.

Goldstein, A. (1964). Wakefulness caused by caffeine. *Archiv für Experimentelle Pathologie und Pharmakologie, 248,* 269-278.

Goldstein, A., Kaizer, S., & Whitby, O. (1969). Psychotropic effects of caffeine in man: IV. Quantitative and qualitative differences associated with habituation to coffee. *Clinical Pharmacology and Therapeutics, 10,* 489-497.

Goldstein, A., & Warren, R. (1962). Passage of caffeine into human gonadal and fetal tissue. *Biochemical Pharmacology, 11,* 166-168.

Goldstein, A., Warren, R., & Kaizer, S. (1965). Psychotropic effects of caffeine in man: I. Individual differences in sensitivity to caffeine-induced wakefulness. *Journal of Pharmacology and Experimental Therapeutics, 149,* 156-159.

Goldstein, H. R. (1982). No association found between coffee and cancer of the pancreas. *New England Journal of Medicine, 306,* 997.

Goldstein, I. B., & Shapiro, D. (1987). The effects of stress and caffeine on hypertensives. *Psychosomatic Medicine, 49,* 226-235.

Goldstein, I. B., Shapiro, D., Hui, K. K., & Yu, J. L. (1990). Blood pressure response to the "second cup of coffee." *Psychosomatic Medicine, 52,* 337-345.

Goldstein, L., Murphree, H. B., & Pfeiffer, C. C. (1963). Quantitative electroencephalography in man as a measure of CNS stimulation. *Annals of the New York Academy of Sciences, 107,* 1045-1056.

Gomez, J., & Rodriguez, A. (1989). An evaluation of the results of a drug sample analysis. *Bulletin on Narcotics, 1-2,* 121-126.

Gondola, J. C., & Tuckman, B. W. (1983). Diet, exercise, and physical discomfort in college students. *Perceptual and Motor Skills, 57,* 559-565.

Gorodischer, R., & Karplus, M. (1982). Pharmacokinetic aspects of caffeine in premature infants with apnoea. *European Journal of Clinical Pharmacology, 22,* 47-52.

Gould, L., Reddy, C. V. R., Oh, K. C., Kim, S. G., & Becker, W. (1979). Electrophysiologic properties of coffee in man. *Journal of Clinical Pharmacology, 11,* 46-55.

Gould, L., Venkataraman, K., Goswami, M., & Gomprecht, R. F. (1973). The cardiac effects of coffee. *Angiology, 24,* 455-463.

Graboys, T. B. (1989). The effect of caffeine on ventricular ectopic activity in patients with malignant ventricular arrhythmia. *Archives of Internal Medicine, 149,* 637-639.

Graboys, T. B., & Lown, B. (1983). Coffee, arrhythmias, and common sense. *New England Journal of Medicine, 308,* 835-836.

Graham, H. N. (1984a). *Maté.* New York: Alan R. Liss.

Graham, H. N. (1984b). *Tea: The plant and its manufacture: Chemistry and consumption of the beverage.* New York: Alan R. Liss.

Graham, H. N. (1992). Green tea composition, consumption, and polyphenol chemistry. *Preventive Medicine, 32,* 334-350.

Graham, T. E., Rush, W. E., & van Soeren, M. H. (1994). Caffeine and exercise: Metabolism and performance. *Canadian Journal of Applied Physiology, 19,* 111-138.

Graham, T. E., & Spriet, L. L. (1991). Performance and metabolic responses to a high caffeine dose during prolonged exercise. *Journal of Applied Physiology, 21,* 2292-2298.

Greden, J. F., Fontaine, P., Lubetsky, M., & Chamberlin, K. (1978). Anxiety and depression associated with caffeinism among psychiatric inpatients. *American Journal of Psychiatry, 135,* 963-966.

Greden, J. F., Victor, B. S., Fontaine, P., & Lubetsky, M. (1980). Caffeine withdrawal headache: A clinical profile. *Psychosomatics, 21,* 411-418.

Green, M. S., & Harari, G. (1992). Association of serum lipoproteins and health-related habits with coffee and tea consumption in free-living subjects examined in the Israeli CORDIS Study. *Preventive Medicine, 21,* 532-545.

Green, P. J., & Suls, J. (1996). The effects of caffeine on ambulatory blood pressure, heart rate, and mood in coffee drinkers. *Journal of Behavioral Medicine, 19,* 111-128.

Greenberg, W., & Shapiro, D. (1987). The effects of caffeine and stress on blood pressure in individuals with and without a family history of hypertension. *Psychophysiology, 24,* 151-156.

Greenland, S. (1980). The effect of misclassification in the presence of covariates. *American Journal of Epidemiology, 112,* 564-569.

Greenland, S. (1993). A meta-analysis of coffee, myocardial infarction, and coronary death. *Epidemiology, 4,* 366-374.

Greenland, S., & Robins, J. M. (1985). Confounding and misclassification. *American Journal of Epidemiology, 122,* 495-506.

Greenstadt, L., Yang, L., & Shapiro, D. (1988). Caffeine, mental stress, and risk for hypertension: A cross-cultural replication. *Psychosomatic Medicine, 50,* 15-22.

Greenwood, K. M., Rich, W. J., & James, J. E. (1996). Sleep hygiene practices and sleep duration in rotating-shift shiftworkers. *Work and Stress, 9,* 262-271.

Griffiths, R. R., Bigelow, G. E., & Liebson, I. A. (1986). Human coffee drinking: Reinforcing and physical dependence producing effects of caffeine. *Journal of Pharmacology and Experimental Therapeutics, 239,* 416-425.

Griffiths, R. R., Bigelow, G. E., & Liebson, I. A. (1989). Reinforcing effects of caffeine in coffee and capsules. *Journal of the Experimental Analysis of Behavior, 52,* 127-140.

Griffiths, R. R., Evans, S. M., Heishman, S. J., Preston, K. L., Sannerud, C. A., Wolf, B., & Woodson, P. P. (1990). Low-dose caffeine physical dependence in humans. *Journal of Pharmacology and Experimental Therapeutics, 255,* 1123-1132.

Griffiths, R. R., & Mumford, G. K. (1995a). Caffeine reinforcement, discrimination, tolerance, and physical dependence in laboratory animals and humans. In C. R. Schuster, S. W. Gust, & M. J. Kuhar (Eds.), *Pharmacological aspects of drug dependence—Toward an integrated neurobehavioral approach—Handbook of experimental pharmacology*. New York: Springer-Verlag.

Griffiths, R. R., & Mumford, G. K. (1995b). Caffeine—a drug of abuse? In F. E. Bloom & D. J. Kupfer (Eds.), *Psychopharmacology: The fourth generation of progress* .New York: Raven Press.

Griffiths, R. R., & Woodson, P. P. (1988a). Reinforcing effects of caffeine in humans. *Journal of Pharmacology and Experimental Therapeutics, 246,* 21-29.

Griffiths, R. R., & Woodson, P. P. (1988b). Reinforcing properties of caffeine: Studies in humans and laboratory animals. *Pharmacology, Biochemistry, and Behavior, 29,* 419-427.

Grobbee, D. E., Rimm, E. B., Giovannucci, E., Colditz, G., Stampfer, M., & Willett, W. (1990). Coffee, caffeine, and cardiovascular disease in men. *New England Journal of Medicine, 323,* 1026-1032.

Grodstein, F., Goldman, M. B., Ryan, L., & Cramer, D. W. (1993). Relation of female infertility to consumption of caffeinated beverages. *American Journal of Epidemiology, 137,* 1353-1360.

Gross, M. D. (1975). Caffeine in the treatment of children with minimal brain dysfunction or hyperkinetic syndrome. *Psychosomatics, 16,* 26-27.

Grounds, A. (1982). Transient psychoses in anorexia nervosa: A report of seven cases. *Psychological Medicine, 12,* 107.

Grundy, S. M. (1982). Rationale of the Diet-Heart Statement of the American Heart Association: Report of Nutrition Committee. *Circulation, 65,* 839A-854A.

Gunn, T. R., Metrakos, K., Riley, P., Willis, D., & Aranda, J. V. (1979). Sequelae of caffeine treatment in preterm infants with apnea. *Journal of Pediatrics, 94,* 106.

Gupta, U. (1991). Differential effects of caffeine on free recall after semantic and rhyming tasks in high and low impulsives. *Psychopharmacology, 105,* 137-140.

Gupta, U. (1993). Effects of caffeine on recognition. *Pharmacology Biochemistry and Behavior, 44,* 393-396.

Gupta, U., Dubey, G. P., & Gupta, B. S. (1994). Effects of caffeine on perceptual judgment. *Neuropsychobiology, 30,* 185-188.

Gyntelberg, F., Hein, H. O., Suadicani, P., & Sorensen, H. (1995). Coffee consumption and risk of ischaemic heart disease—a settled issue? *Journal of Internal Medicine, 237,* 55-61.

Hadeed, A., & Siegel, S. (1993). Newborn cardiac arrhythmias associated with maternal caffeine use during pregnancy. *Clinical Pediatrics, 32,* 45-47.

Haenszel, W., Berg, J. W., Segi, M., Kurihara, M., & Locke, F. B. (1973). Large-bowel cancer in Hawaiian Japanese. *Journal of the National Cancer Institute, 51,* 1765-1779.

Haigh, R. A., Harper, G. D., Fotherby, M., Hurd, J., Macdonald, I. A., & Potter, J. F. (1993). Duration of caffeine abstention influences the acute blood pressure responses to caffeine in elderly normotensives. *European Journal of Clinical Pharmacology, 44,* 549-553.

Hale, K. L., Hughes, J. R., Oliveto, A. H., & Higgins, S. T. (1995). Caffeine self-administration and subjective effects in adolescents. *Experimental and Clinical Psychopharmacology, 3,* 364-370.

Haley, T. J. (1983). Metabolism and pharmacokinetics of theophylline in human neonates, children, and adults. *Drug Metabolism Reviews, 14,* 295.

Hamelin, B. A., Xu, K., Valle, F., Manseau, L., Richer, M., & LeBel, M. (1994). Caffeine metabolism in cystic fibrosis: Enhanced xanthine oxidase activity. *Clinical Pharmacology and Therapeutics, 56,* 521-529.

Hampl, K. F., Schneider, M. C., Ruttimann, U., Ummenhofer, W., & Drewe, J. (1995). Perioperative administration of caffeine tablets for prevention of postoperative headaches. *Canadian Journal of Anaesthesia, 42,* 789-792.

Hansen, S., Ferreira, A., & Selart, M. E. (1985). Behavioral similarities between mother rats and benzodiazepine-treated nonmaternal animals. *Psychopharmacology, 86,* 344-347.

Harris, S. S., & Dawson-Hughes, B. (1994). Caffeine and bone loss in healthy postmenopausal women. *American Journal of Clinical Nutrition, 60,* 573-578.

Harrison, H., Jr. (1992). Apnea of prematurity: Theophylline v. caffeine. *Alaska Medicine, 34,* 173-176.

Harrison, R. F. (1978). Insemination of husband's semen with and without the addition of caffeine. *Fertility and Sterility, 29,* 532-534.

Harrison, R. F., Sheppard, B. L., & Kallizer, M. (1980a). Observation on the motility, ultrastructure, and elemental composition of human spermatozoa incubated with caffeine. *Andrology, 12,* 34-42.

Harrison, R. F., Sheppard, B. L., & Kallizer, M. (1980b). Observation on the motility, ultrastructure, and elemental composition of human spermatozoa incubated with caffeine: II. A time sequence study. *Andrology, 12,* 434-437.

Hart, P., Farrell, G. C., Cooksley, W. G. E., & Powell, L. W. (1976). Enhanced drug metabolism in cigarette smokers. *British Medical Journal, 2,* 147-149.

Hartge, P., Lesher, L. P., McGowan, L., & Hoover, R. (1982). Coffee and ovarian cancer. *International Journal of Cancer, 30,* 531.

Harvey, D. H., & Marsh, R. W. (1978). The effects of decaffeinated coffee versus whole coffee on hyperactive children. *Developmental Medicine and Child Neurology, 20,* 81-86.

Hasenfratz, M., & Bättig, K. (1992). Action profiles of smoking and caffeine: Stroop effect, EEG, and peripheral physiology. *Pharmacology, Biochemistry, and Behavior, 42,* 155-161.

Hasenfratz, M., & Bättig, K. (1994). Acute dose-effect relationships of caffeine and mental performance, EEG, cardiovascular, and subjective parameters. *Psychopharmacology, 114,* 281-287.

Hasenfratz, M., Bunge, A., Dal-Pra, G., & Bättig, K. (1993). Antagonistic effects of caffeine and alcohol on mental performance parameters. *Pharmacology Biochemistry and Behavior, 46,* 463-465.

Hasenfratz, M., Jacober, A., & Bättig, K. (1993). Smoking-related subjective and physiological changes: Pre- to postpuff and pre- to postcigarette. *Pharmacology Biochemistry and Behavior, 46,* 527-534.

Hashiguchi, M., Fujimura, A., Ohashi, K., & Ebihara, A. (1992). Diurnal effect on caffeine clearance. *Journal of Clinical Pharmacology, 32,* 184-187.

Hashimoto, K., Joseph, F., Jr., Falster, A. U., Simmons, W. B., & Nakamoto, T. (1992). Effects of maternal caffeine intake during lactation on molar enamel surfaces in newborn rats. *Archives of Oral Biology, 37,* 105-109.

Hatch, E. E., & Bracken, M. B. (1993). Association of delayed conception with caffeine consumption. *American Journal of Epidemiology, 138,* 1082-1092.

Hawk, P. G. (1929). A study of the physiological and psychological reactions of the human organism to coffee drinking. *American Journal of Physiology, 90,* 380-381.

Heaney, R. P., & Recker, R. R. (1982). Effects of nitrogen, phosphorus, and caffeine on calcium balance in women. *Journal of Laboratory and Clinical Medicine, 99,* 46-55.

Heaney, R. P., & Recker, R. R. (1994). Determinants of endogenous fecal calcium in healthy women. *Journal of Bone and Mineral Research, 9,* 1621-1627.

Heckers, H., Gobel, U., & Kleppel, U. (1994). End of the coffee mystery: Diterpene alcohols raise serum low-density lipoprotein cholesterol and triglyceride levels [Letter to the editor]. *Journal of Internal Medicine, 235,* 192-193.

Heilbrun, L. K., Nomura, A., & Stemmermann, G. N. (1986). Black tea consumption and cancer risk: A prospective study. *British Journal of Cancer, 54,* 677-683.

Heiman-Patterson, T. D., Rosenberg, J., Fletcher, J. E., & Tahmoush, A. J. (1988). Halothane-caffeine contracture testing in neuromuscular disease. *Muscle Nerve, 11,* 453-457.

Heishman, S. J., & Henningfield, J. E. (1992). Stimulus functions of caffeine in humans: Relation to dependence potential. *Neuroscience and Biobehavioral Reviews, 16,* 273-287.

Heishman, S. J., & Henningfield, J. E. (1994). Is caffeine a drug of dependence? Criteria and comparisons. *Pharmacopsychoecologia, 7,* 127-135.

Heishman, S. J., Snyder, F. R., & Henningfield, J. E. (1993). Performance, subjective, and physiological effects of nicotine in nonsmokers. *Drug and Alcohol Dependence, 34,* 11-18.

Hemminki, E., Rahkonen, O., & Rimpelä, M. (1988). Selection to coffee drinking by health—who becomes an adolescent coffee drinker? *American Journal of Epidemiology, 127,* 1088-1090.

Henderson, G. I., & Schenker, S. (1984). Effects of ethanol and/or caffeine on fetal development and placental amino acid uptake in rats. *Developmental Pharmacology and Therapeutics, 7,* 177-187.

Henderson, J. C., O'Connell, F., & Fuller, R. W. (1993). Decrease of histamine-induced bronchoconstriction by caffeine in mild asthma. *Thorax, 48,* 824-826.

Hennekens, C. H., Drolette, M. E., Jesse, M. J., Davies, J. E., & Hutchison, G. B. (1976). Coffee drinking and death due to coronary heart disease. *New England Journal of Medicine, 294,* 633-636.

Henry, J. P., & Stephens, P. M. (1980). Caffeine as an intensifier of stress-induced hormonal and pathophysiologic changes in mice. *Pharmacology, Biochemistry, and Behavior, 13,* 719-727.

Hernandez-Avila, M., Colditz, G. A., Stampfer, M. J., Rosner, B., Speizer, F. E., & Willet, W. C. (1991). Caffeine, moderate alcohol intake, and risk of fractures of the hip and forearm in middle-aged women. *American Journal of Clinical Nutrition, 54,* 157-163.

Hernandez-Avila, M., Stampfer, M. J., Ravnikar, V. A., Willet, W. C., Schiff, I., Francis, M., Longscope, C., & McKinley, S. M. (1993). Caffeine and other predictors of bone density among pre- and perimenopausal women. *Epidemiology, 4,* 128-134.

Hertog, M. G., Feskens, E. J., Hollman, P. C., Katan, M. B., & Kromhout, D. (1993). Dietary antioxidant flavonoids and risk of coronary heart disease: The Zutphen Elderly Study. *Lancet, 342,* 1007-1011.

Heseltine, D., Dakkak, M., Woodhouse, K., Macdonald, I. A., & Potter, J. F. (1991). The effect of caffeine on postprandial hypotension in the elderly. *Journal of the American Geriatrics Society, 39,* 160-164.

Hetzler, R. K., Warhaftig-Glynn, N., Thompson, D. L., Dowling, E., & Weltman, A. (1994). Effects of acute caffeine withdrawal on habituated male runners. *Journal of Applied Physiology, 76,* 1043-1048.

Heuch, I., Kvåle, G., Jacobsen, B. K., & Bjelke, E. (1983). Use of alcohol, tobacco, and coffee and risk of pancreatic cancer. *British Journal of Cancer, 48,* 637-643.

Heuman, J. (1994a). Inside trade associations. *Tea and Coffee Trade Journal, 166*(3), 5-7.

Heuman, J. (1994b). A look back on 1993. *Tea and Coffee Trade Journal, 166*(1), 5-7.

Heyden, S., & Muhlbaier, L. H. (1984). Prospective study of fibrocystic breast disease and caffeine consumption. *Surgery, 96,* 479-484.

184   UNDERSTANDING CAFFEINE

Hicks, R. A., Hicks, G. J., Reyes, J. R., & Cheers, Y. (1983). Daily caffeine use and the sleep of college students. *Bulletin of the Psychonomic Society, 21,* 24-25.

Hicks, R. A., Kilcourse, J., & Sinnott, M. A. (1983). Type A-B behavior and caffeine use in college students. *Psychological Reports, 52,* 338.

Higgins, I., Stolley, P., & Wynder, E. L. (1981). Coffee and cancer of the pancreas. *New England Journal of Medicine, 304,* 1605.

Higginson, J. (1966). Etiological factors in gastrointestinal cancer in man. *Journal of the National Cancer Institute, 37,* 527-545.

Hildebrandt, R., Gundertr, U., & Weber, E. (1983). Transfer of caffeine to breast milk. *British Journal of Clinical Pharmacology, 15,* 612.

Hill, C. (1985). Coffee consumption and cholesterol concentrations. *British Medical Journal, 290,* 1590.

Hinkle, P. E., Coffey, C. E., Weiner, R. D., Cress, M., & Christison, C. (1987). Use of caffeine to lengthen seizures in ECT. *American Journal of Psychiatry, 144,* 1143-1148.

Hire, J. N. (1978). Anxiety and caffeine. *Psychological Reports, 42,* 833-834.

Hirsh, K. (1984). *Central nervous system pharmacology of the dietary methylxanthines.* New York: Alan R. Liss.

Hofman, A., van Laar, A., Klein, F., & Valkenburg, H. A. (1983). Coffee and cholesterol [Letter to the editor]. *New England Journal of Medicine, 309,* 1248-1249.

Hogue, C. J. (1981). Coffee in pregnancy [Letter to the editor]. *Lancet, 1,* 554.

Holck, H. G. O. (1933). Effect of caffeine upon chess problem solving. *Journal of Comparative Psychology, 15,* 301-311.

Holley, J. L., Nespor, S., & Rault, R. (1992). A comparison of reported sleep disorders in patients on chronic hemodialysis and continuous peritoneal dialysis. *American Journal of Kidney Diseases, 19,* 156-161.

Hollingworth, H. L. (1912a). The influence of caffeine on mental and motor efficiency. *Archives of Psychology, 22,* 1-166.

Hollingworth, H. L. (1912b). The influence of caffeine on the speed and quality of performance in typewriting. *Psychological Review, 19,* 66-73.

Holloway, F. A., Modrow, H. E., & Michaelis, R. C. (1985). Methylzanthine discrimination in the rat: Possible benzodiazepine and adenosine mechanisms. *Pharmacology, Biochemistry, and Behavior, 22,* 815-824.

Holloway, W. R., & Thor, D. H. (1983). Caffeine and social investigation in the adult male rat. *Neurobehavioral Toxicology and Teratology, 5,* 119-125.

Holloway, W. R., & Thor, D. H. (1984). Acute and chronic caffeine exposure effects on play fighting in the juvenile rat. *Neurobehavioral Toxicology and Teratology, 6,* 85-91.

Holstege, A., Staiger, M., Haag, K., & Gerok, W. (1989). Correlation of caffeine elimination and Child's classification in liver cirrhosis. *Klinische Wochenschrift, 67,* 6-15.

Holtzman, S. G. (1983). Complete reversible, drug-specific tolerance to stimulation of locomotor activity by caffeine. *Life Sciences, 33,* 779.

Holtzman, S. G., & Finn, I. B. (1988). Tolerance to behavioral effects of caffeine in rats. *Pharmacology, Biochemistry, & Behavior, 29,* 411-418.

Holtzman, S. G., Mante, S., & Minnemen, K. P. (1991). Role of adenosine receptors in caffeine tolerance. *Journal of Pharmacology and Experimental Therapeutics, 256,* 62-68.

Horning, M. G., Butler, C. M., Nowlin, J., & Hill, R. B. (1975). Drug metabolism in the human neonate. *Life Sciences, 16,* 651-671.

Horning, M. G., Stratton, C., Nowlin, J., Wilson, A., Horning, E. C., & Hill, R. M. (1973). *Placental transfer of drugs.* New York: Raven Press.

Horowitz, J. D., Howes, L. G., & Christophidis, N. (1980). Hypertensive responses induced by phenylpropanolamine in anorectic and decongestant preparations. *Lancet, 1*, 60-61.

Horst, K., Buxton, R. E., & Robinson, W. D. (1934). The effect of the habitual use of coffee or decaffeinated coffee upon blood pressure and certain motor reactions of normal young men. *Journal of Pharmacology and Experimental Therapeutics, 52*, 322-337.

Horst, K., & Jenkins, W. L. (1935). The effect of caffeine, coffee, and decaffeinated coffee upon blood pressure, pulse rate, and sample reaction time of men of various ages. *Journal of Pharmacology and Experimental Therapeutics, 53*, 385-398.

Horst, K., Robinson, W. D., Jenkins, W. L., & Bao, D. L. (1934). The effect of caffeine, coffee, and decaffeinated coffee upon blood pressure, pulse rate, and certain motor reactions of normal young men. *Journal of Pharmacology and Experimental Therapeutics, 52*, 307-321.

Horst, K., Wilson, R. J., & Smith, R. G. (1936). The effect of coffee and decaffeinated coffee on oxygen consumption, pulse rate, and blood pressure. *Journal of Pharmacology and Experimental Therapeutics, 58*, 294-304.

Houston, M. C. (1989). New insights and new approaches for the treatment of essential hypertension: Selection of therapy based on coronary heart disease risk factor analysis, hemodynamic profiles, quality of life, and subsets of hypertension. *American Heart Journal, 117*, 911-951.

Houston, T. P. (1991). Official misuse of tobacco industry propoganda: Report of a Trojan horse. *Journal of the American Medical Association, 266*, 2702.

Howell, J., Clozel, M., & Aranda, J. V. (1981). Adverse effects of caffeine and theophylline in the newborn infant. *Seminars in Perinatology, 5*, 359-369.

Hsieh, C.-C., MacMahon, B., Yen, S., Trichopoulos, D., Warren, K., & Nardi, G. (1986). Coffee and pancreatic cancer. *New England Journal of Medicine, 315*, 587-589.

Hsu, L. K. G., Meltzer, E. S., & Crisp, A. H. (1981). Schizophrenia and anorexia nervosa. *Journal of Nervous and Mental Disease, 169*, 273.

Huestos, R. D., Arnold, L. E., & Smeltzer, D. J. (1975). Caffeine versus methyphenidate and d-amphetamine in minimal brain dysfunction: A double-blind comparison. *American Journal of Psychiatry, 132*, 868-870.

Hughes, J. R. (1991). Distinguishing withdrawal relief and direct effects of smoking. *Psychopharmacology, 104*, 409-410.

Hughes, J. R., Higgins, S. T., Bickel, W. K., Hunt, W. K., Fenwick, J. W., Gulliver, S. B., & Mireault, G. C. (1991). Caffeine self-administration, withdrawal, and adverse effects among coffee drinkers. *Archives of General Psychiatry, 48*, 611-617.

Hughes, J. R., Hunt, W. K., Higgins, S. T., Bickel, W. K., Fenwich, J. W., & Pepper, S. L. (1992). Effect of dose on the ability of caffeine to serve as a reinforcer in humans. *Behavioral Pharmacology, 3*, 211-218.

Hughes, J. R., & Oliveto, A. H. (1993). Coffee and alcohol intake as predictors of smoking cessation and tobacco withdrawal. *Journal of Substance Abuse, 5*, 305-310.

Hughes, J. R., Oliveto, A. H., Bickel, W. K., Higgins, S. T., & Badger, G. J. (1993). Caffeine self-administration and withdrawal: Incidence, individual differences, and interrelationships. *Drug and Alcohol Dependence, 32*, 239-246.

Hughes, J. R., Oliveto, A. H., Bickel, W. K., Higgins, S. T., & Badger, G. J. (1995). The ability of low doses of caffeine to serve as reinforcers in humans: A replication. *Experimental and Clinical Psychopharmacology, 3*, 358-363.

Hughes, J. R., Oliveto, A. H., Helzer, J. E., Higgins, S. T., & Bickel, W. K. (1992). Should caffeine abuse, dependence, or withdrawal be added to DSM-IV and ICD-10? *American Journal of Psychiatry, 149*, 33-40.

Hughes, R. N., & Beveridge, I. J. (1991). Behavioral effects of exposure to caffeine during gestation, lactation, or both. *Neurotoxicology and Teratology, 13,* 641-647.

Hull, C. L. (1935). The influence of caffeine and other factors on certain phenomena of rote learning. *Journal of General Psychology, 13,* 249-274.

Humphreys, M. S., & Revelle, W. (1984). Personality, motivation, and performance: A theory of the relationship between individual differences and information processing. *Psychological Review, 91,* 153-184.

IARC. (1991). *Coffee, tea, maté, methylxanthines, and methylglyoxal* (IARC Monograph Evaluating Carcinogenic Risks to Humans). London: WHO.

Imai, K., & Nakachi, K. (1995). Cross-sectional study of effects of drinking green tea on cardiovascular and liver diseases. *British Medical Journal, 310,* 693-696.

Imoedehme, D. A., Sigue, A. B., Pacpaco, E. L., Pacpaco, E. L., & Olazo, A. B. (1992). The effect of caffeine on the ability of spermatozoa to fertilize mature human oocytes. *Journal of Assisted Reproduction and Genetics, 9,* 155-160.

Infante-Rivard, C., Fernandez, A., Gauthier, R., David, M., & Rivard, G. E. (1993). Fetal loss associated with caffeine intake before and during pregnancy. *Journal of the American Medical Association, 270,* 2940-2943.

Institute of Food Technologists' Expert Panel on Food Safety & Nutrition. (1983). Caffeine: A scientific status summary. *Food Technology, 37,* 87-91.

Iqbal, N., Ahmad, B., Janbaz, K. H., Gilani, A. U., & Niazi, S. K. (1995). The effect of caffeine on the pharmacokinetics of acetaminophen in man. *Biopharmaceutics and Drug Disposition, 16,* 481-487.

Isaacs, H., & Badenhorst, M. (1993). False-negative results with muscle caffeine halothane contracture testing for malignant hyperthermia. *Anesthesiology, 79,* 5-9.

Izzo, J. L., Ghosal, A., Kwong, T., Freedman, R. B., & Jaenike, R. (1983). Age and prior caffeine use alter the cardiovascular and adrenomedullary responses to oral caffeine. *American Journal of Cardiology, 52,* 769-773.

Jacobsen, B., Bjelke, E., Kvåle, G., & Heuch, I. (1986). Coffee drinking, mortality, and cancer incidence: Results from a Norwegian prospective study. *Journal of the National Cancer Institute, 76,* 823-831.

Jacobsen, B. K., & Hansen, V. (1988). Caffeine and health [Letter to the editor]. *British Medical Journal [Clinical Research], 296,* 291.

Jacobsen, B. K., & Thelle, D. S. (1987). The Tromso heart study: Is coffee drinking an indicator of a life style with high risk for ischemic heart disease? *Acta Medica Scandinavica, 222,* 215-221.

Jacobson, B. H., & Edgley, B. M. (1987). Effects of caffeine on simple reaction time and movement time. *Aviation, Space, and Environmental Medicine, 58,* 1153-1156.

Jacobson, B. H., & Thurman-Lacey, S. R. (1992). Effect of caffeine on motor performance by caffeine-naive and -familiar subjects. *Perceptual and Motor Skills, 74,* 151-157.

Jacobson, S. W., Fein, G. G., Jacobson, J. L., Schwartz, P. M., & Dowler, J. K. (1984). Neonatal correlates of prenatal exposure to smoking, caffeine, and alcohol. *Infant Behavior and Development, 7,* 253-265.

James, J. E. (1990). The influence of user status and anxious disposition on the hypertensive effects of caffeine. *International Journal of Psychophysiology, 10,* 171-179.

James, J. E. (1991). *Caffeine and health.* London: Academic Press.

James, J. E. (1993). Caffeine and ambulatory blood pressure [Letter; comment]. *American Journal of Hypertension, 6,* 91-92.

James, J. E. (1994a). Caffeine, health, and commercial interests. *Addiction, 89,* 1595-1599.

James, J. E. (1994b). Chronic effects of habitual caffeine consumption on laboratory and ambulatory blood pressure levels. *Journal of Cardiovascular Research, 1,* 159-164.

James, J. E. (1994c). Does caffeine enhance or merely restore degraded psychomotor performance. *Neuropsychobiology, 30,* 124-125.

James, J. E. (1995a). Caffeine and psychomotor performance revisited. *Neuropsychobiology, 31,* 202-203.

James, J. E. (1995b). Caffeine, health, and commercial interests: Reply to Golding. *Addiction, 90,* 989-990.

James, J. E. (1997). Caffeine and blood pressure: Habitual use is a preventable cardiovascular risk factor. *Lancet, 349,* 279-281.

James, J. E., Bruce, M. S., Lader, M. H., & Scott, N. R. (1989). Self-report reliability and symptomatology of habitual caffeine consumption. *British Journal of Clinical Pharmacology, 27,* 507-514.

James, J. E., & Crosbie, J. (1987). Somatic and psychological health implications of heavy caffeine use. *British Journal of Addiction, 82,* 503-509.

James, J. E., Crosbie, J., & Paull, I. (1987). Symptomatology of habitual caffeine use amongst psychiatric patients. *Australian Journal of Psychology, 39,* 139-149.

James, J. E., & Paull, I. (1985). Caffeine and human reproduction. *Reviews on Environmental Health, 7,* 151-167.

James, J. E., Paull, I., Cameron-Traub, E., Miners, J. O., Lelo, A., & Birkett, D. J. (1988). Biochemical validation of self-reported caffeine consumption during caffeine fading. *Journal of Behavioral Medicine, 11,* 15-30.

James, J. E., & Richardson, M. (1991). Pressor effects of caffeine and cigarette smoking. *British Journal of Clinical Psychology, 30,* 276-278.

James, J. E., Sawczuk, D., & Merritt, S. (1989). The effect of chronic caffeine consumption on urinary incontinence in psychogeriatric inpatients. *Psychology and Health, 3,* 297-305.

James, J. E., Stirling, K. P., & Hampton, B. A. M. (1985). Caffeine fading: Behavioral treatment of caffeine abuse. *Behavior Therapy, 16,* 15-27.

Jansen, D. F., Nedeljkovic, S., Feskens, E. J., Ostojic, M. C., Grujic, M. Z., Bloemberg, B. P., & Kromhout, D. (1995). Coffee consumption, alcohol use, and cigarette smoking as determinants of serum total and HDL cholesterol in two Serbian cohorts of the Seven Countries Study. *Arteriosclerosis, Thrombosis, and Vascular Biology, 15,* 1793-1797.

Jansen, R. W., & Lipsitz, L. A. (1995). Postprandial hypotension: Epidemiology, pathophysiology, and clinical management. *Annals of Internal Medicine, 122,* 286-295.

Janson, C., Gislason, T., De-Backer, W., Plaschke, P., Bjornsson, E., Hetta, J., Kristbjarnason, H., Vermeire, P., & Boman, G. (1995). Prevalence of sleep disturbances among young adults in three European countries. *Sleep, 18,* 589-597.

Jarvis, A. P., Greenawalt, J. W., & Fagraeus, L. (1986). Intravenous caffeine for postdural puncture headache [Letter]. *Anesthesia and Analgesia, 65,* 316-317.

Jarvis, M. J. (1993). Does caffeine intake enhance absolute levels of cognitive performance? *Psychopharmacology, 110,* 45-52.

Jefferson, J. (1988). Lithium tremor and caffeine intake: Two cases of drinking less and shaking more. *Journal of Clinical Psychiatry, 49,* 72-73.

Jeong, D., & Dimsdale, J. E. (1990). The effects of caffeine on blood pressure in the work environment. *American Journal of Hypertension, 3,* 749-753.

Jick, H., Miettinen, O. S., Neff, R. K., Shapiro, S., Heinonen, O. P., & Slone, D. (1973). Coffee and myocardial infarction. *New England Journal of Medicine, 289,* 63-67.

Joeres, R., Brachtel, D., Gallenkamp, H., Hofstetter, G., Klinker, H., Zilly, W., & Richter, E. (1993). Caffeine elimination in cirrhotic and noncirrhotic liver disease of different etiology. *Zeitschrift für Gastroenterologie, 2,* 56-61.

Joeres, R., Klinker, H., Heusler, H., Epping, J., & Richter, E. (1987). Influence of mexiletine on caffeine elimination. *Pharmacology and Therapeutics, 33,* 163-169.

Joeres, R., Klinker, H., Heusler, H., Epping, J., Zilly, W., & Richter, E. (1988). Influence of smoking on caffeine elimination in healthy volunteers and in patients with alcoholic liver cirrhosis. *Hepatology, 8,* 575-579.

Joesoef, M. R., Beral, V., Rolfs, R. T., Aral, S. O., & Cramer, D. W. (1990). Are caffeinated beverages risk factors for delayed conception? *Lancet, 335,* 136-137.

Johansen, J. P., & Viskum, S. (1987). Asthma associated with the handling of green coffee beans. *Ugeskrift for Laeger, 149,* 2853.

Johansson, C., Mellström, D., Lerner, U., & Österberg, T. (1992). Coffee drinking: A minor risk factor for bone loss and fractures. *Age and Ageing, 21,* 20-26.

Johnsen, R., Forde, O. H., Straume, B., & Burhol, P. G. (1994). Aetiology of peptic ulcer: A prospective population study in Norway. *Journal of Epidemiology and Community Health, 48,* 156-160.

Johnson, C., & Edleman, K. J. (1992). Malignant hyperthermia: A review. *Journal of Perinatology, 12,* 61-71.

Johnson, L. C., Spinweber, C. L., & Gomez, S. A. (1990). Benzodiazepines and caffeine: Effect on daytime sleepiness, performance, and mood. *Psychopharmacology, 101,* 160-167.

Jokela, S., & Vartiainen, A. (1959). Caffeine poisoning. *Acta Pharmacologica et Toxicologica, 15,* 331-334.

Jorhem, L., & Haegglund, G. (1992). Aluminium in Lebensmitteln und in Nahrung in Schweden [Aluminium in foodstuffs and diets in Sweden]. *Zeitschrift für Lebensmittel Untersuchung und Forschung, 194,* 38-42.

Jossa, F., Krogh, V., Farinaro, E., Panico, S., Giumetti, D., Galasso, R., Celentano, E., Mancini, M., & Trevisan, M. (1993). Coffee and serum lipids: Findings from the Olivetti Heart Study. *Annals of Epidemiology, 3,* 250-255.

Josselyn, S. A., & Beninger, R. J. (1991). Behavioral effects of intrastriatal caffeine mediated by adenosinergic modulation of dopamine. *Pharmacology Biochemistry and Behavior, 39,* 97-103.

Jost, G., Wahllander, A., von Mandach, U., & Preisig, R. (1987). Overnight salivary caffeine clearance: A liver function test suitable for routine use. *Hepatology, 7,* 338-344.

Jung, R. T., Shetty, P. S., James, W. P. T., Barrand, M. A., & Callingham, B. A. (1981). Caffeine: Its effect on catecholamines and metabolism in lean and obese humans. *Clinical Science, 60,* 527.

Kaa, E. (1994). Impurities, adulterants, and diluents of illicit heroin: Changes during a 12-year period. *Forensic Science International, 64,* 171-179.

Kalandidi, A., Tzonou, A., Toupadaki, N., Lan, S. J., Koutis, C., Drogari, P., Notara, V., Hsieh, C. C., Toutouzas, P., & Trichopoulos, D. (1992). A case-control study of coronary heart disease in Athens, Greece. *International Journal of Epidemiology, 21,* 1074-1080.

Kalapothaki, V., Tzonou, A., Hsieh, C. C., Toupadaki, N., Karakatsani, A., & Trichopoulos, D. (1993). Tobacco, ethanol, coffee, pancreatitis, diabetes mellitus, and cholelithiasis as risk factors for pancreatic carcinoma. *Cancer Causes and Control, 4,* 375-382.

Kalow, W., Britt, B. A., Terreau, M. E., & Haist, C. (1970). Metabolic error of muscle metabolism after recovery from malignant hyperthermia. *Lancet, 2,* 895-898.

Kalow, W., & Tang, B. K. (1991). Caffeine as a metabolic probe: Exploration of the enzyme-inducing effect of cigarette smoking. *Clinical Pharmacology and Therapeutics, 49,* 44-48.

Kamimori, G. H., Eddington, N. D., Hoyt, R. W., Fulco, C. S., Lugo, S., Durkot, M. J., Brunhart, A. E., & Cymerman, A. (1995). Effects of altitude (4300 m) on the pharmacokinetics of caffeine and cardio-green in humans. *European Journal of Clinical Pharmacology, 48,* 167-170.

Kannel, W. B., & Schatzkin, A. (1983). Risk factor analysis. *Progress in Cardiovascular Diseases, 26,* 309-332.

Kant, G. J. (1993). Effects of psychoactive drugs or stress on learning, memory, and performance as assessed using a novel water maze task. *Pharmacology, Biochemistry and Behavior, 44,* 287-295.

Karacan, L., Thornby, J. I., Anch, A. M., Booth, G. H., Williams, R. L., & Salis, P. J. (1976). Dose-related sleep disturbances induced by coffee and caffeine. *Clinical Pharmacology and Therapeutics, 20,* 682-689.

Karacan, I., Thornby, J. I., Booth, G. H., Okawa, M., Salis, P. J., Anch, A. M., & Williams, R. L. (1975). *Dose response effects of coffee on objective (EEG) and subjective measures of sleep.* Basel: S. Karger.

Kasanen, A., & Forsström, J. (1966). Eating and smoking habits of patients with myocardial infarction. *Annales Medicinae Internae Fenniae, 55,* 7-11.

Kaus, S. J., & Rockoff, M. A. (1994). Malignant hyperthermia. *Pediatric Clinics of North America, 41,* 221-237.

Kawachi, I., Colditz, G. A., & Stone, C. B. (1994). Does coffee drinking increase the risk of coronary heart disease? Results from a meta-analysis. *British Heart Journal, 72,* 269-275.

Keister, M. E., & McLaughlin, R. J. (1972). Vigilance performance related to extraversion-introversion and caffeine. *Journal of Experimental Research in Personality, 6,* 5-11.

Kelsey, M. C., & Grossberg, G. T. (1995). Safety and efficacy of caffeine-augmented ECT in elderly depressives: A retrospective study. *Journal of Geriatric Psychiatry and Neurology, 8,* 168-172.

Kendrick, Z. V., Affrime, M. B., & Lowenthal, D. T. (1994). Effects of caffeine or ethanol on treadmill performance and metabolic responses of well-trained men. *International Journal of Clinical Pharmacology and Therapeutics, 32,* 536-541.

Kenemans, J. L., & Lorist, M. M. (1995). Caffeine and selective visual processing. *Pharmacology Biochemistry Behavior, 52,* 461-471.

Kerr, J. S., Sherwood, N., & Hindmarch, I. (1991). Separate and combined effects of the social drugs on psychomotor performance. *Psychopharmacology, 104,* 113-119.

Kessler, H. (1981). Coffee and cancer of the pancreas. *New England Journal of Medicine, 304,* 1605.

Khanna, N. A., Somani, S. M., Boyer, A., Miller, J., Chua, C., & Menke, J. A. (1982). Cross-validation of serum to saliva relationships of caffeine, theophylline, and total methylxanthines in neonates. *Developmental Pharmacology and Therapeutics, 4,* 18-27.

Kiel, D. P., Felson, D. T., Hannan, M. T., Anderson, J. J., & Wilson, P. W. (1990). Caffeine and the risk of hip fracture: The Framingham Study [letter to the editor]. *American Journal of Epidemiology, 132,* 675-684.

Kihlman, B. A. (Ed.) (1977). *Caffeine and chromosomes.* New York: Elsevier North-Holland.

Kihlman, B. A., & Andersson, H. C. (1987). Effects of caffeine on chromosomes in cells of higher eukaryotic organisms. *Reviews on Environmental Health, 7,* 279-382.

Kimmel, C. A., Kimmel, G. L., White, C. G., Grafton, T. F., Young, J. F., & Nelson, C. J. (1984). Blood flow changes and conceptual development in pregnant rats in response to caffeine. *Fundamental and Applied Toxicology, 4,* 240-247.

King, D. J., & Henry, G. (1992). The effect of neuroleptics on cognitive and psychomotor function. A preliminary study in healthy volunteers. *British Journal of Psychiatry, 160,* 647-653.

Kinlen, L. J., Willows, A. N., Goldblatt, P., & Yudkin, J. (1988). Tea consumption and cancer. *British Journal of Cancer, 58,* 397-401.

Kirchhoff, M., Torp-Pedersen, C., Hougaard, K., Jacobsen, T. J., Sjol, A., Munch, M., Tingleff, J., Jorgensen, T., Schroll, M., & Olsen, M. E. (1994). Casual blood pressure in a general Danish population: Relation to age, sex, weight, height, diabetes, serum lipids, and consumption of coffee, tobacco and alcohol. *Journal of Clinical Epidemiology, 47,* 469-474.

Kirsch, I., & Rosadino, M. J. (1993). Do double-blind studies with informed consent yield externally valid results? An empirical test. *Psychopharmacology, 110,* 437-442.

Kirsch, I., & Weixel, L. J. (1988). Double-blind versus deceptive administration of a placebo. *Behavioral Neuroscience, 102,* 319-323.

Kivity, S., Ben Aharon, Y., Man, A., & Topilsky, M. (1990). The effect of caffeine on exercise-induced bronchoconstriction. *Chest, 97,* 1083-1085.

Klag, M. J., Mead, L. A., LaCroix, A. Z., Wang, N. Y., Coresh, J., Liang, K. Y., Pearson, T. A., & Levine, D. M. (1994). Coffee intake and coronary heart disease. *Annals of Epidemiology, 4,* 425-433.

Klatsky, A. L., Armstrong, M. A., & Friedman, G. D. (1993). Coffee, tea, and mortality. *Annals of Epidemiology, 3,* 375-381.

Klatsky, A. L., Friedman, G. D., & Armstrong, M. A. (1986). The relationship between alcoholic beverage use and other traits to blood pressure: A new Kaiser Permanente study. *Circulation, 73,* 628-636.

Klatsky, A. L., Friedman, G. D., & Armstrong, M. A. (1990). Coffee use prior to myocardial infarction restudied: Heavier intake may increase the risk. *American Journal of Epidemiology, 132,* 479-488.

Klatsky, A. L., Friedman, G. D., & Siegelaub, A. B. (1973). Coffee drinking prior to acute myocardial infarction. Results from the Kaiser-Permanente epidemiologic study of myocardial infarction. *Journal of the American Medical Association, 226,* 540-543.

Klatsky, A. L., Friedman, G. D., & Siegelaub, A. B. (1974). Habits and sudden cardiac death. *Circulation, 50*(Suppl. 3), 99.

Klein, E., Zohar, J., Geraci, M. F., Murphy, D. L., & Uhde, T. W. (1991). Anxiogenic effects of m-CPP in patients with panic disorder: Comparison to caffeine's anxiogenic effects. *Biological Psychiatry, 30,* 973-984.

Klesges, R. C., Ray, J. W., & Klesges, L. M. (1994). Caffeinated coffee and tea intake and its relationship to cigarette smoking: An analysis of the Second National Health and Nutrition Examination Survey (NHANES II). *Journal of Substance Abuse, 6,* 407-418.

Kling, O. R., & Christensen, H. D. (1979). Caffeine elimination in late pregnancy. *Federation Proceedings, 38,* 266.

Knutti, R., Rothweiler, H., & Schlatter, C. (1981). Effect of pregnancy on the pharmacokinetics of caffeine. *European Journal of Clinical Pharmacology, 21,* 121-126.

Knutti, R., Rothweiler, H., & Schlatter, C. (1982). The effect of pregnancy on the pharmacokinetics of caffeine. *Archives of Toxicology*(Suppl. 5), 187-192.

Koch, G. G., Amara, I. A., & MacMillan, J. (1994). Evaluation of alternative statistical models for crossover studies to demonstrate caffeine adjuvancy in the treatment of tension headache. *Journal of Biopharmaceutical Statistics, 4,* 347-410.

Koczapski, A., Paredes, J., Kogan, C., Ledwidge, B., & Higenbottam, J. (1989). Effects of caffeine on behavior of schizophrenic inpatients. *Schizophrenia Bulletin, 15,* 339-344.

Koot, P., & Deurenberg, P. (1995). Comparison of changes in energy expenditure and body temperatures after caffeine consumption. *Annals of Nutrition and Metabolism, 39,* 135-142.

Koppe, J. G., de Bruijne, J. I., & de Boer, P. (1979). Apneic spells and transcutaneous PO2: Treatment with caffeine, 19 year follow-up. *Birth Defects, 15,* 437-445.

Kotake, A. N., Schoeller, D. A., Lambert, G. H., Baker, A. L., Schaffer, D. D., & Josephs, H. (1982). The caffeine CO_2 breath test: Dose response and route of N-demethylation in smokers and nonsmokers. *Clinical Pharmacology and Therapeutics, 32,* 261-269.

Kovar, M. G., Fulwood, R., & Feinleib, M. (1983). Coffee and cholesterol [Letter to the editor]. *New England Journal of Medicine, 309,* 1249.

Kozlowski, L. T. (1976). Effect of caffeine on coffee drinking. *Nature, 264,* 354-355.

Kozlowski, L. T., Henningfield, J. E., Keenan, R. M., Lei, H., Leigh, G., Jelinek, L. C., Pope, M. A., & Haertzen, C. A. (1993). Patterns of alcohol, cigarette, and caffeine and other drug use in two drug-abusing populations. *Journal of Substance Abuse Treatment, 10,* 171-179.

Krahn, D. D., Hasse, S., Ray, A., Gosnell, B., & Drewnowski, A. (1991). Caffeine consumption in patients with eating disorders. *Hospital and Community Psychiatry, 42,* 313-315.

Kreiger, N., Gross, A., & Hunter, G. (1992). Dietary factors and fracture in postmenopausal women: A case-control study. *International Journal of Epidemiology, 21,* 953-958.

Krivosic-Horber, R., Adnet, P., Krivosic, I., Theunynck, D., Guévart, R., & Adamantidis, M. (1988). Tests de contracture et sensibilité à l'hypothermie anesthésique chez vingt-sept sujets suspects [Tests of contracture and sensitivity to malignant hyperthermia in 27 patients]. *Annales Françaises d'Anesthésie et de Réanimation, 7,* 132-138.

Kulkarni, P. B., & Dorand, R. D. (1979). Caffeine toxicity in the neonate. *Pediatrics, 64,* 254-255.

Kupietz, S. S., & Winsberg, B. G. (1977). Caffeine and inattentiveness in reading-disabled children. *Perceptual and Motor Skills, 44,* 1238.

Kurppa, K., Holmberg, P. C., Kuosma, E., & Saxen, L. (1983). Coffee consumption during pregnancy and selected congenital malformations: A nationwide case-control study. *American Journal of Public Health, 73,* 1397-1399.

Kusanagi, C., Fujii, S., & Inada, S. (1974). Evaluation of doping drugs by treadmill exercise in dogs: I. Caffeine. *Japanese Journal of Veterinary Science, 36,* 81-92.

Kuzemko, J. A., & Paala, J. (1973). Apneic attacks in the newborn treated with aminophylline. *Archives of Disease in Childhood, 48,* 404-406.

Lack, L., Miller, W., & Turner, D. (1988). A survey of sleeping difficulties in an Australian population. *Community Health Studies, 12,* 200-207.

LaCroix, A. Z., Mead, L. A., Liang, K. Y., Thomas, C. B., & Pearson, T. A. (1986). Coffee consumption and the incidence of coronary heart disease. *New England Journal of Medicine, 315,* 977-982.

LaCroix, A. Z., Mead, L. A., Liang, K. Y., Thomas, C. B., & Pearson, T. A. (1987). Coffee consumption and coronary heart disease. *New England Journal of Medicine, 316,* 947.

Lake, C. R., & Quirk, R. S. (1984). CNS stimulants and the look-alike drugs. *Psychiatric Clinics of North America, 7,* 689-701.

Lake, C. R., Rosenberg, D. B., Gallant, S., Zaloga, G., & Chernow, B. (1990). Phenylpropanolamine increases plasma caffeine levels. *Clinical Pharmacology and Therapeutics, 47,* 675-685.

Lake, C. R., Zaloga, G., Bray, J., Rosenberg, D., & Chernow, B. (1989). Transient hypertension after two phenylpropanolamine diet aids and the effects of caffeine: A placebo-controlled follow-up study. *American Journal of Medicine, 86,* 427-432.

Lambrecht, G. L., Malbrain, M. L., Chew, S. L., Baeck, E., & Verbraeken, H. (1993). Intranasal caffeine and amphetamine causing stroke. *Acta Neurologica Belgica, 93,* 146-149.

Lancaster, T., Muir, J., & Silagy, C. (1994). The effects of coffee on serum lipids and blood pressure in a UK population. *Journal of the Royal Society of Medicine, 87,* 506-507.

Lane, E. A. (1988). The aminopyrine breath test for the evaluation of liver function in alcoholic patients: Drug pharmacokinetics and environmental factors. *Advances in Alcohol and Substance Abuse, 7,* 25-32.

Lane, J. D. (1983). Caffeine and cardiovascular responses to stress. *Psychosomatic Medicine, 45,* 447-451.

Lane, J. D. (1994). Neuroendocrine responses to caffeine in the work environment. *Psychosomatic Medicine, 546,* 267-270.

Lane, J. D., Adcock, R. A., Williams, R. B., & Kuhn, C. M. (1990). Caffeine effects on cardiovascular and neuroendocrine responses to acute psychosocial stress and their relationship to level of habitual caffeine consumption. *Psychosomatic Medicine, 52,* 320-336.

Lane, J. D., & Manus, D. C. (1989). Persistent cardiovascular effects with repeated caffeine administration. *Psychosomatic Medicine, 51,* 373-380.

Lane, J. D., Pieper, C. F., Barefoot, J. C., Williams, R. B., & Siegler, I. C. (1994). Caffeine and cholesterol: Interactions with hostility. *Psychosomatic Medicine, 56,* 260-266.

Lane, J. D., & Rose, J. E. (1995). Effects of daily caffeine intake on smoking behavior in the natural environment. *Experimental and Clinical Psychopharmacology, 3,* 49-55.

Lane, J. D., Steege, J. F., Rupp, S. L., & Kuhn, C. M. (1992). Menstrual cycle effects on caffeine elimination in the human female. *European Journal of Clinical Pharmacology, 43,* 543-546.

Lane, J. D., & Williams, R. B., (1985). Caffeine affects cardiovascular responses to stress. *Psychophysiology, 22,* 648-655.

Lane, J. D., & Williams, R. B. (1987). Cardiovascular effects of caffeine and stress in regular coffee drinkers. *Psychophysiology, 24,* 157-164.

Lang, T., Bureau, J. F., Degoulet, P., Salah, H., & Benattar, C. (1983). Blood pressure, coffee, tea, and tobacco consumption: An epidemiological study in Algiers. *European Heart Journal, 4,* 602-607.

Lang, T., Degoulet, P., Aime, F., Fourlaud, C., Jacquinet-Salord, M., Laprugne, J., Main, J., Oeconomos, J., Phalente, J., & Prades, A. (1983). Relation between coffee drinking and blood pressure: Analysis of 6,321 subjects in the Paris region. *American Journal of Cardiology, 52,* 1238-1242.

Larroque, B., Kaminski, M., Lelong, N., Subtil, D., & Dehaene, P. (1993a). Effects on birth weight of alcohol and caffeine consumption during pregnancy. *American Journal of Epidemiology, 137,* 941-950.

Larroque, B., Kaminski, M., Lelong, N., Subtil, D., & Dehaene, P. (1993b). Larroque et al. reply to "Invited commentary: Caffeine and birth outcomes." *American Journal of Epidemiology, 137,* 957-958.

Laska, E. M., Sunshine, A., Mueller, F., Elvers, W. B., Siegel, C., & Rubin, A. (1984). Caffeine as an analgesic adjuvant. *Journal of the American Medical Association, 251,* 1711-1718.

Lau, C. E., & Falk, J. L. (1995). Dose-dependent surmountability of locomotor activity in caffeine tolerance. *Pharmacology, Biochemistry, and Behavior, 52,* 139-143.

La Vecchia, C. (1990). Epidemiological evidence on coffee and digestive tract cancers: A review. *Digestive Diseases, 8,* 281-286.

La Vecchia, C., Ferraroni, M., Negri, E., D'Avanzo, B., Decarli, A., Levi, F., & Franceschi, S. (1989). Coffee consumption and digestive tract cancers. *Cancer Research, 49,* 1049-1051.

La Vecchia, C., Franceschi, S., Decarli, A., Gentile, A., Liati, P., Regallo, M., & Tognoni, G. (1984). Coffee drinking and the risk of epithelial ovarian cancer. *International Journal of Cancer, 33*, 559-562.

La Vecchia, C., Franceschi, S., Decarli, A., Pampallona, S., & Tognoni, G. (1987). Risk factors for myocardial infarction in young women. *American Journal of Epidemiology, 125*, 832-843.

La Vecchia, C., Franceschi, S., Decarli, A., Parazzini, F., & Tognoni, G. (1986). Coffee consumption and the risk of breast cancer. *Surgery, 100*, 477-481.

La Vecchia, C., Franceschi, S., Parazzini, F., Regallo, M., Decarli, A., Gallus, G., Di Pietro, S., & Tognoni, G. (1985). Benign breast disease and consumption of beverages containing methylxanthines. *Journal of the National Cancer Institute, 74*, 995-1000.

La Vecchia, C., Gentile, A., Negri, E., Parazzini, F., & Franceschi, S. (1989). Coffee consumption and myocardial infarction in women. *American Journal of Epidemiology, 130*, 481-485.

La Vecchia, C., Negri, E., Decarli, A., D'Avanzo, B., Gallotti, L., Gentile, A., & Franceschi, S. (1988). A case-control study of diet and colo-rectal cancer in northern Italy. *International Journal of Cancer, 41*, 492-498.

La Vecchia, C., Negri, E., Franceschi, S., D'Avanzo, B., & Boyle, P. (1992). Tea consumption and cancer risk. *Nutrition and Cancer, 17*, 27-31.

Lawson, D. H., Jick, H., & Rothman, K. J. (1981). Coffee and tea consumption and breast disease. *Surgery, 90*, 801-803.

LeBlanc, J., & Soucy, J. (1994). Hormonal dose-response to an adenosine receptor agonist. *Canadian Journal of Physiology and Pharmacology, 72*, 113-116.

Lechat, M. F., Borlee, I., Bouckaert, A., & Misson, C. (1980). Caffeine study. *Science, 207*, 1296.

Lee, B. L., Wong, D., Benowitz, N. L., & Sullam, P. M. (1993). Altered patterns of drug metabolism in patients with acquired immunodeficiency syndrome. *Clinical Pharmacology and Therapeutics, 53*, 529-535.

Lee, M. A., Cameron, O. G., & Greden, J. F. (1985). Anxiety and caffeine consumption in people with anxiety disorders. *Psychiatry Research, 15*, 211-217.

Lee, M. A., Flegel, P., Greden, J. F., & Cameron, O. G. (1988). Anxiogenic effects of caffeine on panic and depressed patients. *American Journal of Psychiatry, 145*, 632-635.

Lee, S. (1993). Carcinogens and mutagens. *Tea and Coffee Trade Journal, 165*(1), pp. 5-6.

Lee, W. C., Neugut, A. I., Garbowski, G. C., Forde, K. A., Treat, M. R., Waye, J. D., & Fenoglio-Preiser, C. (1993). Cigarettes, alcohol, coffee, and caffeine as risk factors for colorectal adenomatous polyps. *Annals of Epidemiology, 3*, 239-244.

LeGrady, D., Dyer, A. R., Shekelle, R. B., Stamler, J., Liu, K., Paul, O., Lepper, M., & Shryock, A. M. (1987). Coffee consumption and mortality in the Chicago Western Electric Company Study. *American Journal of Epidemiology, 126*, 803-812.

Lehmann, H. E., & Csank, J. (1957). Differential screening of phrenotropic agents in man: Psychophysiologic test data. *Journal of Clinical and Experimental Psychopathology, 18*, 222-235.

Leibenluft, E., Fiero, P. L., Bartko, J. J., Moul, D. E., & Rosenthal, N. E. (1993). Depressive symptoms and the self-reported use of alcohol, caffeine, and carbohydrates in normal volunteers and four groups of psychiatric outpatients. *American Journal of Psychiatry, 150*, 294-301.

Lelo, A., Birkett, D. J., Robson, R. A., & Miners, J. O. (1986). Comparative pharmacokinetics of caffeine and its primary demethylated metabolites paraxanthine, theobromine and theophylline in man. *British Journal of Clinical Pharmacology, 22*, 177-182.

Lelo, A., Miners, J. O., Robson, R., & Birkett, D. J. (1986a). Assessment of caffeine exposure: Caffeine content of beverages, caffeine intake, and plasma concentrations of methylxanthines. *Clinical Pharmacology and Therapeutics, 39,* 54-59.

Lelo, A., Miners, J. O., Robson, R. A., & Birkett, D. J. (1986b). Quantitative assessment of caffeine partial clearances in man. *British Journal of Clinical Pharmacology, 22,* 183-186.

Lenders, J. W., Morre, H. L., Smits, P., & Thien, T. (1988). The effects of caffeine on the postprandial fall of blood pressure in the elderly. *Age and Ageing, 17,* 236-240.

Leson, C. L., McGuigan, M. A., & Bryson, S. M. (1988). Caffeine overdose in an adolescent male. *Journal of Toxicology: Clinical Toxicology, 26,* 407-415.

Levi, L. (1967). The effect of coffee on the function of the sympathoadrenomedullary system in man. *Acta Medica Scandinavica, 181,* 431-498.

Lewis, C. E., Caan, B., Funkhouser, E., Hilner, J. E., Bragg, C., Dyer, A., Raczynski, J. M., Savage, P. J., Armstrong, M. A., & Friedman, G. D. (1993). Inconsistent associations of caffeine-containing beverages with blood pressure and with lipoproteins. The CARDIA Study. Coronary Artery Risk Development in Young Adults. *American Journal of Epidemiology, 138,* 502-507.

Lewis, F. W., & Rector, W., Jr. (1992). Caffeine clearance in cirrhosis: The value of simplified determinations of liver metabolic capacity. *Journal of Hepatology, 14,* 157-162.

Lieberman, H. R., Wurtman, R. J., Emde, G. G., & Coviella, I. L. G. (1987). The effects of caffeine and aspirin on mood and performance. *Journal of Clinical Psychopharmacology, 7,* 315-320.

Lieberman, H. R., Wurtman, R. J., Emde, G. G., Roberts, C., & Coviella, I. L. G. (1987). The effects of low doses of caffeine on human performance and mood. *Psychopharmacology, 92,* 308-312.

Lienert, G. A., & Huber, H. P. (1966). Differential effects of coffee on speed and power tests. *Journal of Psychology, 63,* 269-274.

Lima, D. R., Andrade, G. d. N., Santos, R. M., & David, C. N. (1989). Cigarettes and caffeine. *Chest, 95,* 255-256.

Lin, H. J., Perng, C. L., Lee, F. Y., Lee, C. H., & Lee, S. D. (1994). Clinical courses and predictors for rebleeding in patients with peptic ulcers and nonbleeding visible vessels: A prospective study. *Gut, 35,* 1389-1393.

Linde, L. (1995). Mental effects of caffeine in fatigued and nonfatigued female and male subjects. *Ergonomics, 38,* 864-885.

Lindinger, M. I., Graham, T. E., & Spriet, L. L. (1993). Caffeine attenuates the exercise-induced increase in plasma [K+] in humans. *Journal of Applied Physiology, 74,* 1149-1155.

Linn, S., Schoenbaum, S. C., Monson, R. R., Rosner, B., Stubblefield, P. G., & Ryan, K. J. (1982). No association between coffee consumption and adverse outcomes of pregnancy. *New England Journal of Medicine, 306,* 141-145.

Linsted, K. D., Kuzma, J. W., & Anderson, J. L. (1992). Coffee consumption and cause-specific mortality. Association with age at death and compression of mortality. *Journal of Clinical Epidemiology, 45,* 733-742.

Lipinsky, D. P., Black, J. L., Nelson, R. O., & Cimimero, A. R. (1975). The influence of motivational variables on the reactivity and reliability of self-recording. *Journal of Consulting and Clinical Psychology, 43,* 637-646.

Lipsitz, L. A., Jansen, R. W., Connelly, C. M., Kelley-Gagnon, M. M., & Parker, A. J. (1994). Haemodynamic and neurohumoral effects of caffeine in elderly patients with symptomatic postprandial hypotension: A double-blind, randomized, placebo-controlled study. *Clinical Science, 87,* 259-267.

Llopis, A., Morales, M., & Rodriguez, R. (1992). Digestive cancer in relation to diet in Spain. *Journal of Environmental Pathology, Toxicology and Oncology, 11,* 169-175.

Loke, W. H. (1988). Effects of caffeine on mood and memory. *Physiology and Behavior, 44,* 367-372.

Loke, W. H., Hinrichs, J. V., & Ghoneim, M. M. (1985). Caffeine and diazepam: Separate and combined effects on mood, memory, and psychomotor performance. *Psychopharmacology, 87,* 344-350.

Loke, W. H., & Meliska, C. J. (1984). Effects of caffeine use and ingestion on a protracted visual vigilance task. *Psychopharmacology, 84,* 54-57.

Lönnerholm, G., Lindstro, B., Paalzow, L., & Sedin, G. (1983). Plasma theophylline and caffeine and plasma-clearance of theophylline during theophylline treatment in the first year of life. *European Journal of Clinical Pharmacology, 24,* 371-374.

Lopes, J. M., Aubier, M., Jardin, J., Aranda, J. V., & Macklom, P. T. (1983). Effect of caffeine on skeletal muscle function before and after fatigue. *Journal of Applied Physiology: Respiratory, Environmental, and Exercise Physiology, 54,* 1303-1305.

Lorist, M. M., Snel, J., & Kok, A. (1994). Influence of caffeine on information-processing stages in well-rested and fatigued subjects. *Psychopharmacology, 113,* 411-421.

Lovallo, W. R., Pincomb, G. A., Sung, B. H., Everson, S. A., Passey, R. B., & Wilson, M. F. (1991). Hypertension risk and caffeine's effect on cardiovascular activity during mental stress in young men. *Health Psychology, 10,* 236-243.

Lovallo, W. R., Pincomb, G. A., Sung, B. H., Passey, R. B., Sausen, K. P., & Wilson, M. F. (1989). Caffeine may potentiate adrenocortical stress responses in hypertension-prone men. *Hypertension, 14,* 170-176.

Lowe, G. (1988). State-dependent retrieval effects with social drugs. *British Journal of Addiction, 83,* 99-103.

Lubin, F., Ron, E., Wax, Y., & Modan, B. (1985). Coffee and methylxanthines and breast cancer: A case-control study. *Journal of the National Cancer Institute, 74,* 569-573.

Lubin, J. H., Burns, P. E., Blot, W. J., Ziegler, R. G., Lees, A. W., & Fraumeni, J. F. (1981). Dietary factors and breast cancer risk. *International Journal of Cancer, 28,* 685-689.

Lucas, P. B., Pickar, D., Kelsoe, J., Rapoport, M., Pato, C., & Hommer, D. (1990). Effects of the acute administration of caffeine in patients with schizophrenia. *Biological Psychiatry, 28,* 35-40.

Lynn, R. (1973). National differences in anxiety and the consumption of caffeine. *British Journal of Social and Clinical Psychology, 12,* 92-93.

Lyon, J. L., Mahoney, A. W., French, T. K., & Moser, R., Jr. (1992). Coffee consumption and the risk of cancer of the exocrine pancreas: A case-control study in a low-risk population. *Epidemiology, 3,* 164-170.

MacDonald, T. M., Sharpe, K., Fowler, G., Lyons, D., Freestone, S., Lovell, H. G., Webster, J., & Petrie, J. C. (1991). Caffeine restriction: Effect of mild hypertension. *British Medical Journal, 303,* 1235-1238.

Mackay, D. C., & Rollins, J. W. (1989). Caffeine and caffeinism. *Journal of the Royal Navy Medical Service, 75,* 65-67.

MacMahon, B. (1984). *Coffee and cancer of the pancreas: A review.* New York: Cold Spring Harbor Laboratory.

MacMahon, B., Yen, S., Trichopoulos, D., Warren, K., & Nardi, G. (1981a). Coffee and cancer of the pancreas. *New England Journal of Medicine, 304,* 630-633.

MacMahon, B., Yen, S., Trichopoulos, D., Warren, K., & Nardi, G. (1981b). Coffee and cancer of the pancreas [Reply]. *New England Journal of Medicine, 304,* 1605-1606.

MacMahon, S., Peto, R., Cutler, J., Collins, R., Sorlie, P., Neaton, J., Abbott, R., Godwin, J., Dyer, A., & Stamler, J. (1990). Blood pressure, stroke, and coronary heart disease: Part 1, prolonged differences in blood pressure: Prospective observational studies corrected for the regression dilution bias. *Lancet, 335,* 765-774.

Mansel, R. E., Webster, D. J. T., Burr, M., & Leger, S. S. (1982). Is there a relationship between coffee consumption and breast disease? *British Journal of Surgery, 69,* 295-296.

Manuck, S. B., Kasprowicz, A. L., & Muldoon, M. F. (1990). Behaviorally evoked cardiovascular reactivity and hypertension: Conceptual issues and potential associations. *Annals of Behavioral Medicine, 12,* 17-29.

Marangos, P. J., & Boulenger, J. P. (1985). Basic and clinical aspects of adenosinergic neuromodulation. *Neuroscience and Biobehavioral Reviews, 9,* 421-430.

Marangos, P. J., Martino, A. M., Paul, S. M., & Skolnick, P. (1981). The benzodiazepines and inosine antagonize caffeine-induced seizures. *Psychopharmacology, 72,* 269-273.

Marchand, L. L., Kolonel, L. N., Hankin, J. H., & Yoshizawa, C. N. (1989). Relationship of alcohol consumption to diet: A population-based study in Hawaii. *American Journal of Clinical Nutrition, 49,* 567-572.

Marchbanks, C. R. (1993). Drug-drug interactions with fluoroquinolones. *Pharmacotherapy, 13,* 23S-28S.

Marchesini, G., Checchia, G. A., Grossi, G., Lolli, R., Bianchi, G. P., Zoli, M., & Pisi, E. (1988). Caffeine intake, fasting plasma caffeine, and caffeine clearance in patients with liver diseases. *Liver, 8,* 241-246.

Marks, V., & Kelly, J. F. (1973). Absorption of caffeine from tea, coffee, and Coca Cola. *Lancet, 1,* 827.

Marshall, J., Graham, S., & Swanson, M. (1982). Caffeine consumption and benign breast disease: A case-control comparison. *American Journal of Public Health, 72,* 610-612.

Marshall, W. R., Epstein, L., & Green, S. B. (1980a). Coffee drinking and cigarette smoking: I. Coffee, caffeine, and cigarette smoking behavior. *Addictive Behaviors, 5,* 389-394.

Marshall, W. R., Epstein, L., & Green, S. B. (1980b). Coffee drinking and cigarette smoking: II. Coffee, urinary pH, and cigarette smoking behavior. *Addictive Behaviors, 5,* 395-400.

Martin, J. B., Annegers, J. F., Curb, J. D., Heyden, S., Howson, C., Lee, E. S., & Lee, M. (1988). Mortality patterns among hypertensives by reported level of caffeine consumption. *Preventive Medicine, 17,* 310-320.

Martin, T. R., & Bracken, M. B. (1987). The association between low birth weight and caffeine consumption during pregnancy. *American Journal of Epidemiology, 126,* 813-821.

Massey, L. K., Bergman, E. A., Wise, K. J., & Sherrard, D. J. (1994). Interactions between dietary caffeine and calcium on calcium and bone metabolism in older women. *Journal of the American College of Nutrition, 13,* 592-606.

Massey, L. K., & Whiting, S. J. (1993). Caffeine, urinary calcium, calcium metabolism, and bone. *Journal of Nutrition, 123,* 1611-1614.

Massey, L. K., & Wise, K. J. (1984). The effect of dietary caffeine on urinary excretion of calcium, magnesium, sodium, and potassium in healthy young females. *Nutrition Research, 4,* 43-50.

Masterson, J. (1983). Trends in coffee consumption. *Tea and Coffee Trade Journal, March,* pp. 24-25, 44-45.

Mathew, R. J., & Wilson, W. H. (1985). Caffeine consumption, withdrawal, and cerebral blood flow. *Headache, 25,* 305-309.

Mathew, R. J., & Wilson, W. H. (1990). Behavioral and cerebrovascular effects of caffeine in patients with anxiety disorders. *Acta Psychiatrica Scandinavica, 82,* 17-22.

Mattila, M. E., Mattila, M. J., & Nuotto, E. (1992). Caffeine moderately antagonizes the effects of triazolam and zopiclone on the psychomotor performance of healthy subjects. *Pharmacology and Toxicology, 70,* 286-289.

Mattila, M. J., Palva, E., & Savolainen, K. (1982). Caffeine antagonizes Diazepam effects in man. *Medical Biology, 60,* 121-123.

Mau, G., & Netter, P. (1974). Kaffee- und Alkoholkonsum—Risikofaktoren in der Schwangerschaft? [Are coffee and alcohol consumption risk factors in pregnancy?]. *Geburtshilfe und Frauenheilkunde, 34,* 1018-1022.

May, D. C., Jarboe, C. H., Vanbakel, A. B., & Williams, W. M. (1982). Effects of cimetidne on caffeine disposition in smokers and nonsmokers. *Clinical Pharmacology and Therapeutics, 31,* 656-661.

May, D. C., Long, T., Madden, R., Hurst, H. E., & Jarboe, C. H. (1981). Caffeine toxicity secondary to street drug ingestion. *Annals of Emergency Medicine, 10,* 549.

Mayo, K. M., Falkowski, W., & Jones, C. A. (1993). Caffeine: Use and effects in long-stay psychiatric patients. *British Journal of Psychiatry, 162,* 543-545.

McArthur, K., Hogan, D., & Isenberg, J. I. (1982). Relative stimulatory effects of commonly ingested beverages on gastric acid secretion in humans. *Gastroenterology, 83,* 199-203.

McCall, W. V., Reid, S., Rosenquist, P., Foreman, A., & Kiesow-Webb, N. (1993). A reappraisal of the role of caffeine in ECT. *American Journal of Psychiatry, 150,* 1543-1545.

McDonald, A. D., Armstrong, B. G., & Sloan, M. (1992a). Cigarette, alcohol, and coffee consumption and congenital defects. *American Journal of Public Health, 82,* 91-93.

McDonald, A. D., Armstrong, B. G., & Sloan, M. (1992b). Cigarette, alcohol, and coffee consumption and prematurity. *American Journal of Public Health, 82,* 87-90.

McGee, M. B. (1980). Caffeine poisoning in a 19-year-old female. *Journal of Forensic Science, 25,* 29-32.

McGowan, J. D., Altman, R. E., & Kanto, W. P., Jr. (1988). Neonatal withdrawal symptoms after chronic maternal ingestion of caffeine. *Southern Medical Journal, 81,* 1092-1094.

McKim, W. A. (1980). The effect of caffeine, theophylline, and amphetamine on operant responding of the mouse. *Psychopharmacology, 68,* 135-138.

McLaughlin, C. C., Mahoney, M. C., Nasca, P. C., Metzger, B. B., Baptiste, M. S., & Field, N. A. (1992). Breast cancer and methylxanthine consumption. *Cancer Causes and Control, 3,* 175-178.

McNanamy, M. C., & Schube, P. G. (1936). Caffeine intoxication: Report of a case the symptoms of which amounted to psychosis. *New England Journal of Medicine, 215,* 616-620.

McQuilkin, S. H., Nierenberg, D. W., & Bresnick, E. (1995). Analysis of within-subject variation of caffeine metabolism when used to determine cytochrome P4501A2 and N-acetyltransferase-2 activities. *Cancer Epidemiology, Biomarkers, and Prevention, 4,* 139-146.

Medeiros, D. M. (1982). Caffeinated beverage consumption and blood pressure in Mississippi young adults. *Nutrition Reports International, 26,* 563-568.

Meliska, C. J., & Brown, R. E. (1982). Effects of caffeine on schedule-controlled responding in the rat. *Pharmacology, Biochemistry, and Behavior, 16,* 745-750.

Mensink, G. B., Kohlmeier, L., Rehm, J., & Hoffmeister, H. (1993). The relationship between coffee consumption and serum cholesterol under consideration of smoking history. *European Journal of Epidemiology, 9,* 140-150.

Mester, R., Toren, P., Mizrachi, I., Wolmer, L., Karni, N., & Weizman, A. (1995). Caffeine withdrawal increases lithium blood levels. *Biological Psychiatry, 37,* 348-350.

Meyer, F. P., Walther, T., & Walther, H. (1983). Über den Einfluß von Persönlichkeitsmerkmalen auf die Reaktionsleistungen friewilliger Probanden nach einmaliger Applikation von Plazebo, Crotylbarbital und Coffein [Influence of personality traits on reaction performance in volunteers after single application of placebo, crotylbarbital, and caffeine]. *Pharmacopsychiatry, 16,* 13-18.

Meyer, L. C., Peacock, J. L., Bland, J. M., & Anderson, H. R. (1994). Symptoms and health problems in pregnancy: Their association with social factors, smoking, alcohol, caffeine, and attitude to pregnancy. *Paediatric and Perinatal Epidemiology, 8,* 145-155.

Migliardi, J. R., Armellino, J. J., Friedman, M., Gillings, D. B., & Beaver, W. T. (1994). Caffeine as an analgesic adjuvant in tension headache. *Clinical Pharmacology and Therapeutics, 56,* 576-586.

Mikkelsen, E. S. (1978). Caffeine and schizophrenia. *Journal of Clinical Psychiatry, 39,* 732-736.

Mills, J. L., Holmes, L. B., Aarons, J. H., Simpson, J. L., Brown, Z. A., Jovanovic-Peterson, L. G., Conley, M. R., Graubard, B. I., Knopp, R. H., & Metzger, B. E. (1993). Moderate caffeine use and the risk of spontaneous abortion and intrauterine growth retardation. *Journal of the American Medical Association, 269,* 593-597.

Miner, M. H., McKinney, M. E., Witte, H., Buell, J. C., & Eliot, R. S. (1985). Regular caffeine consumption: Effect on resting cardiovascular function and cardiovascular changes induced by mental challenge. *Nebraska Medical Journal, 70,* 43-48.

Minton, J. P., Abou-Issa, H., Foecking, M. K., & Sriram, M. G. (1983). Caffeine and unsaturated fat diet significantly promotes DMBA-induced breast cancer in rats. *Cancer, 51,* 1249-1253.

Minton, J. P., Abou-Issa, H., Reiches, N., & Roseman, J. M. (1981). Clinical and biochemical studies on methylxanthine-related fibrocystic breast disease. *Surgery, 90,* 229-304.

Minton, J. P., Foecking, M. K., Webster, D. J. T., & Matthews, R. H. (1979a). Caffeine, cyclic nucleotides, and breast disease. *Surgery, 86,* 105.

Minton, J. P., Foecking, M. K., Webster, D. J. T., & Matthews, R. H. (1979b). Response of fibrocystic disease to caffeine withdrawal and correlation of cyclic nucleotides with breast disease. *American Journal of Obstetrics and Gynecology, 135,* 157-158.

Mitchell, P. J., & Redman, J. R. (1992). Effects of caffeine, time of day, and user history on study-related performance. *Psychopharmacology, 109,* 121-126.

Mitchell, V. E., Ross, S., & Hurst, P. M. (1974). Drugs and placebos: Effects of caffeine on cognitive performance. *Psychological Reports, 35,* 875-883.

Miura, S., Watanabe, J., Tomita, T., Sano, M., & Tomita, I. (1994). The inhibitory effects of tea polyphenols (flavan-3-ol derivatives) on $Cu2+$ mediated oxidative modification of low density lipoprotein. *Biological and Pharmaceutical Bulletin, 17,* 1567-1572.

Modest, G. (1983). Coffee and cholesterol [Letter to the editor]. *New England Journal of Medicine, 309,* 1248.

Mohr, U., Althoff, J., Ketkar, M. B., Conradt, P., & Morgareidge, K. (1984). The influence of caffeine on tumor incidence in Sprague-Dawley rats. *Food and Chemical Toxicology, 22,* 377-382.

Molinengo, L., Scordo, I., & Pastorello, B. (1994). Action of caffeine, L-PIA, and their combination on memory retention in the rat. *Life Sciences, 54,* 1247-1250.

Momas, I., Daures, J. P., Festy, B., Bontoux, J., & Gremy, F. (1994). Relative importance of risk factors in bladder carcinogenesis: Some new results about Mediterranean habits. *Cancer Causes and Control, 5,* 326-332.

Montague, T. J., McPherson, D. D., MacKenzie, B. R., Spencer, C. A., Nanton, M. A., & Horacek, B. M. (1983). Frequent ventricular ectopic activity without underlying cardiac disease: Analysis of 45 subjects. *American Journal of Cardiology, 52,* 980-984.

Morewood, G. H. (1993). A rational approach to the cause, prevention, and treatment of postdural puncture headache. *Canadian Medical Association Journal, 149,* 1087-1093.

Morgan, K. J., Stuits, V. J., & Zabik, M. E. (1982). Amount and food sources of caffeine and saccharin consumption. *Federation Proceedings, 41,* 952.

Morton, J. F. (1992). Widespread tannin intake via stimulants and masticatories, especially guarana, kola nut, betel vine, and accessories. In R. W. Hemingway & P. E. Laks (Eds.), *Plant polyphenols (pp. 739-765). New York: Plenum.*

Moskowitz, H., & Burns, M. (1981). The effects of alcohol and caffeine, alone and in combination, on skills performance. In L. Goldberg (Ed.), *Alcohol, drugs, and traffic safety* (pp. 969-983). Stockholm: Almqvist & Wiksell.

Moussa, M. M. (1983). Caffeine and sperm motility. *Fertility and Sterility, 39,* 845.

Mueller, S. M., Muller, J., & Asdell, S. M. (1984). Cerebral hemorrhage associated with phenylpropanolamine in combination with caffeine. *Stroke, 15,* 119-123.

Mukhtar, H., Katiyar, S. K., & Agarwal, R. (1994). Green tea and skin—anticarcinogenic effects. *Journal of Investigative Dermatology, 102,* 3-7.

Mukhtar, H., Wang, Z. Y., Katiyar, S. K., & Agarwal, R. (1992). Tea components: Antimutagenic and anticarcinogenic effects. *Preventive Medicine, 21,* 351-360.

Murat, I., Moriette, G., Blin, D., Couchard, M., Flouvat, B., De Gamarra, E., Relier, J. P., & Dreyfus-Brisac, C. (1981). The efficacy of caffeine in the treatment of recurrent ideopathic apnea in premature infants. *Journal of Pediatrics, 99,* 984-989.

Myasnikov, A. L. (1958). Influence of some factors on development of experimental cholesterol atherosclerosis. *Circulation, 17,* 99-113.

Myers, M. G. (1988). Caffeine and cardiac arrhythmias [Editorial]. *Chest, 94,* 4-5.

Myers, M. G., & Basinski, A. (1992). Coffee and coronary heart disease. *Archives of Internal Medicine, 152,* 1767-1772.

Myers, M. G., & Harris, L. (1990). High dose caffeine and ventricular arrhythmias. *Canadian Journal of Cardiology, 6,* 95-98.

Myers, M. G., Harris, L., & Leenen, F. H. H. (1987). Caffeine as a possible cause of ventricular arrhythmias during the healing phase of acute myocardial infarction. *American Journal of Cardiology, 59,* 1024-1028.

Myers, M. G., & Reeves, R. A. (1991). The effect of caffeine on daytime ambulatory blood pressure. *American Journal of Hypertension, 4,* 427-431.

Myers, M. G., Shapiro, D., McClure, F., & Daimes, R. H. (1989). Caffeine and stress reactivity in black and white males. *Health Psychology, 8,* 248-256.

Nagesh, R. V., & Murphy, K. A., Jr. (1988). Caffeine poisoning treated by hemoperfusion. *American Journal of Kidney Diseases, 12,* 316-318.

Naismith, D. J., Akinyanju, P. A., Szanto, S., & Yudkin, J. (1970). The effect in volunteers of coffee and decaffeinated coffee on blood glucose, insulin, plasma lipids, and some factors involved in blood clotting. *Nutrition and Metabolism, 12,* 144-151.

Nakajima, S., Otsuka, K., Yamanaka, T., Omori, K., Kubo, Y., Toyoshima, T., Watanabe, Y., & Watanabe, H. (1992). Ambulatory blood pressure and postprandial hypotension [Letter to the editor]. *American Heart Journal, 124,* 1669-1671.

Nakamoto, T., Cheuk, S. L., Yoshino, S., Falster, A. U., & Simmons, W. B. (1993). Cariogenic effect of caffeine intake during lactation on first molars of newborn rats. *Archives of Oral Biology, 38,* 919-922.

Nakamoto, T., Hartman, A. D., & Joseph, F. J. (1989). Interaction between caffeine intake and nutritional status on growing brains in newborn rats. *Annals of Nutrition and Metabolism, 33,* 92-99.

Nakamoto, T., Roy, G., Gottschalk, S. B., Yazdani, M., & Rossowska, M. (1991). Lasting effects of early chronic caffeine feeding on rats' behavior and brain in later life. *Physiology and Behavior, 49,* 721-727.

Nash, H. (1966). Psychological effects and alcohol-antagonizing properties of caffeine. *Quarterly Journal of Studies on Alcohol, 27,* 727-734.

Nehlig, A., & Debry, G. (1994). Potential genotoxic, mutagenic, and antimutagenic effects of coffee: A review. *Mutation Research, 317,* 145-162.

Neil, J. F., Himmelhoch, J. M., Mallinger, A. G., Mallinger, J., & Israel, H. (1978). Caffeinism complicating hypersomnic depressive syndromes. *Comprehensive Psychiatry, 19,* 377-385.

Neims, M. D., Bailey, J., & Aldridge, A. (1979). Disposition of caffeine during and after pregnancy. *Clinical Research, 27,* 236A.

Nelson, R. O., Lipinsky, D. P., & Black, J. L. (1975). The effects of expectancy on the reactivity of self-recoding. *Behavior Therapy, 6,* 337-349.

Neuberger, M. B. (1963). *Smoke screen: Tobacco and the public welfare.* Englewood Cliffs, NJ: Prentice Hall.

Newcombe, P. F., Renton, K. W., Rautaharju, P. M., Spencer, C. A., & Montague, T. J. (1988). High-dose caffeine and cardiac rate and rhythm in normal subjects. *Chest, 94,* 90-94.

Newman, H. W., & Newman, E. J. (1956). Failure of dexedrine and caffeine as practical antagonists of the depressant effect of ethyl alcohol in man. *Quarterly Journal of Studies on Alcohol, 17,* 406-410.

Nicholson, A. N., & Stone, B. M. (1980). Heterocyclic amphetamine derivatives and caffeine on sleep in man. *British Journal of Clinical Pharmacology, 9,* 195-203.

Nicolau, D. P., Nightingale, C. H., Tessier, P. R., Fu, Q., Xuan, D. W., Esguerra, E. M., & Quintiliani, R. (1995). The effect of fleroxacin and ciprofloxacin on the pharmacokinetics of multiple dose caffeine. *Drugs, 2,* 357-359.

Nikodijevic, O., Jacobson, K. A., & Daly, J. W. (1993). Locomotor activity in mice during chronic treatment with caffeine and withdrawal. *Pharmacology, Biochemistry, and Behavior, 44,* 199-216.

Nikolajsen, L., Larsen, K. M., & Kierkegaard, O. (1994). Effect of previous frequency of headache, duration of fasting, and caffeine abstinence on perioperative headache. *British Journal of Anaesthesia, 72,* 295-297.

Nishi, M., Ohba, S., Hirata, K., & Miyake, H. (1996). Dose-response relationship between coffee and the risk of pancreas cancer. *Japanese Journal of Clinical Oncology, 26,* 42-48.

Nishimura, H., & Nakai, K. (1960). Congenital malformations in offspring of mice treated with caffeine. *Proceedings of the Society for Experimental Biology and Medicine, 104,* 140-142.

Noerr, B. (1989). Caffeine citrate: Pointers in practical pharmacology. *Neonatal Network, 7,* 86-87.

Nolen, G. A. (1981). The effect of brewed and instant coffee on reproduction and teratogenesis in the rat. *Toxicology and Applied Pharmacology, 58,* 171-183.

Nolen, G. A. (1982). A reproduction/teratology study of brewed and instant decaffeinated coffees. *Journal of Toxicology and Environmental Health, 10,* 769-783.

Nomura, A., Heilbrun, L. K., & Stemmermann, G. N. (1986). Prospective study of coffee consumption and the risk of cancer. *Journal of the National Cancer Institute, 76,* 587-590.

Nomura, A., Stemmerman, G. N., & Heilbrun, L. K. (1981). Coffee and pancreatic cancer. *Lancet, 2,* 415.

Norell, S. E., Ahlbom, A., Erwald, R., Jacobson, G., Lindberg-Navier, I., Olin, R., Törnberg, B., & Wiechel, K. L. (1986). Diet and pancreatic cancer: A case-control study. *American Journal of Epidemiology, 124,* 894-902.

Nuotto, E., Mattila, M. J., Seppälä, T., & Konno, K. (1982). Coffee and caffeine and alcohol effects on psychomotor function. *Clinical Pharmacology Therapy, 23,* 68-76.

Nylander, P. O., Asplund, K., Beckman, L., Stegmayr, B., & Johansson, I. (1993). Population studies in northern Sweden: 18. Geographical covariates between hypercholesterolemia and Finnish genetic influence. *Human Heredity, 43,* 147-154.

Oberman, Z., Harell, A., Herzberg, M., Hoerer, E., Jaskolka, H., & Laurian, L. (1975). Changes in plasma cortisol, glucose, and free fatty acids after caffeine ingestion in obese women. *Israel Journal of Medical Sciences, 11,* 33-36.

Oborne, D. J., & Rogers, Y. (1983). Interactions of alcohol and caffeine on human reaction time. *Aviation, Space, and Environmental Medicine, 54,* 528-553.

Ockene, I. S., Ockene, J. K., Goldberg, R., & Dalen, J. E. (1983). Brief correspondence. *New England Journal of Medicine, 309,* 1248.

Odenheimer, D. J., Zunzunegui, M. V., King, M. C., Shipler, C. P., & Friedman, G. D. (1984). Risk factors for benign breast disease: A case-control study of discordant twins. *American Journal of Epidemiology, 120,* 565-571.

Okuma, T., Matsuoka, H., Matsue, Y., & Toyomura, K. (1982). Model insomnia by methylphenidate and caffeine and use in the evaluation of temazepam. *Psychopharmacology, 76,* 201-208.

Oliveto, A. H., Bickel, W. K., Hughes, J. R., & Shea, P. J. (1992). Caffeine drug discrimination in humans: Acquisition, specifity, and correlation with self-reports. *Journal of Pharmacology and Experimental Therapeutics, 261,* 885-894.

Oliveto, A. H., Bickel, W. K., Hughes, J. R., Terry, S. Y., Higgins, S. T., & Badger, G. J. (1993). Pharmacological specificity of the caffeine discriminative stimulus in humans: Effects of theophylline, methylphenidate, and buspirone. *Behavioral Pharmacology, 4,* 237-246.

Olsen, J. (1991). Cigarette smoking, tea and coffee drinking, and subfecundity. *American Journal of Epidemiology, 133,* 734-739.

Olsen, J., & Kronborg, O. (1993). Coffee, tobacco, and alcohol as risk factors for cancer and adenoma of the large intestine. *International Journal of Epidemiology, 22,* 398-402.

Olsen, J., Overvad, K., & Frische, G. (1991). Coffee consumption, birth weight, and reproductive failures. *Epidemiology, 2,* 370-374.

Onrot, J., Goldberg, M. R., Biaggioni, I., Hollister, A. S., Kincaid, D., & Robertson, D. (1985). Hemodynamic and humoral effects of caffeine in autonomic failure: Therapeutic implications for postprandial hypotension. *New England Journal of Medicine, 313,* 549-554.

Ørding, H. (1988). Diagnosis of susceptibility to malignant hyperthermia in man. *British Journal of Anaesthesia, 60,* 287-302.

Ossip, D. J., Epstein, L. H., & McKnight, D. (1980). Modeling, coffee drinking, and smoking. *Psychological Reports, 47,* 408-410.

Overton, D. A. (1973). State-dependent learning produced by addicting drugs. In S. Fisher & A. M. Freedman (Eds.), *Opiate addiction: Origins and treatment* (pp. 61-75). Washington, DC: Winston.

Ozasa, K., Watanabe, Y., Higashi, A., Liang, H., Hayashi, K., Shimouchi, A., Aoike, A., & Kawai, K. (1994). [Reproducibility of a self-administered questionnaire for dietary habits, smoking, and drinking.] *Nippon Eiseigaku Zasshi, 48,* 1048-1057.

Pagano, R., Negri, E., Decarli, A., & La Vecchia, C. (1988). Coffee drinking and prevalence of bronchial asthma. *Chest, 94,* 386-399.

Page, R. M. (1987). Perceived consequences of drinking caffeinated beverages. *Perceptual and Motor Skills, 65,* 765-767.

Palm, P. E., Arnold, E. P., Rachwall, P. C., Leyczeik, J. C., Teague, K. W., & Kensler, C. J. (1978). Evaluation of the teratogenic potential of fresh-brewed coffee and caffeine in the rat. *Toxicology and Applied Pharmacology, 44,* 1-16.

Palmer, J. R., Rosenberg, L., Rao, R. S., & Shapiro, S. (1995). Coffee consumption and myocardial infarction in women. *American Journal of Epidemiology, 141,* 724-731.

Pantelios, G., Lack, L., & James, J. E. (1989). Caffeine consumption and sleep. *Sleep Research, 18,* 65.

Parazzini, F., Chatenoud, L., & La Vecchia, C. (1994). Fetal loss and caffeine intake [Letter; comments]. *Journal of the American Medical Association, 272,* 28-29.

Parker, A. C., Preston, T., Heaf, D., Kitteringham, N. R., & Choonara, I. (1994). Inhibition of caffeine metabolism by ciprofloxacin in children with cystic fibrosis as measured by the caffeine breath test. *British Journal of Clinical Pharmacology, 38,* 573-576.

Parrott, A. C. (1991a). Performance tests in human psychopharmacology (1): Test reliability and standardization. *Human Psychopharmacology, 6,* 1-9.

Parrott, A. C. (1991b). Performance tests in human psychopharmacology (2): Content validity, criterion validity, and face validity. *Human Psychopharmacology, 6,* 91-98.

Parrott, A. C. (1991c). Performance tests in human psychopharmacology (3): Construct validity and test interpretation. *Human Psychopharmacology, 6,* 197-207.

Parsons, W. D., & Neims, A. H. (1981). Prolonged half-life of caffeine in healthy term newborn infants. *Journal of Pediatrics, 98,* 640-641.

Parsons, W. D., & Neims, M. D. (1978). Effect of smoking on caffeine clearance. *Clinical Pharmacology and Therapeutics, 24,* 40-45.

Parsons, W. D., & Pelletier, J. G. (1982). Delayed elimination of caffeine by women in the last 2 weeks of pregnancy. *Canadian Medical Association Journal, 127,* 377-380.

Parsons, W. D., Pelletier, J. G., & Neims, A. H. (1976). Caffeine elimination in pregnancy. *Clinical Research, 24,* 652A.

Passmore, A. P., Kondowe, G. B., & Johnston, G. D. (1987). Renal and cardiovascular effects of caffeine: A dose-response study. *Clinical Science, 72,* 749-756.

Pastore, L. M., & Savitz, D. A. (1995). Case-control study of caffeinated beverages and preterm delivery. *American Journal of Epidemiology, 141,* 61-69.

Patton, G. C., Hibbert, M., Rosier, M. J., Carlin, J. B., Caust, J., & Bowes, G. (1995). Patterns of common drug use in teenagers. *Australian Journal of Public Health, 19,* 393-399.

Patwardhan, R. V., Desmond, P. V., Johnson, R. F., & Schenker, S. (1980). Impaired elimination of caffeine by oral contraceptive steroids. *Journal of Laboratory and Clinical Medicine, 95,* 603-608.

Paul, O., Leper, M. H., Phelan, W. H., Dupertuis, G. W., MacMillan, A., McKean, H., & Park, H. (1963). A longitudinal study of coronary heart disease. *Circulation, 28,* 20-31.

Paul, S., Kurunwune, B., & Biaggioni, I. (1993). Caffeine withdrawal: Apparent heterologous sensitization to adenosine and prostacyclin actions in human platelets. *Journal of Pharmacology and Experimental Therapeutics, 267,* 838-843.

Peacock, J. L., Bland, J. M., & Anderson, H. R. (1991). Effects on birth weight of alcohol and caffeine consumption in smoking women. *Journal of Epidemiology and Community Health, 45,* 159-163.

Pearlman, S. A., Duran, C., Wood, M. A., Maisels, M. J., & Berlin, C. M., Jr. (1989). Caffeine pharmacokinetics in preterm infants older than 2 weeks. *Developmental Pharmacology and Therapeutics, 12,* 65-69.

Penetar, D., McCann, U., Thorne, D., Kamimori, G., Galinski, C., Sing, H., Thomas, M., & Belenky, G. (1993). Caffeine reversal of sleep deprivation effects on alertness and mood. *Psychopharmacology, 112,* 359-365.

Pentel, P. R., Mikell, F. L., & Zavoral, J. H. (1982). Myocardial injury after phenylpropanolamine ingestion. *British Heart Journal, 47,* 51-54.

Periti, M., Salvaggio, A., Quaglia, G., & Di Marzio, L. (1987). Coffee consumption and blood pressure: An Italian study. *Clinical Science, 72,* 443-447.

Perkins, K. A., Sexton, J. E., Epstein, L. H., DiMarco, A., Fonte, C., Stiller, R. L., Scierka, A., & Jacob, R. G. (1994). Acute thermogenic effects of nicotine combined with caffeine during light physical activity in male and female smokers. *American Journal of Clinical Nutrition, 60,* 312-319.

Perkins, K. A., Sexton, J. E., Stiller, R. L., Fonte, C., DiMarco, A., Goettler, J., & Scierka, A. (1994). Subjective and cardiovascular responses to nicotine combined with caffeine during rest and casual activity. *Psychopharmacology, 113,* 438-444.

Perng, C. L., Lin, H. J., Chen, C. J., Lee, F. Y., Lee, S. D., & Lee, C. H. (1994). Characteristics of patients with bleeding peptic ulcer requiring emergency endoscopy and aggressive treatment. *American Journal of Gastroenterology, 89,* 1811-1814.

Petrek, J. A., Sandberg, W. A., Cole, M. N., Silberman, M. S., & Collins, D. S. (1985). The inhibitory effect of caffeine on hormone-induced rat breast cancer. *Cancer, 56,* 1977-1981.

Petridou, E., Katsouyanni, K., Spanos, E., Skalkidis, Y., Panagiotopoulou, K., & Trichopoulos, D. (1992). Pregnancy estrogens in relation to coffee and alcohol intake. *Annals of Epidemiology, 2,* 241-247.

Petridou, E., Panagiotopoulou, K., Katsouyanni, K., Spanos, E., & Trichopoulos, D. (1990). Tobacco smoking, pregnancy estrogens, and birth weight. *Epidemiology, 1,* 247-250.

Pettijohn, T. F. (1979). Effects of alcohol and caffeine on wheel-running activity in the Mongolian gerbil. *Pharmacology, Biochemistry, and Behavior, 10,* 339-341.

Pfeifer, R. W., & Notari, R. E. (1988). Predicting caffeine plasma concentrations resulting from consumption of food or beverages: A simple method and its origin. *Drug Intelligence and Clinical Pharmacy, 22,* 953-959.

Phillips, B. A., & Danner, F. J. (1995). Cigarette smoking and sleep disturbance. *Archives of Internal Medicine, 155,* 734-737.

Phillis, J. W., Wu, P. H., & Coffin, V. L. (1983). Inhibition of adenosine uptake into rat brain synaptosomes by prostaglandins, benzodiazepines, and other centrally active compounds. *General Pharmacology, 14,* 475-479.

Pianosi, P., Grondin, D., Desmond, K., Coates, A. L., & Aranda, J. V. (1994). Effect of caffeine on the ventilatory response to inhaled carbon dioxide. *Respiration Physiology, 95,* 311-320.

Pickering, T. G., Mann, S. J., & James, G. D. (1991). Clinic and ambulatory blood pressure measurements for the evaluation of borderline hypertension in smokers and nonsmokers. *Archives des Maladies du Coeur et des Vaisseaux, 84*(Spec), 17-19.

Pincomb, G. A., Lovallo, W. R., Passey, R. B., Brackett, D. J., & Wilson, M. F. (1987). Caffeine enhances the physiological response to occupational stress in medical students. *Health Psychology, 6,* 101-112.

Pincomb, G. A., Lovallo, W. R., Passey, R. B., & Wilson, M. F. (1988). Effect of behavior state on caffeine's ability to alter blood pressure. *American Journal of Cardiology, 61,* 798-802.

Pincomb, G. A., Sung, B. H., Lovallo, W. R., & Wilson, M. F. (1993). Consistency of cardiovascular response pattern to caffeine across multiple studies using impedance and nuclear cardiography. *Biological Psychology, 36,* 131-138.

Pincomb, G. A., Wilson, M. F., Sung, B. H., Passey, R. B., & Lovallo, W. R. (1991). Effects of caffeine on pressor regulation during rest and exercise in men at risk for hypertension. *American Heart Journal, 122,* 1107-1115.

Pintos, J., Franco, E. L., Oliveira, B. V., Kowalski, L. P., Curado, M. P., & Dewar, R. (1994). Maté, coffee, and tea consumption and risk of cancers of the upper aerodigestive tract in southern Brazil. *Epidemiology, 5,* 583-590.

Podboy, J. W., & Mallory, W. A. (1977). Caffeine reduction and behavior change in the severely retarded. *Mental Retardation, 15,* 40.

Poehlman, E. T., LaChance, P., Tremblay, A., Nadequ, A., Dussault, J., Theriault, G., Despres, J. P., & Bouchard, C. (1989). The effect of prior exercise and caffeine ingestion on metabolic rate and hormones in young adult males. *Canadian Journal of Physiology and Pharmacology, 67,* 10-16.

Pola, J., Subiza, J., Armentia, A., Zapata, C., Hinojosa, M., Losada, E., & Valdivieso, R. (1988). Urticaria caused by caffeine. *Annals of Allergy, 60,* 207-208.

Pollard, I., Jabbour, H., & Mehrabani, P. A. (1987). Effects of caffeine administered during pregnancy on fetal development and subsequent function in the adult rat: Prolonged effects on a second generation. *Journal of Toxicology and Environmental Health, 22,* 1-15.

Polonovski, M., Donzelot, E., Briskas, S., & Doziopoulos, T. (1952). The comparative effects of coffee and soluble extracts of coffee on normal persons and on cardiacs. *Cardiologia, 21,* 809-816.

Polychronopoulou, A., Tzonou, A., Hsieh, C. C., Kaprinis, G., Rebelakos, A., Toupadaki, N., & Trichopoulos, D. (1993). Reproductive variables, tobacco, ethanol, coffee, and soma-tometry as risk factors for ovarian cancer. *International Journal of Cancer, 55,* 402-407.

Powell, J. J., Greenfield, S. M., Parkes, H. G., Nicholson, J. K., & Thompson, R. P. (1993). Gastro-intestinal availability of aluminium from tea. *Food and Chemical Toxicology, 31,* 449-454.

Powers, S. K., Byrd, R. J., Tulley, R., & Callender, T. (1983). Effects of caffeine ingestion on metabolism and performance during graded-exercise. *European Journal of Applied Physiology and Occupational Physiology, 50,* 301-307.

Prineas, R. J., Jacobs, D. R., Crow, R. S., & Blackburn, H. (1980). Coffee, tea, and VPB. *Journal of Chronic Diseases, 33,* 67-72.

Pritchard, W. S., Robinson, J. H., deBethizy, J. D., Davis, R. A., & Stiles, M. F. (1995). Caffeine and smoking: Subjective, performance, and psychophysiological effects. *Psychophysiology, 32,* 19-27.

Procter, A. W., & Greden, J. F. (1982). Caffeine and benzodiazepine use. *American Journal of Psychiatry, 139,* 132.

Rall, T. W. (1985). Central nervous system stimulants. In L. S. Goodman & A. Gilman (Eds.), *Pharmacological basis of therapeutics* (pp. 589-603). New York: Macmillan.

Rall, T. W. (1990a). Drugs used in the treatment of asthma: The methylxanthines, cromolyn sodium, and other agents. In A. G. Gilman, T. W. Rall, A. S. Nies, & P. Taylor (Eds.), *Goodman and Gilman's the pharmacological basis of therapeutics* (pp. 618-637). New York: Pergamon.

Rall, T. W. (1990b). Oxytocin, prostaglandins, ergot alkaloids, and other drugs: Tocolytic agents. In A. G. Gilman, T. W. Rall, A. S. Nies, & P. Taylor (Eds.), *Goodman and Gilman's the pharmacological basis of therapeutics* (pp. 939-947). New York: Pergamon.

Rapoport, J. L., Berg, C. J., Ismond, D. R., Zahn, T. P., & Neims, A. (1984). Behavioral effects of caffeine in children: Relationship between dietary choice and effects of caffeine challenge. *Archives of General Psychiatry, 41,* 1073-1079.

Rapoport, J. L., Jensvold, M., Elkins, R., Buchsbaun, M. S., Weingartner, H., Ludlow, C., Zahn, T. P., Berg, C. J., & Neims, A. H. (1981). Behavioral and cognitive effects of caffeine in boys and adult males. *Journal of Nervous and Mental Disease, 169,* 726-732.

Ratliff-Crain, J., O'Keefe, M. K., & Baum, A. (1989). Cardiovascular reactivity, mood, and task performance in deprived and nondeprived coffee drinkers. *Health Psychology, 8,* 427-447.

Ratnayake, W. M., Hollywood, R., O'Grady, E., & Stavric, B. (1993). Lipid content and composition of coffee brews prepared by different methods. *Food and Chemical Toxicology, 31,* 263-269.

Ratnayake, W. M., Pelletier, G., Hollywood, R., Malcolm, S., & Stavric, B. (1995). Investigation of the effect of coffee lipids on serum cholesterol in hamsters. *Food and Chemical Toxicology, 33,* 195-201.

Ray, R. L., Nellis, M. J., Brady, J. V., & Foltin, R. W. (1986). Nicotine and caffeine effects on the task-elicited blood pressure response. *Addictive Behaviors, 11,* 31-36.

Regestein, Q. R. (1989). Pathologic sleepiness induced by caffeine. *American Journal of Medicine, 87,* 586-588.

Regina, E. G., Smith, G. M., Keiper, C. G., & McKelvey, R. K. (1974). Effects of caffeine on alertness in simulated automobile driving. *Journal of Applied Psychology, 59,* 483-489.

Reichart, P. A., Philipsen, H. P., Mohr, U., Geerlings, H., & Srisuwan, S. (1988). Miang chewing in northern Thai villagers. *Tropical and Geographical Medicine, 40,* 39-44.

Reichert, E. (1890). Action of caffeine on tissue metamorphosis and heat phenomena. *New York Medical Journal, 51,* 456-464.

Rejent, T., Michaleck, M., & Krajewski, M. (1981). Caffeine fatality with coincident ephedrine. *Bulletin of the International Association of Forensic Toxicology, 16,* 18.

Renneker, M. (Ed.). (1988). *Understanding cancer* (3rd ed.). Palo Alto, CA: Bull.

Renner, E., Wietholtz, H., Huguenin, P., Arnaud, M. J., & Preisig, R. (1984). Caffeine: A model compound for measuring liver function. *Hepatology, 4,* 38-46.

Revelle, W., Amaral, P., & Turriff, S. (1976). Intraversion/extraversion, time-stress, and caffeine: Effect on verbal performance. *Science, 192,* 149-150.

Revelle, W., Humphreys, M. S., Simon, L., & Gilliland, K. (1980). The interactive effect of personality, time of day, and caffeine: A test of the arousal model. *Journal of Experimental Psychology: General, 109,* 1-31.

Richards, G. (1994). Tea in 1993. *Tea and Coffee Trade Journal, 166,* 42-50.

Richardson, N. J., Rogers, P. J., Elliman, N. A., & O'Dell, R. J. (1995). Mood and performance effects of caffeine in relation to acute and chronic caffeine deprivation. *Pharmacology, Biochemistry, and Behavior, 52,* 313-320.

Riechert, M., Lipowsky, G., Stöckl, H., & Stiegler, H. (1981). Pharmakokinetik von Theophyllin und Coffein bei Frühgeborenen mit Apnoen [Pharmacokinetics of theophylline and caffeine in premature infants with apnea]. *Monatsschrift für Kinderheilkunde, 129,* 697-702.

Ritchie, J. M. (1975). The xanthines. In L. S. Goodman & A. Gilman (Eds.), *Pharmacological basis of therapeutics* (pp. pp. 367-376). New York: Macmillan.

Ritter, E. J., Scott, W. J., & Bruce, L. M. (1982). Caffeine potentiation of hydroxyurea (HU) teratogenesis in the rat— Mechanistic studies. *Teratology, 25,* A70.

Rizzo, A. A., Stamps, L. E., & Fehr, L. A. (1988). Effects of caffeine withdrawal on motor performance and heart rate changes. *International Journal of Psychophysiology, 6,* 9-14.

Roache, J. D., & Griffiths, R. R. (1987). Interactions of diazepam and caffeine: Behavioral and subjective dose effects in humans. *Pharmacology, Biochemistry, and Behavior, 26,* 801-812.

Robertson, D., Frölich, J. C., Carr, R. K., Watson, J. T., Hollifield, J. W., Shand, D. G., & Oates, J. A. (1978). Effects of caffeine on plasma renin activity, catecholamines, and blood pressure. *New England Journal of Medicine, 298,* 181-186.

Robertson, D., Wade, D., Workman, R., Woosley, R. L., & Oates, J. A. (1981). Tolerance to the humoral and hemodynamic effects of caffeine in man. *Journal of Clinical Investigation, 67,* 1111-1117.

Rodvold, K. A., & Piscitelli, S. C. (1993). New oral macrolide and fluoroquinolone antibiotics: An overview of pharmacokinetics, interactions, and safety. *Clinical Infectious Diseases, 17*(Suppl. 1), S192-S199.

Roeckel, I. E. (1983). Brief correspondence. *New England Journal of Medicine, 309,* 1248.

Rogers, P. J., & Richardson, N. J. (1993). Why do we like drinks that contain caffeine? *Trends in Food Science and Technology, 4,* 108-111.

Rogers, P. J., Richardson, N. J., & Elliman, N. A. (1995). Overnight caffeine abstinence and negative reinforcement of preference for caffeine-containing drinks. *Psychopharmacology, 120,* 457-462.

Rohan, T. E., & McMichael, A. J. (1988). Methylxanthines and breast cancer. *International Journal of Cancer, 41,* 390-393.

Romano, C., Sulotto, F., Piolatto, G., Ciacco, C., Capellaro, E., Falagiani, P., Constable, D. W., Verga, A., & Scansetti, G. (1995). Factors related to the development of sensitization to green coffee and castor bean allergens among coffee workers. *Clinical and Experimental Allergy, 25,* 643-650.

Rose, J. E., & Behm, F. M. (1991). Psychophysiological interactions between caffeine and nicotine. *Pharmacology, Biochemistry, and Behavior, 38,* 333-337.

Rosenberg, L., Miller, D. R., Helmrich, S. P., Kaufman, D. W., Schottenfeld, D., Stolley, P. D., & Shapiro, S. (1985). Breast cancer and the consumption of coffee. *American Journal of Epidemiology, 122,* 391-399.

Rosenberg, L., Mitchell, A. A., Shapiro, S., & Slone, D. (1982). Selected birth defects in relation to caffeine-containing beverages. *Journal of the American Medical Association, 247,* 1429-1432.

Rosenberg, L., Palmer, J. R., Kelly, J. P., Kaufman, D. W., & Shapiro, S. (1988). Coffee drinking and nonfatal myocardial infarction in men under 55 years of age. *American Journal of Epidemiology, 128,* 570-578.

Rosenberg, L., Slone, D., Shapiro, S., Kaufman, D. W., & Miettinen, O. S. (1981). Case-control studies on the acute effects of coffee upon the risk of myocardial infarction: Problems in the selection of a hospital control series. *American Journal of Epidemiology, 113,* 646-652.

Rosenberg, L., Werler, M. M., Kaufman, D. W., & Shapiro, S. (1987). Coffee drinking and myocardial infarction in young women: An update. *American Journal of Epidemiology, 126,* 147-149.

Rosenquist, P. B., McCall, W. V., Farah, A., & Reboussin, D. M. (1994). Effects of caffeine pretreatment on measures of seizure impact. *Convulsive Therapy, 10,* 181-185.

Rosenthal, L., Roehrs, T., Zwyghuizen-Doorenbos, A., Plath, D., & Roth, T. (1991). Alerting effects of caffeine after normal and restricted sleep. *Neuropsychopharmacology, 4,* 103-108.

Rosmarin, P. C., Applegate, W. B., & Somes, G. W. (1990). Coffee consumption and serum lipids: A randomized, crossover clinical trial. *American Journal of Medicine, 88,* 349-356.

Rowland, D., & Mace, J. (1976). Caffeine poisoning in childhood. *Western Journal of Medicine, 124,* 52-53.

Rush, C. R., Higgins, S. T., Bickel, W. K., & Hughes, J. R. (1994). Acute behavioral effects of lorazepam and caffeine, alone and in combination, in humans. *Behavioral Pharmacology, 5,* 245-254.

Rush, C. R., Higgins, S. T., Hughes, J. R., & Bickel, W. K. (1994). Acute behavioral effects of triazolam and caffeine, alone and in combination, in humans. *Experimental and Clinical Pharmacology, 2,* 211-222.

Ruzich, J. V., Gill, H., Wein, A. J., Van Arsdelen, K., Hypolite, J., & Levin, R. M. (1987). Objective assessment of the effect of caffeine on sperm motility and velocity. *Fertility and Sterility, 48,* 891-893.

Ryall, J. E. (1984). Caffeine and ephidrine fatality. *Bulletin of the International Association of Forensic Toxicology, 17,* 13-14.

Sadzuka, Y., Mochizuki, E., & Takino, Y. (1993). Caffeine modulates the antitumor activity and toxic side effects of adriamycin. *Japanese Journal of Cancer Research, 84,* 348-353.

Sadzuka, Y., Mochizuki, E., & Takino, Y. (1995). Mechanism of caffeine modulation of the antitumor activity of adriamycin. *Toxicology Letters, 75,* 39-49.

Salvaggio, A., Periti, M., Miano, L., & Zambelli, C. (1990). Association between habitual coffee consumption and blood pressure levels. *Journal of Hypertension, 8,* 585-590.

Salvaggio, A., Periti, M., Quaglia, G., Marzorati, D., & Tavanelli, M. (1992). The independent effect of habitual cigarette and coffee consumption on blood pressure. *European Journal of Epidemiology, 8,* 776-782.

Samuels, B., & Glantz, S. A. (1991). The politics of local tobacco control. *Journal of the American Medical Association, 266,* 2110-2117.

Sanders, T. A., & Sandaradura, S. (1992). The cholesterol-raising effect of coffee in the Syrian hamster. *British Journal of Nutrition, 68,* 431-434.

Sanguigni, V., Gallu, M., Ruffini, M. P., & Strano, A. (1995). Effects of coffee on serum cholesterol and lipoproteins: The Italian brewing method (Italian Group for the Study of Atherosclerosis and Dismetabolic Diseases, Rome II Center). *European Journal of Epidemiology, 11,* 75-78.

Sansone, M., Battaglia, M., & Castellano, C. (1994). Effect of caffeine and nicotine on avoidance learning in mice: Lack of interaction. *Journal of Pharmacy and Pharmacology, 46,* 765-767.

Sasaki, H., Maeda, J., Usui, S., & Ishiko, T. (1987). Effect of sucrose and caffeine ingestion on performance of prolonged strenuous running. *International Journal of Sports Medicine, 8,* 261-265.

Sawynok, J., & Yaksh, T. L. (1993). Caffeine as an analgesic adjuvant: A review of pharmacology and mechanisms of action. *Pharmacological Reviews, 45,* 43-85.

Scanlon, J. E., Chin, K. C., Morgan, M. E., Durbin, G. M., Hale, K. A., & Brown, S. S. (1992). Caffeine or theophylline for neonatal apnoea? *Archives of Disease in Childhood, 67,* 425-428.

Schaafsma, G. (1992). The scientific basis of recommended dietary allowances for calcium. *Journal of International Medicine, 231,* 187-194.

Schaafsma, G., van Beresteyn, E. C. H., Raymakers, J. A., & Duursma, S. A. (1987). *Nutritional aspects of osteoporosis.* Basel: Karger.

Schackenberg, R. (1973). Caffeine as a substitute for schedule II stimulants in hyperkinetic children. *American Journal of Psychiatry, 130,* 796-798.

Schachtel, B. P., Fillingim, J. M., Lane, A. C., Thoden, W. R., & Baybutt, R. I. (1991). Caffeine as an analgesic adjuvant: A double-blind study comparing aspirin with caffeine to aspirin and placebo in patients with sore throat. *Archives of Internal Medicine, 151,* 733-737.

Schairer, C., Brinton, L. A., & Hoover, R. N. (1987). Methylxanthines and breast cancer. *International Journal of Cancer, 40,* 469-473.

Schiffman, S. S., Diaz, C., & Beeker, T. G. (1986). Caffeine intensifies taste of certain sweeteners: Role of adenosine receptor. *Pharmacology, Biochemistry, and Behavior, 24,* 429-432.

Schiffman, S. S., & Warwick, Z. S. (1989). *Use of flavor-amplified foods to improve nutritional status in elderly persons.* New York: The New York Academy of Sciences.

Schilling, W. (1921). The effect of caffeine and acetanilid on simple reaction time. *Psychological Review, 28,* 72-79.

Schreiber, G. B., Maffeo, C. E., Robins, M., Masters, M. N., & Bond, A. P. (1988). Measurement of coffee and caffeine intake: Implications for epidemiologic research. *Preventive Medicine, 17,* 280-294.

Schreiber, G. B., Robins, M., Maffeo, C. E., Masters, M. N., Bond, A. P., & Morganstein, D. (1988). Confounders contributing to the reported associations of coffee or caffeine with disease. *Preventive Medicine, 17,* 295-309.

Schwartz, J., & Weiss, S. T. (1992). Caffeine intake and asthma symptoms. *Annals of Epidemiology, 2,* 627-635.

Schwarz, B., Bischof, H. P., & Kunze, M. (1994). Coffee, tea, and lifestyle. *Preventive Medicine, 23,* 377-384.

Scott, L., & Smith, S. (1995). Human sperm motility-enhancing agents have detrimental effects on mouse oocytes and embryos. *Fertility and Sterility, 63,* 166-175.

Scott, N. R., Stambuk, D., Chakraborty, J., Marks, V., & Morgan, M. Y. (1988). Caffeine clearance and biotransformation in patients with chronic liver disease. *Clinical Science, 74,* 377-384.

Scott, N. R., Stambuk, D., Chakraborty, J., Marks, V., & Morgan, M. Y. (1989). The pharmacokinetics of caffeine and its dimethylxanthine metabolites in patients with chronic liver disease. *British Journal of Clinical Pharmacology, 27,* 205-213.

Searle, G. F. (1994). The effect of dietary caffeine manipulation on blood caffeine, sleep, and disturbed behavior. *Journal of Intellectual Disability Research, 38,* 383-391.

Seashore, R. H., & Ivy, A. C. (1953). The effects of analeptic drugs in relieving fatigue. *Psychological Monographs: General and Applied, 67,* 1-16.

Sechzer, P. H. (1979). Post spinal anesthesia headache treated with caffeine: Part II. Intracranial vascular distension, a key factor. *Current Therapeutic Research, 26,* 440-448.

Sechzer, P. H., & Abel, L. (1978). Post-spinal anesthesia headache treated with caffeine: Evaluation with demand method, Part I. *Current Therapeutic Research, 24,* 307-312.

Seger, D., & Schwartz, G. (1994). Chloral hydrate: A dangerous sedative for overdose patients? *Pediatric Emergency Care, 10,* 349-350.

Setchell, K. D. R., Welsh, M. B., Klooster, M. J., & Balistrerei, W. F. (1987). Rapid high-performance liquid chromatography assay for salivary and serum caffeine following an oral load. *Journal of Chromatography, 385,* 267-274.

Severson, R. K., Davis, S., & Polissar, L. (1982). Smoking, coffee, and cancer of the pancreas. *British Medical Journal, 285,* 214.

Shapira, B., Lerer, B., Gilboa, D., Drexler, H., Kugelmass, S., & Calev, A. (1987). Facilitation of ECT by caffeine pretreatment. *American Journal of Psychiatry, 144,* 1199-1202.

Shaul, P. W., Farrell, M. K., & Maloney, M. J. (1984). Caffeine toxicity as a cause of acute psychosis in anorexia nervosa. *Journal of Pediatrics, 105,* 493-495.

Shedlofsky, S. (1981). Coffee and cancer of the pancreas. *New England Journal of Medicine, 304,* 1604.

Shekelle, R. B., Gale, M., Paul, O. F., & Stamler, J. (1983). Coffee and cholesterol [Letter to the editor]. *New England Journal of Medicine, 309,* 1249-1250.

Shekelle, R. B., Shryock, A. M., Paul, O., Lepper, M., Stamler, J., Liu, S., & Raynor, W. J. (1981). Diet serum cholesterol and death from coronary heart disease: The Western Electric Study. *New England Journal of Medicine, 304,* 65-70.

Shen, W., & D'Souza, T. (1979). Cola-induced psychotic organic brain syndrome. *Rocky Mountain Medical Journal, 76,* 312-313.

Shi, D., Nikodijevic, O., Jacobson, K. A., & Daly, J. W. (1993). Chronic caffeine alters the density of adenosine, adrenergic, cholinergic, GABA, and serotonin receptors and calcium channels in mouse brain. *Cellular and Molecular Neurobiology, 13,* 247-261.

Shi, J., Benowitz, N. L., Denaro, C. P., & Sheiner, L. B. (1993). Pharmacokinetic-pharmacodynamic modeling of caffeine: Tolerance to pressor effects. *Clinical Pharmacology and Therapeutics, 53,* 6-14.

Shi, S. T., Wang, Z. Y., Smith, T. J., Hong, J. Y., Chen, W. F., Ho, C. T., & Yang, C. S. (1994). Effects of green tea and black tea on 4-(methylnitrosamino)-1-(3-pyridyl)-1-butanone bioactivation, DNA methylation, and lung tumorigenesis in A/J mice. *Cancer Research, 54,* 4641-4647.

Shibata, A., Mack, T. M., Paganini-Hill, A., Ross, R. K., & Henderson, B. E. (1994). A prospective study of pancreatic cancer in the elderly. *International Journal of Cancer, 58,* 46-49.

Shiono, P. H., & Klebanoff, M. A. (1993). Invited commentary: Caffeine and birth outcomes. *American Journal of Epidemiology, 137,* 951-954.

Shirai, T., Sato, A., & Hara, Y. (1994). Epigallocatechin gallate: The major causative agent of green tea-induced asthma. *Chest, 106,* 1801-1805.

Shiraki, M., Hara, Y., Osawa, T., Kumon, H., Nakayama, T., & Kawakishi, S. (1994). Antioxidative and antimutagenic effects of theaflavins from black tea. *Mutation Research, 323,* 29-34.

Shirlow, M. J., Berry, G., & Stokes, G. (1988). Caffeine consumption and blood pressure: An epidemiological study. *International Journal of Epidemiology, 17,* 90-97.

Shirlow, M. J., & Mathers, C. D. (1985). A study of caffeine consumption and symptoms: Indigestion, palpitations, headache, and insomnia. *International Journal of Epidemiology, 14,* 239-248.

Shisslak, C. M., Beutler, L. E., Scheiber, S., Gaines, J. A., La Wall, J., & Crago, M. (1985). Patterns of caffeine use and prescribed medications in psychiatric inpatients. *Psychological Reports, 57,* 39-42.

Shomer, N. H., Mickelson, J. R., & Louis, C. F. (1994). Caffeine stimulation of malignant hyperthermia-susceptible sarcoplasmic reticulum Ca2 + release channel. *American Journal of Physiology, 267,* C1253-C1261.

Shu, X. O., Hatch, M. C., Mills, J., Clemens, J., & Susser, M. (1995). Maternal smoking, alcohol drinking, caffeine consumption, and fetal growth: Results from a prospective study. *Epidemiology, 6,* 115-120.

Silverman, D. T., Hoover, R. N., Swanson, G. M., & Hartge, P. (1983). The prevalence of coffee drinking among hospitalized and population-based control groups. *Journal of the American Medical Association, 249,* 1877-1880.

Silverman, K., Evans, S. M., Strain, E. C., & Griffiths, R. R. (1992). Withdrawal syndrome after the double-blind cessation of caffeine consumption. *New England Journal of Medicine, 327,* 1109-1114.

Silverman, K., & Griffiths, R. R. (1992). Low-dose caffeine discrimination and self-reported mood effects in normal volunteers. *Journal of the Experimental Analysis of Behavior, 57,* 91-107.

Silverman, K., Mumford, G. K., & Griffiths, R. R. (1994). Enhancing caffeine reinforcement by behavioral requirements following drug ingestion. *Psychopharmacology, 114,* 424-432.

Sinton, C. M., & Petitjean, F. (1989). The influence of chronic caffeine administration on sleep parameters in the cat. *Pharmacology, Biochemistry, and Behavior, 32,* 459-462.

Skinner, B. F., & Heron, W. T. (1937). Effects of caffeine and benzedrine upon conditioning and extinction. *Psychological Record, 1,* 340-346.

Slattery, M. L., West, D. W., Robison, L. M., French, T. K., Ford, M. H., Schuman, K. L., & Sorenson, A. W. (1990). Tobacco, alcohol, coffee, and caffeine as risk factors for colon cancer in a low-risk population. *Epidemiology, 1,* 141-145.

Smith, A. P. (1995). Caffeine and psychomotor performance: A reply to James [letter to the editor]. *Addiction, 90,* 1261-1265.

Smith, A. P., Brockman, P., Flynn, R., Maben, A. L., & Thomas, M. (1993). Investigation of the effects of coffee on alertness and performance and mood during the day and night. *Neuropsychobiology, 27,* 217-223.

Smith, A. P., Kendrick, A. M., & Maben, A. L. (1992). Effects of breakfast and caffeine on performance and mood in the late morning and after lunch. *Neuropsychobiology, 26,* 198-204.

Smith, A. P., Kendrick, A., Maben, A., & Salmon, J. (1994). Effects of breakfast and caffeine on cognitive performance, mood, and cardiovascular functioning. *Appetite, 22,* 39-55.

Smith, A. P., Maben, A., & Brockman, P. (1993). The effects of caffeine and evening meals on sleep and performance, mood, and cardiovascular functioning the following day. *Journal of Psychopharmacology, 7,* 203-206.

Smith, A. P., Maben, A., & Brockman, P. (1994). Effects of evening meals and caffeine on cognitive performance, mood, and cardiovascular functioning. *Appetite, 22,* 57-65.

Smith, A. P., Rusted, J. M., Eaton-Williams, P., Savory, M., & Leathwood, P. (1990). Effects of caffeine given before and after lunch on sustained attention. *Neuropsychobiology, 23,* 160-163.

Smith, A. P., Rusted, J. M., Savory, M., Eaton-Williams, P., & Hall, S. R. (1991). The effects of caffeine, impulsivity, and time of day on performance, mood, and cardiovascular function. *Journal of Psychopharmacology, 5,* 120-128.

Smith, B. D., Davidson, R. A., & Green, R. L. (1993). Effects of caffeine and gender on physiology and performance: Further tests of a biobehavioral model. *Physiology and Behavior, 54,* 415-422.

Smith, D. L., Tong, J. E., & Leigh, G. (1977). Combined effects of tobacco and caffeine on the components of choice reaction-time, heart rate, and hand steadiness. *Perceptual and Motor Skills, 45,* 635-639.

Smith, R. (1987). Caffeine withdrawal headache. *Journal of Clinical Pharmacy and Therapeutics, 12,* 53-57.

Smith, S. E., McElhatton, P. R., & Sullivan, F. M. (1987). Effects of administering caffeine to pregnant rats either as a single daily dose or as divided doses four times a day. *Food and Chemical Toxicology, 25,* 125-133.

Smith, S. J., Deacon, J. M., & Chilvers, C. E. (1994). Alcohol, smoking, passive smoking, and caffeine in relation to breast cancer risk in young women (UK National Case-Control Study Group). *British Journal of Cancer, 70,* 112-119.

Smits, P., Boekema, P., De Abreu, R., Thien, T., & van't Laar, A. (1987). Evidence for an antagonism between caffeine and adenosine in the human cardiovascular system. *Journal of Cardiovascular Pharmacology, 10,* 136-143.

Smits, P., Hoffman, H., Thien, T., Houben, H., & van't Laar, A. (1983). Hemodynamic and humoral effects of coffee after β1-selective and no selective β-blockade. *Clinical Pharmacology and Therapeutics, 34,* 153-158.

Smits, P., Pieters, G., & Thien, T. (1986). The role of epeniphrine in the circulatory effects of coffee. *Clinical Pharmacology and Therapeutics, 40,* 431-437.

Smits, P., Schouten, J., & Thien, T. (1989). Cardiovascular effects of two xanthines and the relation to adenosine antagonism. *Clinical Pharmacology and Therapeutics, 45,* 593-599.

Smits, P., Temme, L., & Thien, T. (1993). The cardiovascular interaction between caffeine and nicotine in humans. *Clinical Pharmacology and Therapeutics, 54,* 194-204.

Smits, P., Thien, T., & van't Laar, A. (1985a). The cardiovascular effects of regular and decaffeinated coffee. *British Journal of Clinical Pharmacology, 19,* 852-854.

Smits, P., Thien, T., & van't Laar, A. (1985b). Circulatory effects of coffee in relation to the pharmacokinetics of caffeine. *American Journal of Cardiology, 56,* 958-963.

Snel, J. (1993). Coffee and caffeine: Sleep and wakefulness. In S. Garattini (Ed.), *Caffeine, coffee, and health* (pp. 255-290). New York: Raven Press.

Snowdon, D. A., & Phillips, R. L. (1984). Coffee consumption and risk of fatal cancers. *American Journal of Public Health, 74,* 820-823.

Snyder, S. H., & Sklar, P. (1984). Behavioral and molecular actions of caffeine: Focus on adenosine. *Journal of Psychiatric Research, 18,* 91-106.

Soeken, K. L., & Bausell, R. B. (1989). Alcohol use and its relationship to other addictive and preventive behaviors. *Addictive Behaviors, 14,* 459-464.

Somani, S. M., & Gupta, P. (1988). Caffeine: A new look at an age-old drug. *International Journal of Clinical Pharmacology, Therapy, and Toxicology, 26,* 521-533.

Somani, S. M., Khanna, N. N., & Bada, H. S. (1980). Caffeine and theophylline: Serum/CSF correlation in premature infants. *Journal of Pediatrics, 96,* 1091-1093.

Soto, J., Sacristan, J. A., & Alsar, M. J. (1994). Cerebrospinal fluid concentrations of caffeine following oral drug administration: Correlation with salivary and plasma concentrations. *Therapeutic Drug Monitoring, 16,* 108-110.

Sours, J. A. (1983). Case reports of anorexia nervosa and caffeinism. *American Journal of Psychiatry, 140,* 235-236.

Spielman, W. S., & Thompson, C. I. (1982). A proposed role for adenosine in the regulation of renal hemodynamics and renin release. *American Journal of Physiology, 242,* F423.

Spiller, M. A. (1984). *The chemical components of coffee.* New York: Liss.

Spindel, E. (1984). *Action of the methylxanthines on the pituitary and pituitary-dependent hormones.* New York: Alan R. Liss.

Spindel, E. R., Wurtman, R. J., McCall, A., Carr, D., Conlay, L., Griffith, L., & Arnold, M. A. (1984). Neuroendocrine effects of caffeine in normal subjects. *Clinical Pharmacology and Therapeutics, 36,* 402-407.

Spinillo, A., Capuzzo, E., Nicola, S. E., Colonna, L., Egbe, T. O., & Zara, C. (1994). Factors potentiating the smoking-related risk of fetal growth retardation. *British Journal of Obstetrics and Gynaecology, 101,* 954-958.

Spriet, L., MacLean, D. A., Dyck, D. J., Hultman, E., Cederblad, G., & Graham, T. E. (1992). Caffeine ingestion and muscle metabolism during prolonged exercise in humans. *American Journal of Physiology, 262*(6, Pt. 1), E891-E898.

Srisuphan, W., & Bracken, M. B. (1986). Caffeine consumption during pregnancy and association with late spontaneous abortion. *American Journal of Obstetrics and Gynecology, 154,* 14-20.

Stachecki, J. J., Ginsburg, K. A., & Armant, D. R. (1994). Stimulation of cryopreserved epididymal spermatozoa of the domestic cat using the motility stimulants caffeine, pentoxifylline, and 2'-deoxyadenosine. *Journal of Andrology, 15,* 157-164.

Stamler, J. S., Goldman, M. E., Gomes, J., Matza, D., & Horowitz, S. F. (1992). The effect of stress and fatigue on cardiac rhythm in medical interns. *Journal of Electrocardiology, 25,* 333-338.

Stanton, M. F., Ahrens, R. A., & Douglas, L. W. (1978). Coffee and cola beverage consumption as heart disease risk factors in man. *Experientia, 34,* 1182-1183.

Statland, B. E., & Demas, T. J. (1980). Serum caffeine half-lives—healthy subjects vs. patients having alcoholic hepatic disease. *American Journal of Clinical Pathology, 73,* 390-393.

Stavchansky, S., Combs, A., Sagraves, R., Delgado, M., & Joshi, A. (1988). Pharmacokinetics of caffeine in breast milk and plasma after single oral administration of caffeine to lactating mothers. *Biopharmaceutics and Drug Disposition, 9,* 285-299.

Stavric, B. (1988a). Methylxanthines: Toxicity to humans: 2. Caffeine. *Food and Chemical Toxicology, 26,* 645-662.

Stavric, B. (1988b). Methylxanthines: Toxicity to humans: 3. Theobromine, paraxanthine, and the combined effects of methylxanthines. *Food and Chemical Toxicology, 26,* 725-733.

Stavric, B., Klassen, R., Watkinson, B., Karpinski, K., Stapley, R., & Fried, P. (1988). Variability in caffeine consumption from coffee and tea: Possible significance for epidemiological studies. *Food and Chemical Toxicology, 26,* 111-118.

Stein, M. B., & Uhde, T. W. (1989). Depersonalization disorder: Effects of caffeine and response to pharmacotherapy. *Biological Psychiatry, 26,* 315-320.

Stein, Z., & Susser, M. (1991). Miscarriage, caffeine, and the epiphenomena of pregnancy: The causal model. *Epidemiology, 2,* 163-167.

Steinke, J. (1973). Coffee drinking and acute myocardial infarction. *Lancet, 1,* 258.

Stensvold, I., & Jacobsen, B. K. (1994). Coffee and cancer: A prospective study of 43,000 Norwegian men and women. *Cancer Causes and Control, 5,* 401-408.

Stensvold, I., Tverdal, A., & Foss, O. P. (1989). The effect of coffee on blood lipids and blood pressure: Results from a Norwegian cross-sectional study, men and women, 40-42 years. *Journal of Clinical Epidemiology, 42,* 877-884.

Stensvold, I., Tverdal, A., Solvoll, K., & Foss, O. P. (1992). Tea consumption: Relationship to cholesterol, blood pressure, and coronary and total mortality. *Preventive Medicine, 22,* 546-553.

Stepanski, E., Faber, M., Zorick, F., Basner, R., & Roth, T. (1995). Sleep disorders in patients on continuous ambulatory peritoneal dialysis. *Journal of the American Society of Nephrology, 6,* 192-197.

Stern, K. N., Chait, L. D., & Johanson, C. E. (1989). Reinforcing and subjective effects of caffeine in normal human volunteers. *Psychopharmacology, 98,* 81-88.

Stillner, V., Popkin, M. K., & Pierce, C. M. (1978). Caffeine-induced delirium during prolonged competitive stress. *American Journal of Psychiatry, 135,* 855-856.

Stocks, P. (1970). Cancer mortality in relation to national consumption of cigarettes, solid fuel, tea, and coffee. *British Journal of Cancer, 24,* 215-225.

Strain, E. C., Mumford, G. K., Silverman, K., & Griffiths, R. R. (1994). Caffeine dependence syndrome: Evidence from case histories and experimental evaluations. *Journal of the American Medical Association, 272,* 1043-1048.

Streissguth, A., Martin, D. C., Barr, H. M., & Sandman, B. (1984). Intrauterine alcohol and nicotine exposure: Attention and reaction time in 4-year old children. *Developmental Psychology, 20,* 533-541.

Streissguth, A. P., Barr, H. M., Martin, D. C., & Herman, C. S. (1980). Effects of maternal alcohol, nicotine, and caffeine use during pregnancy on infant mental and motor development at eight months. *Alcoholism: Clinical and Experimental Research, 4,* 152-164.

Strickland, T. L., Myers, H. F., & Lahey, B. B. (1989). Cardiovascular reactivity with caffeine and stress in black and white normotensive females. *Psychosomatic Medicine, 51,* 381-389.

Sullivan, J. L. (1977). Caffeine poisoning in an infant. *Journal of Pediatrics, 90,* 1022-1023.

Sung, B. H., Lovallo, W. R., Pincomb, G. A., & Wilson, M. F. (1990). Effects of caffeine on blood pressure response during exercise in normotensive healthy young men. *American Journal of Cardiology, 65,* 909-913.

Sung, B. H., Whitsett, T. L., Lovallo, W. R., al'Absi, M., Pincomb, G. A., & Wilson, M. F. (1994). Prolonged increase in blood pressure by a single oral dose of caffeine in mildly hypertensive men. *American Journal of Hypertension, 7,* 755-758.

Superko, H. R., Bortz, W. J., Williams, P. T., Albers, J. J., & Wood, P. D. (1991). Caffeinated and decaffeinated coffee effects on plasma lipoprotein cholesterol, apolipoproteins, and lipase activity: A controlled, randomized trial. *American Journal of Clinical Nutrition, 54,* 599-605.

Superko, H. R., Myll, J., DiRicco, C., Williams, P. T., Bortz, W. M., & Wood, P. D. (1994). Effects of cessation of caffeinated-coffee consumption on ambulatory and resting blood pressure in men. *American Journal of Cardiology, 73,* 780-784.

Sutherland, D. J., McPherson, D. D., Renton, K. W., Spencer, C. A., & Montague, T. J. (1985). The effect of caffeine on cardiac rate, rhythm, and ventricular repolarization. *Chest, 87,* 319-324.

Svensson, E., Persson, L.-O., & Sjöberg, L. (1980). Mood effect of diazepam and caffeine. *Psychopharmacology, 67,* 73-80.

Takayama, S., & Kuwabara, N. (1982). Long-term study on the effect of caffeine in Wistar rats. *Gann, 73,* 365-371.

Takayama, S., Nagao, M., Suwa, Y., & Sugimura, T. (1984). *Long-term carcinogenicity studies on caffeine, instant coffee, and methylglyoxal in rats.* New York: Cold Spring Harbor Laboratory.

Tarnopolsky, M. A. (1993). Protein, caffeine, and sports. *Physician and Sportsmedicine, 21,* 137-149.in

Tarnopolsky, M. A., Atkinson, S. A., MacDougall, J. D., Sale, D. G., & Sutton, R. J. (1989). Physiological responses to caffeine during endurance running habitual caffeine users. *Medicine and Science in Sports and Exercise, 21,* 418-424.

Tarrus, E., Cami, J., Roberts, D. J., Spickett, R. G. W., Celdran, E., & Segura, J. (1987). Accumulation of caffeine in healthy volunteers treated with furafylline. *British Journal of Clinical Pharmacology, 23,* 9-18.

Tassaneeyakul, W., Birkett, D. J., McManus, M. E., Tassaneeyakul, W., Veronese, M. E., Andersson, T., Tukey, R. H., & Miners, J. O. (1994). Caffeine metabolism by human hepatic cytochromes P450: Contributions of 1A2, 2E1 and 3A isoforms. *Biochemical Pharmacology, 47,* 1767-1776.

Tavani, A., Negri, E., Franceschi, S., Talamini, R., & La Vecchia, C. (1994). Coffee consumption and risk of non-Hodgkin's lymphoma. *European Journal of Cancer Prevention, 3,* 351-356.

Tavani, A., Negri, E., & La Vecchia, A. (1995). Coffee intake and risk of hip fracture in women in northern Italy. *Preventive Medicine, 24,* 396-400.

Terada, M., & Nishimura, H. (1975). Mitigation of caffeine-induced teratogenicity in mice by prior chronic caffeine ingestion. *Teratology, 12,* 79-82.

Terry, W. S., & Phifer, B. (1986). Caffeine and memory performance on the AVLT. *Journal of Clinical Psychology, 42,* 860-863.

Thayer, P., & Palm, P. (1975). A current assessment of mutagenic and teratogenic effects of caffeine. *CRC Critical Reviews in Toxicology, 5,* 345-380.

Thayer, P. S., & Kensler, C. J. (1973). Exposure of four generations of mice to caffeine in drinking water. *Toxicology and Applied Pharmacology, 25,* 169-179.

Thelle, D. S. (1988). Coffee, alcohol, and coronary risk factors. *Sozial und Preventivmedizin, 33,* 223-225.

Thelle, D. S. (1988). Coffee, alcohol, and coronary risk factors. *Sozial-und Praventiumedizih, 33,* 223-225.

Thelle, D. S., Arnesen, E., & Førde, O. H. (1983a). Coffee and cholesterol [Letter to the editor]. *New England Journal of Medicine, 309,* 1250.

Thelle, D. S., Arnesen, E., & Førde, O. H. (1983b). The Tromsø heart study: Does coffee raise serum cholesterol? *New England Journal of Medicine, 308,* 1454-1457.

Thomas, D. B. (1988). Neonatal abstinence syndrome [Letter to the editor]. *Medical Journal of Australia, 148,* 598.

Thomas, R. B., Luber, S. A., & Smith, J. A. (1977). A survey of alcohol and drug use in medical students. *Diseases of the Nervous System, 38,* 41-43.

Thornton, G. R., Holck, H. G. O., & Smith, E. L. (1939). The effect of benzedrine and caffeine upon performance in certain psychomotor tasks. *Journal of Abnormal Psychology, 34,* 96-113.

Timson, J. (1977). Caffeine. *Mutation Research, 47,* 1-52.

Tola, M. R., Granieri, E., Malagu, S., Caniatti, L., Casetta, I., Govoni, V., Paolino, E., Cinzia-Monetti, V., Canducci, E., & Panatta, G. B. (1994). Dietary habits and multiple sclerosis: A retrospective study in Ferrara, Italy. *Acta Neurologica Napoli, 16,* 189-197.

Tomita, K., & Tsuchiya, H. (1989). Caffeine enhancement of the effect of anticancer agents on human sarcoma cells. *Japanese Journal of Cancer Research, 80,* 83-88.

Tondo, L., & Rudas, N. (1991). The course of a seasonal bipolar disorder influenced by caffeine. *Journal of Affective Disorders, 22,* 249-251.

Tonkin, A. L. (1995). Postural hypotension. *Medical Journal of Australia, 162,* 436-438.

Toubro, S., Astrup, A., Breum, L., & Quaade, F. (1993a). The acute and chronic effects of ephedrine/caffeine mixtures on energy expenditure and glucose metabolism in humans. *International Journal of Obesity and Related Metabolic Disorders, 17*(Suppl. 3), S73-S77.

Toubro, S., Astrup, A. V., Breum, L., & Quaade, F. (1993b). Safety and efficacy of long-term treatment with ephedrine, caffeine, and an ephedrine/caffeine mixture. *International Journal of Obesity and Related Metabolic Disorders, 17*(Suppl. 1), S69-S72.

Touitou, E., Junginger, H. E., Weiner, N. D., Nagai, T., & Mezei, M. (1994). Liposomes as carriers for topical and transdermal delivery. *Journal of Pharmaceutical Sciences, 83,* 1189-1203.

Traub, A. I., Earnshaw, J. C., Branniga, P. D., & Thompson, W. (1982). A critical assessment of the response to caffeine of human-sperm motility. *Fertility and Sterility, 37,* 436-437.

Trichopoulos, D., Papapostolou, M., & Polychronopoulou, A. (1981). Coffee and ovarian cancer. *International Journal of Cancer, 28,* 691-693.

Trichopoulos, D., Tzonou, A., Polychronopoulou, A., & Day, N. E. (1984). *A case-control investigation of a possible association between coffee consumption and ovarian cancer in Greece.* New York: Cold Spring Harbor Laboratory.

Troyer, R. J., & Markle, G. E. (1984). Coffee drinking: An emerging social problem? *Social Problems, 31,* 403-416.

Turmen, T., Davis, J., & Aranda, J. V. (1981). Relationship of dose and plasma concentrations of caffeine and ventilation in neonatal apnea. *Seminars in Perinatology, 5,* 326.

Turner, J. E., & Cravey, R. H. (1977). A fatal ingestion of caffeine. *Clinical Toxicology, 10,* 341-344.

Tye, K., Pollard, I., Karlsson, L., Scheibner, V., & Tye, G. (1993). Caffeine exposure in utero increases the incidence of apnea in adult rats. *Reproductive Toxicology, 7,* 449-452.

Tzonou, A., Day, N. E., Trichopoulos, D., Walker, A., Saliaraki, M., Papapostolou, M., & Polychronopoulou, A. (1984). The epidemiology of ovarian cancer in Greece: A case control study. *European Journal of Cancer and Clinical Oncology, 20,* 1045-1052.

Uematsu, T., Mizuno, A., Itaya, T., Suzuki, Y., Kanamaru, M., & Nakashima, M. (1987). Psychomotor performance tests using a microcomputer: Evaluation of effects of caffeine and chlorpheniramine in healthy human subjects. *Japanese Journal of Psychopharmacology, 4,* 427-432.

Uhde, T. W., Tancer, M. E., Black, B., & Brown, T. M. (1991). Phenomenology and neurobiology of social phobia: Comparison with panic disorder. *Journal of Clinical Psychiatry, 52,* 31-40.

Ullrich, D., Compagnone, D., Munch, B., Brandes, A., Hille, H., & Bircher, J. (1992). Urinary caffeine metabolites in man: Age-dependent changes and pattern in various clinical situations. *European Journal of Clinical Pharmacology, 43,* 167-172.

Ungemack, J. A. (1994). Patterns of personal health practice: Men and women in the United States. *American Journal of Preventive Medicine, 10,* 38-44.

Uragoda, C. G. (1988). Acute symptoms in coffee workers. *Journal of Tropical Medicine and Hygiene, 91,* 169-172.

Urgert, R., Schulz, A. G., & Katan, M. B. (1995). Effects of cafestol and kahweol from coffee grounds on serum lipids and serum liver enzymes in humans. *American Journal of Clinical Nutrition, 61,* 149-154.

U.S. Food and Drug Administration, Office of the Federal Register, National Archives, and Records Administration. (1995). *Title 21, Code of Federal Regulations, 170.22. Safety factors to be considered* (Title 21, Code of Federal Regulations, Parts 170 to 1995). Washington, DC: Government Printing Office.

Vainer, J. L., & Chouinard, G. (1994). Interaction between caffeine and clozapine [Letter to the editor]. *Journal of Clinical Psychopharmacology, 14,* 284-285.

van den Berg, B. J. (1977). *Epidemiologic observations of prematurity: Effects of tobacco, coffee, and alcohol.* Baltimore, MD: Urban and Schwarzenberg.

Van der Merwe, P. J., Müller, F. R., & Müller, F. O. (1988). Caffeine in sport: Urinary excretion of caffeine in healthy volunteers after intake of common caffeine-containing beverages. *South African Medical Journal, 74,* 163-164.

Van Deventer, G., Kamemoto, E., Kuznicki, J. T., Heckert, D. C., & Schulte, M. C. (1992). Lower esophageal sphincter pressure, acid secretion, and blood gastrin after coffee consumption. *Digestive Diseases and Sciences, 37,* 558-569.

van Dusseldorp, M., & Katan, M. B. (1990). Headache caused by caffeine withdrawal among moderate coffee drinkers switched from ordinary to decaffeinated coffee: A 12-week double-blind trial. *British Medical Journal, 300,* 1558-1559.

van Dusseldorp, M., Katan, M. B., & Demacker, P. N. M. (1990). Effect of decaffeinated versus regular coffee on serum lipoproteins. *American Journal of Epidemiology, 132,* 33-40.

van Dusseldorp, M., Katan, M. B., van Vliet, T., Demacker, O. N., & Stalenhoef, A. F. (1991). Cholesterol-raising factor from boiled coffee does not pass a paper filter. *Arteriosclerosis and Thrombosis, 11,* 586-593.

van Dusseldorp, M., Smits, P., Thien, T., & Katan, M. B. (1989). Effect of decaffeinated versus regular coffee on blood pressure: A 12-week, double-blind trial. *Hypertension, 14,* 563-569.

Van Soeren, M. H., Sathasivam, P., Spriet, L. L., & Graham, T. E. (1993). Caffeine metabolism and epinephrine responses during exercise in users and nonusers. *Journal of Applied Physiology, 75,* 805-812.

Van't Hoff, W. (1982). Caffeine in pregnancy. *Lancet, 2,* 1020.

Viani, R. (1988). *Physiologically active substances in coffee.* London: Elsevier Applied Science.

Victora, C. G., Muñoz, N., Day, N. E., Barcelos, L. B., Peccin, A., & Braga, N. M. (1987). Hot beverages and oesophageal cancer in southern Brazil: A case control study. *International Journal of Cancer, 39,* 710-716.

Virtanen, S. M., Rasanen, L., Aro, A., Ylonen, K., Lounamaa, R., Akerblom, H. K., & Tuomilehto, J. (1994). Is children's or parents' coffee or tea consumption associated with the risk for type 1 diabetes mellitus in children? (Childhood Diabetes in Finland Study Group). *European Journal of Clinical Nutrition, 48,* 279-285.

Viscoli, C. M., Lachs, M. S., & Horwitz, R. I. (1993). Bladder cancer and coffee drinking: A summary of case control research. *Lancet, 341,* 1432-1437.

Vistisen, K., Poulsen, H. E., & Loft, S. (1992). Foreign compound metabolism capacity in man measured from metabolites of dietary caffeine. *Carcinogenesis, 13,* 1561-1568.

Vogt, M. T., Cauley, J. A., Kuller, L. H., & Hulley, S. B. (1993). Prevalence and correlates of lower extremity arterial disease in elderly women. *American Journal of Epidemiology, 137,* 559-568.

von Borstel, R. W., & Wurtman, R. J. (1982). Caffeine withdrawal enhances sensitivity to physiologic level of adenosine in vivo. *Federation Proceedings, 41,* 1669.

von Borstel, R. W., Wurtman, R. J., & Conlay, L. A. (1983). Chronic caffeine consumption potentiates the hypotensive action of circulating adenosine. *Life Sciences, 32,* 1151-1158.

Wahrburg, U., Martin, H., Schulte, H., Walek, T., & Assmann, G. (1994). Effects of two kinds of decaffeinated coffee on serum lipid profiles in healthy young adults. *European Journal of Clinical Nutrition, 48,* 172-179.

Walker, S., Fine, A., & Kryger, M. H. (1995). Sleep complaints are common in a dialysis unit. *American Journal of Kidney Diseases, 26,* 751-756.

Walsh, I., Wasserman, G. S., Mestad, P., & Lanman, R. C. (1987). Near-fatal caffeine intoxication treated with peritoneal dialysis. *Pediatric Emergency Care, 3,* 244-249.

Walsh, J. K., Muelbach, M. J., Humm, T. M., Dickens, Q. S., & Sugerman, J. L. (1990). Effect of caffeine on physiological sleep tendency and ability to sustain wakefulness at night. *Psychopharmacology, 101,* 271-273.

Walther, H., Banditt, P., & Kohler, E. (1983). The relevance of caffeine levels assessed in serum, saliva, and urine—Noninvasive methods for a simultaneous determination of pharmacokinetic variables along with psychometric measurements. *Pharmacopsychiatria, 16,* 166.

Wang, Z. Y., Huang, M. T., Lou, Y. R., Xie, J. G., Reuhl, K. R., Newmark, H. L., Ho, C. T., Yang, C. S., & Conney, A. H. (1994). Inhibitory effects of black tea, green tea, decaffeinated black tea, and decaffeinated green tea on ultraviolet B light-induced skin carcinogenesis in 7,12-dimethylbenz[a]anthracene-initiated SKH-1 mice. *Cancer Research, 54,* 3428-3435.

Warburton, D. M. (1995). Effects of caffeine on cognition and mood without caffeine abstinence. *Psychopharmacology, 119,* 66-70.

Ward, N., Whitney, C., Avery, D., & Dunner, D. (1991). The analgesic effects of caffeine in headache. *Pain, 44,* 151-155.

Warner, K. E. (1991). Tobacco industry scientific advisors: Serving society or selling cigarettes? *American Journal of Public Health, 81,* 839-842.

Watkinson, B., & Fried, P. A. (1985). Maternal caffeine use before, during, and after pregnancy and effects upon offspring. *Neurobehavioral Toxicology and Teratology, 7,* 9-17.

Watt, A. H., Bayer, A., Routledge, P. A., & Swift, C. G. (1989). Adenosine-induced respiratory and heart rate changes in young and elderly adults. *British Journal of Clinical Pharmacology, 27,* 265-267.

Wayner, M. J., Jolicoeur, F. B., Rondeau, D. B., & Barone, F. C. (1976). Effects of acute and chronic administration of caffeine on schedule-dependent and schedule-induced behavior. *Pharmacology, Biochemistry, and Behavior, 5,* 343-348.

Weathersbee, P. S., & Lodge, J. R. (1977). Caffeine: Its direct and indirect influence on reproduction. *Journal of Reproductive Medicine, 19,* 55-63.

Weathersbee, P. S., Olsen, G. K., & Lodge, J. R. (1977). Caffeine and pregnancy: A retrospective survey. *Postgraduate Medicine, 62,* 64-69.

Webb, D., & Levine, T. E. (1978). Effects of caffeine on DRL performance in the mouse. *Pharmacology, Biochemistry, and Behavior, 9,* 7-10.

Weber, J. G., Ereth, M. H., & Danielson, D. R. (1993). Perioperative ingestion of caffeine and postoperative headache. *Mayo Clinic Proceedings, 368,* 842-845.

Weill, J., & Le-Bourhis, B. (1994). Factors predictive of alcohol consumption in a representative sample of French male teenagers: A five-year prospective study. *Drug and Alcohol Dependence, 35,* 45-50.

Weiss, B., & Laties, V. G. (1962). Enhancement of human performance by caffeine and the amphetamines. *Pharmacological Reviews, 14,* 1-36.

Welborn, L. G., de Soto, H., Hannallah, R. S., Fink, R., Ruttimann, U. E., & Boeckx, R. (1988). The use of caffeine in the control of post-anesthetic apnea in former premature infants. *Anesthesiology, 68,* 796-798.

Welborn, L. G., & Greenspun, J. C. (1994). Anesthesia and apnea: Perioperative considerations in the former preterm infant. *Pediatric Clinics of North America, 41,* 181-198.

Welsch, C. W., Scieszka, K. M., Senn, E. R., & DeHoog, J. V. (1983). Caffeine (1,2,3-trimethylxanthine), a temperate promotor of DMBA-induced rat mammary gland carcinogenesis. *International Journal of Cancer, 32,* 479-484.

Wendl, B., Pfeiffer, A., Pehl, C., Schmidt, T., & Kaess, H. (1994). Effect of decaffeination of coffee or tea on gastro-oesophageal reflux. *Alimentary Pharmacology and Therapeutics, 8,* 283-287.

Wennmalm, Å., & Wennmalm, M. (1989). Coffee, catecholamines, and cardiac arrhythmia. *Clinical Physiology, 9,* 201-206.

Wenzel, D. G., & Rutledge, C. O. (1962). Effects of centrally acting drugs on human motor and psychomotor performance. *Journal of Pharmaceutical Sciences, 51,* 631-644.

Weusten-Van der Wouw, M. P., Katan, M. B., Viani, R., Huggett, A. C., Liardon, R., Lund-Larsen, P. G., Thelle, D. S., Ahola, I., Aro, A., Meyboom, S., & Beynen, A. G. (1994). Identity of the cholesterol-raising factor from boiled coffee and its effects on liver function enzymes. *Journal of Lipid Research, 35,* 721-733.

Wharrad, J. J., Birmingham, A. T., MacDonald, I. A., Inch, P. J., & Mead, J. L. (1985). The influence of fasting and of caffeine intake on finger tremor. *European Journal of Clinical Pharmacology, 29,* 37-43.

Whitaker, L., & Kelleher, A. (1994). Raynaud's syndrome: Diagnosis and treatment. *Journal of Vascular Nursing, 12,* 10-13.

Whitsett, T. L., Manion, C. V., & Christensen, H. D. (1984). Cardiovascular effects of coffee and caffeine. *American Journal of Cardiology, 53,* 918-922.

218   UNDERSTANDING CAFFEINE

Whittemore, A. S., Paffenbarger, R. S., Jr., Anderson, K., & Halpern, J. (1983). Early precursors of pancreatic cancer in college men. *Journal of Chronic Diseases, 36,* 251.

Whittemore, A. S., Wu, M. L., Paffenbarger, R. S., Jr., Sarles, D. L., Kampert, J. B., Grosser, S., Jung, D. L., Ballon, S., & Hendrickson, M. (1988). Personal and environmental characteristics related to epithelial ovarian cancer: II. Exposures to talcum powder, tobacco, alcohol, and coffee. *American Journal of Epidemiology, 128,* 1228-1240.

Wilairatani, P., Looareeswan, S., Vanijanonta, S., Charoenlarp, P., & Wittayalertpanya, S. (1994). Hepatic metabolism in severe falciparum malaria: Caffeine clearance study. *Annals of Tropical Medicine and Parasitology, 8,* 13-19.

Wilcox, A., Weinberg, C., & Baird, D. (1988). Caffeinated beverages and decreased fertility. *Lancet, 2,* 1453-1456.

Williams, J. H., Barnes, W. S., & Gadberry, W. L. (1987). Influence of caffeine on force and EMG in rested and fatigued muscle. *American Journal of Physical Medicine, 66,* 169-183.

Williams, J. H., Signorile, J. F., Barnes, W. S., & Henrich, T. W. (1988). Caffeine, maximal power output, and fatigue. *British Journal of Sports Medicine, 22,* 132-134.

Williams, M. A., Mittendorf, R., Stubblefield, P. G., Lieberman, E., Schoenbaum, S. C., & Monson, R. R. (1992). Cigarettes, coffee, and preterm premature rupture of the membranes. *American Journal of Epidemiology, 135,* 895-903.

Williams, M. A., Monson, R. R., Goldman, M. B., & Mittendorf, R. (1990). Coffee and delayed conception. *Lancet, 335,* 1603.

Williams, M. H. (1992). Ergogenic and ergolytic substances. *Medicine and Science in Sports and Exercise, 24*(Suppl. 9), S344-S348.

Wilson, J. G., & Scott, W. J., Jr. (1984). *The teratogenic potential of caffeine in laboratory animals.* Berlin: Springer-Verlag.

Wilson, P. W., Garrison, R. J., Kannel, W. B., McGee, D. L., & Castelli, W. P. (1989). Is coffee consumption a contributor to cardiovascular disease? Insights from the Framingham Study. *Archives of Internal Medicine, 149,* 1169-1172.

Winstead, D. K. (1976). Coffee consumption among psychiatric inpatients. *American Journal of Psychiatry, 133,* 1447-1450.

Wrenn, K. D., & Oschner, I. (1989). Rhabdomyolysis induced by a caffeine overdose. *Annals of Emergency Medicine, 18,* 94-97.

Würl, P. (1994). Lebensgefährliche Coffeinintoxikation unter Verwendung von Kaffee als Rauchsmittel [Acute caffeine intoxication after ingestion of a potentially lethal amount of coffee. A case report]. *Wiener Klinische Wochenschrift, 106,* 359-361.

Würzner, H. P. (1988). *Animal feeding studies with coffee.* London: Elsevier Applied Science.

Wyshak, G., & Frisch, R. E. (1994). Carbonated beverages, dietary calcium, the dietary calcium/phosphorus ratio, and bone fractures in girls and boys. *Journal of Adolescent Health, 15,* 210-215.

Yakar, D. (1981). Coffee and cancer of the pancreas. *New England Journal of Medicine, 304,* 1605.

Yang, C. S., & Wang, Z. Y. (1993). Tea and cancer. *Journal of the National Cancer Institute, 85,* 1038-1049.

Yazdani, M., Joseph, F., Grant, S., Hartman, A. D., & Nakamoto, T. (1990). Various levels of maternal caffeine injection during gestation affects biochemical parameters of fetal rat brain differently. *Developmental Pharmacology and Therapeutics, 14,* 52-61.

Yazdani, M., Tran, T. H., Conley, P. M., Laurent, J. J., & Nakamoto, T. (1987). Effect of protein malnutrition and maternal caffeine intake on the growth of fetal rat brain. *Biology of the Neonate, 52,* 86-92.

Yerkes, R. M., & Dodson, J. D. (1908). The relation of strength of stimulus to rapidity of habit-formation. *Journal of Comparative Neurology and Psychology, 18,* 459-482.

Yesair, D. W., Branfman, A. R., & Callahan, M. M. (1984). *Human disposition and some biochemical aspects of methylxanthines.* New York: Alan R. Liss.

Yoshida, T., Sakane, N., Umekawa, T., & Kondo, M. (1994). Relationship between basal metabolic rate, thermogenic response to caffeine, and body weight loss following combined low calorie and exercise treatment in obese women. *International Journal of Obesity, 18,* 345-350.

Yoshino, S., Narayanan, C. H., Joseph, F., Jr., Saito, T., & Nakamoto, T. (1994). Combined effects of caffeine and malnutrition during pregnancy on suckling behavior in newborn rats. *Physiology and Behavior, 56,* 31-37.

Yu, G., Maskray, V., Jackson, S. H., Swift, C. G., & Tiplady, B. (1991). A comparison of the central nervous system effects of caffeine and theophylline in elderly subjects. *British Journal of Clinical Pharmacology, 32,* 341-345.

Zahn, T. P., & Rapoport, J. L. (1987). Autonomic nervous system effects of acute doses of caffeine in caffeine users and abstainers. *International Journal of Psychophysiology, 5,* 33-41.

Zaslove, M. O., Beal, M., & McKinney, R. E. (1991). Changes in behaviors of inpatients after a ban on the sale of caffeinated drinks. *Hospital and Community Psychiatry, 42,* 84-85.

Zatonski, W. A., Boyle, P., Przewozniak, K., Maisonneuve, P., Drosik, K., & Walker, A. M. (1993). Cigarette smoking, alcohol, tea, and coffee consumption and pancreas cancer risk: A case control study from Opole, Poland. *International Journal of Cancer, 53,* 601-607.

Zavela, K. J., Barnett, J. E., Smedi, K. J., Istvan, J. A., & Matarazzo, J. D. (1990). Concurrent use of cigarettes, alcohol, and coffee. *Journal of Applied Social Psychology, 20,* 835-845.

Zheng, W., McLaughlin, J. K., Gridley, G., Bjelke, E., Schuman, L. M., Silverman, D. T., Wacholder, S., Co-Chien, H. T., Blot, W. J., & Fraumeni, J., Jr. (1993). A cohort study of smoking, alcohol consumption, and dietary factors for pancreatic cancer (United States). *Cancer Causes and Control, 4,* 477-482.

Ziebell, J., & Shaw-Stiffel, T. (1995). Update on the use of metabolic probes to quantify liver function: Caffeine versus lidocaine. *Digestive Diseases, 13,* 239-250.

Zimmerberg, B., Carr, K. L., Scott, A., Lee, H. H., & Weider, J. M. (1991). The effects of postnatal caffeine exposure in growth, activity and learning in rats. *Pharmacology, Biochemistry and Behavior, 39,* 883-888.

Zimmerman, P. M., Pulliam, J., & Schwengels, J. (1985). Caffeine intoxication: A near fatality. *Annals of Emergency Medicine, 14,* 1227-1229.

Zock, P. L., Katan, M. B., Merkus, M. P., van Dusseldorp, M., & Harryvan, J. L. (1990). Effect of a lipid-rich fraction from boiled coffee on serum cholesterol. *Lancet, 335,* 1235.

Zoumas, B. L., Kreiser, W. R., & Martin, R. A. (1980). Theobromine and caffeine content of chocolate products. *Journal of Food Science, 45,* 314-316.

Zuskin, E., Schachter, E. N., Kanceljak, B., Witek, T., Jr., & Fein, E. (1993). Organic dust disease of airways. *International Archives of Occupational and Environmental Health, 65,* 135-140.

Zwyghuizen-Doorenbos, A., Roehrs, T. A., Lipschutz, L., Timms, V., & Roth, T. (1990). Effects of caffeine on alertness. *Psychopharmacology, 100,* 36-39.

Zylber-Katz, E., Granit, L., Pharm, B., & Levy, M. (1984). Relationship between caffeine concentrations in plasma and saliva. *Clinical Pharmacology and Therapeutics, 36,* 133-137.

Index

About the Author

Jack E. James is Professor of Behavioral Health Sciences at La Trobe University, Melbourne, Australia. He has been actively engaged in caffeine research for about 15 years, and has published widely on the subject. He is a psychologist, with extensive training and experience in both experimental and applied psychology. He has taught extensively in professional areas of psychology, including clinical psychology, health psychology, and behavioral medicine, and has a substantial record of research publications in these fields. At present, he is at the forefront of initiatives to develop health psychology as an area of professional practice and research in Australia. Professor James's work is strongly influenced by the belief that human problems require multidisciplinary solutions, and this viewpoint is evident in the structure and content of *Understanding Caffeine: A Biobehavioral Analysis*.

SUNY BROCKPORT

3 2815 00809 9080

RC 567 .5   .J15 1997

James, Jack E.

Understanding caffeine

DATE DUE

OCT 18 2000	DEC 1 4 2012
OCT 0 6 2000	DEC 1 2 2012
MAR 1 5 ~~~~ ILL	
APR 1 2 2001	
MAR 2 3 2005	
MAY 0 8 2007	
MAY 0 2 2007	
JUN 0 4 2007	
MAY 0 7 2008	
APR 3 0 2008	
MAY 2 8 2008	
MAY 1 0 2008	
MAY 0 6 2009	
MAY 1 1 2009	
OCT 1 4 2010	
MAY 1 2 2011	
MAY 1 0 2011	

DRAKE MEMORIAL LIBRARY
WITHDRAWN
THE COLLEGE AT BROCKPORT

GAYLORD   PRINTED IN U.S.A.